D0521260

THE CYCLIST'S SOURCEBOOK

THE
CYCLIST'S
SOURCEBOOK

Peter Nye

A PERIGEE BOOK

Perigee Books
are published by
The Putnam Publishing Group
200 Madison Avenue
New York, NY 10016

The prices and availability of the tours and items
listed in this book are accurate at the time of
publication in 1991, but, of course, these listings are
subject to change.

Copyright © 1991 by Robert R. McCord, Inc.

All rights reserved. This book, or parts thereof, may
not be reproduced in any form without permission.

Published simultaneously in Canada

Library of Congress Cataloging-in-Publication Data

Nye, Peter, date.
    The cyclist's sourcebook / Peter Nye.
      p.   cm.
    Includes index.
    ISBN 0–399–51705–7 (alk. paper)
      1. Cycling—Catalogs.   2. Bicycle racing—
Catalogs.   3. Bicycles—Catalogs.   I. Title.
  GV1041.N94   1991   91–3150 CIP
796.6—dc20

Front cover design © 1991 by Mike McIver

Printed in the United States of America

1 2 3 4 5 6 7 8 9 10

This book is printed on acid-free paper.
                ∞

To Alf Goullet,
On your 100th birthday:
April 5, 1991

CONTENTS

Adult men and women cyclists are taking to the road and to country trails on their bicycles to make cycling the sport of the nineties— remarkably similar to a century ago when cycling was a booming sport and bicycle riding was the sport of the nineties. Industry figures show that today there are 48 million adult cyclists, from age sixteen and up, 42 million under sixteen. Among adults, 55 percent are women. Sales of bicycles, clothing, and related equipment in the United States make cycling a $3.1 billion industry.

Baron Karl von Drais figured out a machine that beat walking and made him a walk-and-roller. Cranks and pedals were added to the front wheel for the "boneshaker," which led to the highwheeler and then to the modern "safety" bicycle with its chain drive and diamond frame. Thomas Stevens of England, the patron saint of cycling, pedaled a highwheeler around the world. From San Francisco in August 1884 he went east to Boston and then Eastward Ho! until he returned to San Francisco in January 1887.

Stevens's spirit lives in Iowa, where RAGBRAI draws 7,500 who ride 500 miles across the state in a week. Other mass rides include the Ride the Rockies in Colorado, Bicycle Ride Across Georgia, and many more. In Texas, the Hotter'n Hell Hundred out of Wichita Falls has become known as the Woodstock of Cycling, with 12,000 men and women of all ages braving the August heat just to say they rode the HHH. Montreal's Tour de l'Ile has 38,000 people riding forty miles, usually in the rain, every June, to make it the largest recreation ride in the world.

cross-country ride to a full-time-education association with 20,000 members. Pedal for Power. National Bicycle League. The Wheelmen, preservers of cycling and transportation heritage.

7. PUBLICATIONS 127

The American dream is fulfilled in publishing: How *Bicycling Magazine* grew from a mimeographed newsletter out of a Berkeley, California, bike shop to an ad-rich East Coast magazine with covers that boast, "World's No. 1 cycling magazine." Why *Bicycle Guide, Winning, VeloNews, Mountain Bike Action, BMX Plus!*, and *American Bicyclist and Motorcyclist* succeeded where others failed. Regional publications. Books, including some out of print, of interest to the novice as well as the afficionado.

8. BICYCLING ON FILM 156

Videos giving instruction, fitness techniques, tactics, covering major events in the United States and Europe. Radio plays on cassettes. The story behind the 1979 Academy Award–winning movie *Breaking Away*.

9. HOW TO WATCH A BICYCLE RACE 167

What to look for, best vantage points to see the action for criterium races, stage races, track, and off-road events. Got the bug? How to get started. World Champion Jeannie Longo of France gives her views on racing for women. What a professional cyclist's life is like. Racing as a team sport and its unique division of labor. Philadelphia's Manayunk Wall. Ernest Hemingway, Red Smith, and writing about bicycle races.

10. ULTRAFAST, ULTRALONG—CYCLING'S RECORD HOLDERS 184

Alf Goullet, hailed as the king of six-day bicycle racers in the teens and twenties, has lived long and lived well. His achievements have earned him inductions into four Halls of Fame in the United States and Australia. Connie Young, the fastest woman cyclist in the world. Art Longsjo, the first to compete in two U.S. Olympic teams in the same year, 1956—as a speed skater and a cyclist. Marcus Hurley, winner of four national amateur sprint championships, four Olympic gold medals, a world amateur sprint championship who led Columbia University to intercollegiate basketball championships on teams he captained. John Howard pedaling his bicycle 152 miles an hour. Michael Secrest crossing the United States alone in less than eight days and his plan to make it under three.

ACKNOWLEDGMENTS

When Bob McCord telephoned to suggest this book, his call was well timed. I had gone through five years of writing projects that included a book and reams of free-lance newspaper and magazine articles for publications such as *USA Today, The Washington Post, Denver Post, Sports Illustrated*, and *Women's Sports & Fitness*. The variety of these publications occasionally prompted concerned friends to inquire politely, "Do you have a job yet or are you just writing?"

As often happens, my assignments generated more stories than my editors wanted. Stories are important. Good ones are brought out and presented for appreciation—again and again. Who doesn't want to stop what they're doing just to hear a good story? Or tell one?

Stories I wrote and ones that didn't get the chance all lived in my notebooks. Bob telephoned to offer the opportunity to let my fount of stories make it into print. As he outlined what he had in mind, I could see that his idea was a book waiting to be written, and I was ready to write it.

The only catch was the deadline, which was the moral equivalent of Wednesday.

Somehow we met it. Part of the reason was that I am fortunate to have the joy of cycling instilled in me from Ray and Louise Blum. They showed through example that riding is a way of life, and on occasion is a measure of character. More recently, I am grateful for the friendship that Russell Mamone gave along with insight into cycling in the late nineteenth century and its relevance to twentieth-century transportation.

Also contributing to making the deadline was help from so many of the ride leaders whom I called upon for information which they gave generously out of love for the sport. With their dedication and enthusiasm, American cycling has a solid grassroots foundation.

Bob McCord served me the assignment and backed me all the way with encouragement and helpful suggestions. Others who contributed in encouragement and support are Ann and Gust Svenson, Peter Swan, Rich Carlson, Richard Rosenthal, Kathryn Clark, and Stephanie Drea. As always, I especially appreciate constant help from Clint Page, only a telephone call away, and Valerie Rice, even closer.

Arlington, Virginia
February 1991

11

INTRODUCTION

by Davis Phinney

As we drove to the race site for the Olympics cycling road race on July 29, 1984, I could not have been more surprised. Long used to throngs of spectators in European events but seldom in America, I was not prepared for the several hundred thousand spectators who lined the 9.4-mile circuit to observe their own piece of Olympics history. The 118-mile road race was free to the public, one of the few free Olympic events, which helped to draw the enormous crowd to the race circuit around Mission Viejo, about fifty miles south of downtown Los Angeles. Fans, many of whom obviously had camped overnight to have a spot for the best view on race day, lined the streets waving American flags. To see this was overwhelming. I was prepared for the race, but unprepared for the vociferous and supportive crowd. It was wonderful and frightening.

The women were racing when we arrived. My wife, Connie Carpenter Phinney, entered the event as a favorite. Her race was fifty miles—five laps around the rolling circuit. She was in the lead group of six as they sprinted for the gold medal. I watched on a little black-and-white television from the team pit area just a few hundred meters past the finish.

She started her sprint a little late. I was yelling at the TV, "Go now! Go now!" She caught her teammate, Rebecca Twigg of Seattle, and looked like she just passed her at the finish. It was *so* close. I couldn't tell who won. The crowd went beserk with a one-two United States finish. When she rounded the turn, I asked her above the thundering din of joyous spectators who won. She said, "I did." We fell to the ground laughing.

Wow. So the stage was set for me and my race a few hours away. So much rode on the outcome. We had lived and dreamed and planned for this day, knowing exactly what to expect, yet knowing not at all what to expect. Cycling in the United States had come so far in those first eight years that I had been in the sport.

I saw my first bicycle race in my hometown of Boulder, Colorado, when the Red Zinger Bicycle Classic was created in 1975. Nobody knew much about bike racing then, but it was fast and flashy and it looked like a lot of fun. At the time, I was running on the track team at Boulder High school, but I was looking for something else. My father had competed in some ultra-marathon bike races when he was young, but I never really made the connection that cycling might be something I might want to try. We skied a lot when I was growing up in Colorado, but I never made the connection between training and performance. I was a lazy kid, preferring Saturday morning cartoons to the family hikes in the mountains. But when I fell in love with bicycling, all that changed. I finally had made the connection, and it was liberating.

When I began to ride seriously, few of my friends understood what I was up to. But I persevered. I cut classes sometimes to suit my riding schedule. I loved the challenges that each day brought.

My riding partner was named Tony Comfort, but as a result of the prevalent Italian cycling influence, or maybe the 1979 movie *Breaking Away*, Tony became Antonio Comforte. He was always perfectly decked out—his bike and his clothes—and I pumped him for as much information as I could. Beyond that, I would pore through the English cycling magazine, *International Cycle Sport*, which recounted all the great races of Europe in detail. I would read them and reread them, dream about the great races, and imagine that one day I would be among the ranks of the great riders. Never did I even dare to believe it actually would happen.

But it did. To prepare for the Olympics road race, I had spent many months on rigorous campaigns through Europe as an amateur on the U.S. national team. My results went from dismal in the late 1970s to creditable by the spring of 1984. I was fighting it out with the best Italians, East Germans, French, and Soviets, and I won a few races against them.

In the Olympics road race in Mission Viejo, I was racing over my head. I felt like an animal, covering the first laps easily and making the crucial lead group toward the end of the race. But it was too easy, or I was working too hard, because I faded on the last lap after more than one hundred miles of racing. Steve Bauer of Canada got away with my teammate Alexi Grewal of Aspen, Colorado, shattering the lead group and leaving me to struggle for the finish. I was wasted and rolled in for fifth place. All four of our team had finished in the top ten, with Alexi taking the gold. It was amazing and disappointing at the same time.

But the next week with my teammates Ron Kiefel, Roy Knickman, and Andy Weaver in the 100-kilometer (62.5 miles) team time trial, we won a bronze medal. That helped the U.S. Olympics cycling team collect a total of nine medals, including four golds.

Since 1982 I had raced for the 7-Eleven team, and when the majority of the riders turned professional in 1985, I went with them. We had no idea what we were in for. The glamour of the European scene quickly faded behind the incredibly hard work and often dismal racing conditions: rain, snow, sleet, and too many eight-hour races. It was such difficult work, unimaginably hard riding.

But there were highlights, like when my teammate Kiefel won a race in Italy that first year. We knew we could make it with the established teams in Europe. It was just a matter of time. And, of course, Greg LeMond was starting to really tear up the European scene. Americans were in vogue. We were the new cowboys—at first something to laugh at, but our performances quickly generated respect.

In 1986, when I became the first American to win a road stage in the Tour de France (LeMond had won a time trial stage previously), I felt I finally had arrived. The next year I won another Tour de France stage. In 1988 I won the overall title of the Coors Classic, which had started as the Red Zinger and inspired me a decade earlier. Winning the

Coors Classic was the highlight of my career. I had come full circle.

Meanwhile, cycling had become more popular in the United States because of attention from the 1984 Olympics, the ever-increasing interest in triathlons, and greater coverage of the Tour de France on television. The roads around my hometown have become filled with casual and serious cyclists. On the weekends it is not unusual to see large groups of them cruising the roads. Cycling has come of age. What makes it so popular is the participatory nature of cycling. Besides, who doesn't know how to ride a bike?

Popularity can be measured in many ways, and one measure is the tremendous growth in charity bike-tour participation. Connie and I are involved in the National Multiple Sclerosis Society's Bike Tour program. In only a few years, it has grown into a multimillion-dollar fund-raiser. Tours that drew fewer than one hundred participants in the first year would draw a few hundred the second and a few thousand the third. It was fun to see so many people on their bikes.

Our own Carpenter/Phinney Cycling Camps, now at Beaver Creek Resort in Colorado, have shown us the depth of interest in cycling—from young teenagers to serious cyclists in their sixties.

In the fifteen years that I have raced, I have experienced many highlights, and a few low points, but in all it has really been some ride. I have probably ridden one-quarter of a million miles, and I'm still going strong. Cycling is my avocation—part true business and part true love. I hope you can find some motivation in the pages of this book to get you out on the road. Trust me: You will be happy you did.

THE
CYCLIST'S
SOURCEBOOK

CHAPTER 1

THE SPORT OF THE NINETIES—AGAIN

"THIS YEAR cycling is really going to take off," proclaimed one of the sport's elder statesmen, James Armando. "More people are getting into the sport. Cycling is really going to take off."

That was in 1960. President Dwight Eisenhower was in the White House, a four-cent stamp was all a letter needed to go first class, and the typical American bicycle was a heavy hunk of hardware with balloon tires, made for kids too young to get a driver's license.

Racing bicycles with narrow tires and ten-speed derailleurs were distinctly European, like soccer, and were obscure on this side of the Atlantic. American racing was a small, underground sport with a spirited following. Information on the sport here circulated by word of mouth or personal letters. There was no national team, there were only 1,000 registered amateur racers nationwide, and there were no professionals.

Yet several of the sport's veterans, like

James Armando, a member of the 1924 U.S. Olympic cycling team that competed in Paris, recalled their youth when cycling enjoyed popularity among men and women of all social classes, and racers were as big as top names in baseball, football, and boxing. Oil baron John D. Rockefeller and painter Frederic Remington were recreation cyclists. The Dodge brothers made bicycles before they went into the car business; the Wright brothers had a bike shop before they made airplanes. Albert Champion was a racer before he went on to make the spark plug that bears his name. Champion raced against Walter Marmon, who later shifted gears to make race cars that included the Marmon Wasp, winner of the first Indianapolis 500. Principal founders of the Indianapolis Motor Speedway were Carl Fisher, a local bike-shop entrepreneur, and Arthur Newby, a local bicycle track operator and race organizer.

Armando, a Hartford native, was a wiz-

James Armando, shown here in 1930, was predicting in the 1960s that cycling's popularity was going to take off. (Ed Bieber photo)

ened, gray-haired man still pedaling the bicycle he had ridden in the Olympics when he went to watch New England races in 1960. He was such a regular that events didn't seem official until he rolled up.

Each spring, year after year, Armando would boldly predict that the new season was going to be the biggest for the sport. He liked to tell—whether or not you wanted to listen—about the heyday of cycling, a century ago when he had just come into this world himself, when thousands of men and women cyclists took over city streets on Sunday afternoons to ride for recreation. Back then cycling was a national craze, the way swing music, the Hula-Hoop, and Rubik's Cube became to later generations.

Like today's computers, bicycles were the new technology of the day that made life easier. When chain transmissions became available in the early 1890s, the front and rear wheels became of equal size and were mounted in the diamond frame, as they are today. These new bicycles were such a technical marvel that they were called *extraordinary*, which meant that the highwheelers that first drew people to ride bicycles in large numbers were dubbed *ordinary*.

The final decade of the nineteenth century was a time of great excitement and change. People started talking over great distances to one another on telephones. Electricity was being introduced. Soon there would be so many lights on Broadway in New York City that the famous theater boulevard would become known as The Great White Way. Bicycles were part of the new advances. Fitness buffs pointed out the health benefits—rigorous cardiovascular exercise that didn't pound muscles or jar joints. Environmentalists cited cycling as a quiet, nonpolluting means of transportation. Cycling was advertised as the sport of the nineties.

After the turn of the century, however, cycling's general popularity waned, although bicycle racing thrived as a spectator sport in the Northeast. Armando enjoyed describing the crowds that paid to watch the races on steeply banked outdoor board tracks called velodromes in Newark, Boston, New York, Providence, and Philadelphia. The Super Bowl of bicycle racing was the international six-day bike races in New York City's Madison Square Garden, held every March and December. The Garden was often so packed that the fire marshal would order his men to form a cordon around the massive building to keep more fans from sneaking inside.

Armando's youth was a time when bicycle racers were the best-paid athletes in the country. In 1924, when Armando competed in the Paris Olympics, National Football League franchises sold for a few hundred dollars each; the purse for the Garden's spring and winter six-day events were $50,000 each. Alf Goullet, who lives today in Red Bank, New Jersey, had so many fans eager to watch him ride around the saucerlike track against top international competition that he was paid an appearance fee of $1,000 a day. Goullet's annual earnings were topping $30,000 when major-league baseball players were averaging less than $10,000.

A major difference between cycling's popularity in Armando's youth and the lean years the sport endured after the Depression and World War II was something he attributed in large part to the requirement that riders wear leather hairnet helmets in races, which the sport's governing body mandated in the mid-1940s.

"Helmets should never be required in

A group of women and some men dressed up in their cycling uniforms to take advantage of a nice day, circa 1892, when cycling was the sport of the nineties. (Russell Mamone collection)

Members of the Bay State Wheelmen on an April morning in 1894 in front of their bicycle club in Cambridge ready for a group ride. (Russell Mamone collection)

races," was one of Armando's frequent protests. "When the public sees a rider wearing protective headgear, they see the sport as dangerous and they stay away. That keeps cycling from gaining in this country."

Armando believed that the greatest aspiration anyone could have was to be an athlete, particularly a cyclist. When his younger brother fell in love, Armando tried to dissuade him from marrying, on the assumption that once married, an athlete was finished. Using the same stubborn logic that prevailed in his protest against helmets, Armando contended that a spouse would take away from mental concentration and intense physical training. After marriage came settling down and raising a family—dangerous diversions to an athlete's career. But the younger brother was too much in love to listen: He married, and Armando never spoke to him again.

In the 1920s and 1930s, Armando won many races, but he was best remembered for setting the record for riding up Pikes Peak in 1938. He was past his prime then, but he set the record for riding eighteen miles on dirt roads up to the top of Colorado's 14,110-foot Pikes Peak in 3 hours, 35 minutes. His feat drew the attention of *The New York Times*, which reported that his September ride took him through a snowstorm near the summit. The storm hampered newsreel photographers lugging heavy equipment in cars, but not Armando. He cut thirty-five minutes from the previous best time.

His record ride up Pikes Peak was characteristic of the tenacious way he held to his convictions. Nothing like age, gravity, or even a snowstorm could shake them. His faith paid off. In the 1960s he was still being introduced before the start of New England races as the record holder for that ride up Pikes Peak.

Armando did not live to see the founding of the U.S. Olympic Training Center in Colorado Springs in the 1970s, or see the formation of the national cycling team, or watch newsstands become inundated with new cycling magazines published in America. Nor did he witness his Olympic descendants break the seventy-two-year U.S. Olympic cycling medal drought at the 1984 Los Angeles Olympics with nine medals, including four golds.

He would have been quite vocal in expressing admiration for Greg LeMond's victory in two world professional road-racing championships and three-time triumph in the race of races, the three-week Tour de France. It would have been interesting to hear how Armando would react to LeMond, the superstar athlete, who is a married man with two sons and a daughter. Or to hear Armando's reaction to today's hard-shell helmets that are worn not only by racers but by most recreation riders as well.

Seven presidents have succeeded Eisenhower to the White House, first-class postage has risen 725 percent to 29 cents, but American cycling has finally taken off. Now cycling is a booming sport, the way running was in the 1970s. People of all ages and social strata are riding bicycles for recreation and health benefits as well as for transportation. Once again, cycling is the sport of the nineties.

Cycling's current revival started in the 1960s, when fitness-conscious adults began riding the lightweight ten-speed bicycles that had become popular and were being imported in unprecedented numbers. Interest in two-wheelers began to surge when the

THE U.S. BICYCLE MARKET (IN MILLIONS OF UNITS)

Year	Domestic Shipments	Imports	Total
1960	2.6	1.1	3.7
1965	4.6	1.0	5.6
1970	5.0	1.9	6.9
1971	6.6	2.3	8.9
1972	8.8	5.1	13.9
1973	10.1	5.1	15.2
1974	10.1	4.0	14.1
1975	5.6	1.7	7.3
1976	6.4	1.7	8.1
1977	7.5	1.9	9.4
1978	7.5	1.9	9.4
1979	9.0	1.8	10.8
1980	7.0	2.0	9.0
1981	6.8	2.1	8.9
1982	5.2	1.6	6.8
1983	6.3	2.7	9.0
1984	5.9	4.2	10.1
1985	5.8	5.6	11.4
1986	5.3	7.0	12.3
1987	5.2	7.4	12.6
1988	4.5	5.4	9.9
1989	5.3	5.4	10.7
1990	5.7	5.0	10.7

SOURCE: Bicycle Manufacturers Association of America

Middle East oil-exporting countries quadrupled the price of oil in 1973. More men and women began turning to bicycles for recreation as well as for alternative transportation. Figures from the Bicycle Manufacturers Association in Washington, DC, show the sale of bicycles in the United States jumped from 6.9 million in 1970 to 15.2 million in 1973.

A Gallup Organization poll in early 1990 showed that bicycle riding was among the top three most common recreational activities pursued by Americans aged eighteen and older. Cycling came after swimming and fishing, and was followed by bowling, camping, pool and billiards, hiking, and running.

Gallup's opinion poll, which has been conducted on leisure activities annually since 1959, was based on in-person interviews with 2,053 adults in more than 300 scientifically selected sites nationwide, between November 10, 1989, and January 15, 1990. The survey showed that 28 percent of those polled had ridden a bicycle in the past year, compared with 29 percent who had gone fishing and 38 percent who swam.

The survey noted significant differences between men and women in their preferences, but cycling rated among the top three for both genders. Among men surveyed, cycling placed after fishing and swimming as the most popular. After cycling came hiking, bowling, running, softball, basketball, motorboating, golf, and volleyball. Women in the survey liked swimming best, followed by cycling, then bowling, aerobics, camping, and hiking.

The Gallup poll showed that bicycling is most prevalent among middle-income groups, and more common among those with college degrees.

For the last two years Americans have

BICYCLE USE IN 1989

Total U.S. Bicyclists	90 million
Adults (persons 16 and older)	48 million (53 percent)
Children	42 million (47 percent)
Male/Female ratio for adults	45 percent/55 percent

Category of Use	1989 Level	Increase 1989 to 1990
Adults cycling regularly (average once a week)	23 million	+20 percent
Bicycle commuters	3.2 million	+20 percent
Adults cycling in competition (racing)	200,000	+20 percent
Mountain-bike users	11 million	+30 percent
People touring or vacationing by bike	1.1 million	+10 percent
Recreational event participants	2.7 million	+10 percent

SUMMARY: 1983–1989 (IN MILLIONS)

	1983	1984	1985	1986	1987	1988	1989
Total U.S. bicyclists	72.0	75.0	78.0	82.0	85.0	88.0	90.0
Adults riding regularly	10.0	11.0	12.0	14.0	17.0	20.0	23.0
Bicycle commuters	1.5	1.6	1.8	2.0	2.2	2.7	3.2
Racing (in thousands)	40K	75K	100K	120K	150K	180K	200K
Mountain-bike users	0.2	0.5	1.1	2.6	5.0	7.5	11.0
Touring and vacations	0.50	0.55	0.60	0.75	0.85	1.0	1.1
Event participants	n.a.	1.0	1.2	1.5	1.8	2.4	2.7

SOURCE: Bicycle Institute of America

Wide-tired bicycles with upright handlebars were designed for rugged off-road riding. (Photo by John Kelly/ Pearl Izumi)

been spending more than $3 billion annually on bicycles and related products—from clothing to books and magazines to bike racks for cars. The Bicycle Institute of America, a nonprofit clearing house for cycling information based in Washington, DC, estimates that there are 90 million bicyclists in the country—48 million (53 percent) are adults, aged sixteen and up, and 42 million (47 percent) are children. Women make up a majority of the adult cyclists, 55 percent (26.4 million) and 45 percent of riders (21.6 million) are men.

Sales of bicycles in the United States dropped after the peak year of 1973, but have been holding steady for the last two years at 10.7 million in 1989 and 1990, according to the Bicycle Manufacturers Association of America. The industry's current growth is in mountain bicycles, which have existed only since the mid-1970s. With wide tires, fifteen to eighteen speeds, and straight, upright handlebars, mountain bicycles chiefly grew out of the West Coast, followed soon after by the riders in Colorado's Rocky Mountains, where they were ideal for rugged off-road riding.

Their numbers grew slowly and accounted

Greg LeMond won the world road-racing championship twice and the Tour de France three times to catapult the sport of cycling back into America's consciousness. (Beth Schneider photo)

for only 5 percent of bicycle sales in 1985. Then their popularity soared. People found mountain bicycles were easy to pedal up hills. The fat tires made smooth riding out of rough and bumpy dirt roads and adapted just as easily to paved city streets. The fat tires also were more resistant to punctures than the skinny tires on lightweight bicycles. In 1989 sales of mountain bicycles edged past other bicycles, and in 1990 swept ahead to make up about 65 percent of all sales.

Bicycle racing also has grown considerably. From 1,000 registered amateur cyclists in 1960, the numbers have steadily increased to 9,000 in 1980, 19,000 in 1985, and 35,000 in 1990. The number of professionals has risen to about 100, with many riding on top teams on both sides of the Atlantic.

Interest in bicycle racing has been piqued by Greg LeMond's three victories in the Tour de France, the biggest sports event in the world. LeMond's triumphs were avidly reported in major daily newspapers and on network television. His second Tour victory, in July 1989, catapulted him to superstar status in the United States, where the media were for the most part unfamiliar with the sport.

When *Forbes* magazine listed the thirty highest-paid athletes in the world in August 1990, LeMond was ranked 27th, with $4.2 million in salary and product endorsements. The sums of money are exponentially greater than in Goullet's day, but LeMond is following in Goullet's tiremarks as a cyclist among the best-paid athletes.

Armando was right. Cycling did take off. He was just ahead of his time.

CHAPTER 2

RECREATION CYCLING: A TOUR D'HORIZON

WHAT BEGAN as a convenience in 1818 for Karl von Drais of Mannheim, Germany, a way to tour the forest and garden as chief groundskeeper for the Grand Duke of Baden, gave cycling the push that started it rolling. A quarter-century earlier, Count Médé de Sivrac of Paris had commissioned a carpenter to join two wooden wheels at the hubs with a carved bridge shaped like a horse's back as a toy for his children. This was called a *vélocifère*, and it soon became popular in Europe. Youngsters rolled around by pushing their feet on the ground. Von Drais added a crude but adequate steering device over the front wheel to create what is regarded as the first bicycle. Called the *draisine*, it was made entirely of wood and featured a banana-shaped seat. Von Drais did his inspection tours as a walk-and-roller.

Other draisines were made. Riders started showing up on draisines in London, Vienna, Paris, and other European cities. Two years later, von Drais went to France to demonstrate his invention. He rode it over dirt roads between Dijon and Beaune, about twenty miles, at an average speed of 9.3 miles an hour, to set the world's first cycling record. For a human-powered vehicle in the early days of the Industrial Revolution, this was considered a hot pace, and was appropriately set in France's mustard-growing region.

In 1855 Frenchman Pierre Michaux attached pedals to short cranks that fit to the front wheel of a three-wheeler. Soon after his fourteen-year-old son, Ernest, adapted his father's invention to a two-wheeler, called the *velocipede*.

A decade later, a French carriage maker named Pierre Lallement was in New Haven, Connecticut, early in the summer, demonstrating his velocipede on the village green to get backing for a patent in the United States so he could market the invention.

Right after Karl Von Drais created his draisine around 1818, imitations quickly proliferated, such as this English hobbyhorse, circa 1819. (Smithsonian Institution illustration)

Yankee ingenuity, however, quickly led to several imitations that showed up around town. Lallement returned to France patentless at the end of the summer.

Americans hailed the velocipede because it was a novelty, but the jarring ride on iron-rimmed wooden wheels prompted people to call it a "boneshaker." Despite the rough ride, people were eager to ride the boneshakers. Newspaper reporters and writers disparaged cycling as "a new scourge" and the velocipedes as "an awful vehicle," but all the press did was pique interest further.

Innovations followed. Hard rubber tires on metal wheels replaced iron rims. In the 1870s, the velocipede's front wheel grew considerably larger to give the rider a bigger gear, determined by the rider's leg length, while the rear wheel was made smaller for balance. This bicycle was the highwheeler, what the English referred to as a penny-farthing, for the disparity in size the two-wheelers shared with the two coins.

Highwheelers inspired one intrepid adventurer to show just what the bicycle could do. Thomas Stevens was a native of England who had emigrated to America in 1871. Stevens, then seventeen years old, and his parents headed for Missouri where the family settled to farm. Stevens was an energetic young man who avidly read travel books and soon set out to see the country. He went to Laramie, Wyoming, where he worked in a steel mill for two years, then roamed west to work in the Colorado silver mines.

In late 1883 Stevens was in Denver where he heard about several people's failed attempts to cross the country on a bicycle. The challenges were unlimited: mountains were natural barriers, streams too numerous to be mapped lacked bridges, deserts were impossible to ride across, and vast stretches of the landscape didn't even have a path to follow.

The feat of being the first to cross the continent on a bicycle, the ultimate technical advancement in personal transportation, fascinated twenty-nine-year-old Stevens. The fact that he never had been on a bicycle and was yet to learn to ride one didn't daunt him. Stevens made his way to San Francisco where he bought a Columbia high-wheeler with a fifty-inch wheel, which would indicate that he was about five feet six inches tall. He taught himself to ride in Golden Gate Park.

On April 22, 1884, Stevens waved his broad-brimmed slouch hat to a small gathering of other cyclists and curious onlookers at the Oakland pier and was on his way to becoming the patron saint of American cycling. For the next one hundred three and a half days, Stevens faced tasks equal to the labors of Hercules. Nevada, Utah, and Wyoming had no roads or even maps. Over the course of

3,700 miles, he had to walk, push, or carry his bicycle one-third of the distance.

He crossed streams by using his bicycle as a vaulting pole. For rivers, he got into a routine in which he took off his clothes and swam to the other bank, where he left his clothes, then swam back, found driftwood or fence posts to float his bicycle across, and then swam with this raft to the other bank. His biggest scare was in Nevada, where he was following railroad tracks that took him around a bend where he suddenly encountered a mountain lion. Stevens jumped off his bicycle and took cover behind it as though the wheels were a calvary horse. He fired his revolver and missed, and the animal fled into the bush and disappeared.

In Nebraska he had to ride between

High-wheelers featured hard rubber tires in the late 1880s and opened individual transportation to new possibilities. They led in the early 1890s to pneumatic tires on new safety bicycles. (Russell Mamone collection)

Thomas Stevens often passed westbound wagon trains in 1884 as he rode east from Oakland, California, to Boston. (Bikecentennial illustration by Brian Walker)

wagon-wheel ruts, which made for a precarious ride as the highwheelers toppled over easily. Frequently gusts whipped off the prairie "that blows me and the bicycle square over," he recounted.

Stevens persevered and by July 4th he reached Chicago. The city was raucous with the Democratic Party holding its quadrennial convention, nominating Grover Cleveland for the presidency. Chicago was still close to its founding as a trading post but it was already on its way to becoming what Carl Sandburg would later describe as the "city of the big shoulders." Stevens stayed a week and had his bicycle repaired.

After Chicago, Stevens still found the going arduous. In Indiana "ruthless, relentless mosquitoes" assaulted him. Ohio was better for a while, but he was arrested in Cleveland for riding on the sidewalks, which were smoother than the roads. Local cyclists who followed his progress in newspapers

heard of his predicament and rescued him from the police. After Cleveland, Stevens discovered the roads were better. As he made his way east, local bicycle clubs hosted him with fêtes.

He arrived in Boston on August 4, 1884. He was a hero, as he put it, for being the first "to imprint the rubber hoofmarks of the popular steed of the day" from coast to coast. It was a happy ending—and it proved to be only the beginning for Stevens.

Upon his arrival in Boston, Stevens made the acquaintance of Colonel A. Pope, a distinguished Civil War veteran and founder of the Columbia Bicycle Manufacturing Company. Colonel Pope realized a way to combine Stevens's spirit of adventure and the public's fascination with his bicycle trip. Pope had founded a cycling publication, *The Wheelman*, in 1882, under the editorship of S. S. McClure, who would go on to become a nationally prominent muckraking editor and publisher at the turn of the century. In 1883 Pope had merged *The Wheelman* into *Outing*, a broader-based publication he owned, and in 1884 he hired Stevens as a correspondent for the first round-the-world bicycle trip.

In the spring of 1885 Stevens shipped out to Liverpool, pedaled across his native England, then went east to France and southern Germany. He rode on roads adjacent to the Danube, following much of the same route that the First Crusaders took to Constantinople (today called Istanbul) in 1096. He kept pedaling through Asia Minor and spent the winter of 1885–86 in Teheran.

Political interference kept him from riding through the Russian Empire, but after boat and rail transfers through southern Russia, he continued riding his highwheeler across India during the hot season. The last country he visited, Japan, made for good riding and a pleasant way to end his trip in the harbor of Yokohama for the Pacific crossing. He arrived in San Francisco in January 1887, having ridden 13,500 miles.

Stevens was a national hero when he rode across the United States. As the first to ride around the globe, he achieved even greater stature. Newspapers all over America featured his story on the front page. At numerous banquets and receptions he was called "The Cycling Hero of the Decade," and was hailed the way aviators and astronauts would be in later generations. Stevens was even compared to Jules Verne and Sindbad the Sailor.

His dispatches in *Outing* were devoured by a public eager to follow his progress and read about what he saw and experienced in exotic lands where people were seeing a bicycle rider for the first time. A Turkish pasha announced that Stevens was doing something so extraordinary that "Americans must build him a monument!" In 1886 and 1887 Stevens's dispatches were collected and pub-

lished in the United States and England in the two-volume *Around the World on a Bicycle*, replete with detailed engravings.

By the end of the 1880s, bicycles with chain drive that allowed both wheels to be the same size in a diamond frame were available in growing numbers. The new "safety" bicycles began taking over the roads from the highwheelers. In 1892 Irish chemist John Boyd Dunlop invented pneumatic tires to fit on wooden rims for a more comfortable ride. General interest in cycling exploded. Publications like *Bicycling World* and *Bearings* were devoted to the industry, and other publications like *Scientific American* regularly ran features on leading racers and new technical advances. Bicycle trade shows in New York City and Chicago in the winter months when the next year's product lines were introduced generated big news items.

Prosperity characterized the Gay Nineties, and that prosperity was reflected in the boom of adult bicycle sales for men and women who rode for recreation. In 1896 Susan B. Anthony, one of the best-known women in America for her work in women's suffrage, was asked in an interview with Nellie Bly of *The New York World* what she thought of the social effect of women riding bicycles.

"Let me tell you what I think of bicycling," Anthony said. At seventy-six, Anthony wasn't going to gain anything from cycling but she liked what the bicycle represented to women. "I think it has done more to emancipate women than anything else in the world. I stand and rejoice every time I see a woman ride on a wheel. It gives women a feeling of freedom and self-reliance."

One woman whose action that year illustrated the suffragette's words was Margaret Valentine Le Long, a nineties "new woman" who proclaimed her independence of traditional roles for women by embarking on a solo ride from Chicago to San Francisco. Friends and relatives admonished her not to do it. Roads remained as bad as they were in Stevens's ride the decade before, and commercial accommodations were scarce.

Le Long declared she was not the fragile dilettante that friends and relatives depicted. Her bicycle was a modern safety bicycle with the diamond frame, its top tube dropped to enable her—and other women— to pedal while wearing a dress. All she packed was a small bag that strapped to her handlebars and contained a pistol, curl-papers, makeup box, and underwear.

Her trip took two months. She had to wade across marshes, endure clouds of mosquitoes, and keep pedaling on roads that were sometimes just traces. From Salt Lake City she followed the transcontinental railroad through the rest of Utah and most of Nevada. "The wagon road has a habit of disappearing in the most unaccountable manner," she wrote, "and if you are out of sight of the telegraph poles you are lost."

Hotels were chiefly big-city enterprises, and motels still were to come. Le Long sought food and accommodations in station houses of the railroad. Often railroad workers slammed the door in her face when they saw she was traveling alone. But other railroad workers and ranchers were helpful and courteous.

After Reno, Nevada, Le Long found the going considerably easier all the way to San Francisco. She reached the city of her destination unscathed and showed what women could do.

Victorian constraints relaxed in the Gay Nineties. Bicycles, manufactured in mass quantities and priced at $100 and less, heralded a new age of freedom. Bicycle industry estimates of the 1890s put the number of bicycles at 10 million in a country of 75 million people, most of whom lived in rural America, an average of two bicycles for every fifteen people. With the safety bicycle, cyclists in the 1890s were riding essentially the

Suffragette Susan B. Anthony praised the bicycle: "It gives women a feeling of freedom and self-reliance." (Russell Mamone collection)

same bicycle we have today, although today's machines are lighter due to improved components.

Clubs proliferated to every state in the Union. Club members wore uniforms on regular weekend club runs. They engaged in drills carried out to the sound of bugles, adopted from the mounted calvary. And, most important, clubs used their strength in membership to lobby state legislatures to spend money to improve the quality of roads.

Bicycle races caught the public's fascination with speed. Only baseball rivaled bicycle races as a spectator sport. But the overwhelming majority of cyclists were adults riding to enjoy the outdoors as well as for fitness.

Boxing champion Jim Corbett liked to work out on a bicycle to strengthen his legs and improve his wind. In the summer of 1897 he was speeding in a pack of racers around an outdoor dirt track in Asbury Park, New Jersey, when he touched another rider's rear wheel and crashed. The next day the *Asbury Park Shore Press*'s headline blared, CORBETT KNOCKED OUT (CHAMPION BESTED BY INNOCENT BICYCLE).

By the turn of the century, however, the novelty of bicycles faded and interest in cycling declined rapidly. In the first decade of the twentieth century, bicycle companies in the United States went out of business by the dozens. Dealers were stuck with inventories they couldn't sell; distributors went bankrupt. Colonel Pope was among those who fell on hard times. His numerous companies—including publications, the Columbia Bicycle Company and the Pope-Hartford Automobile Company—went into receivership, contributing to his death at sixty-six in 1909. His protégé, Stevens, who had had flings as a *New York World* correspondent in Africa and Russia, by then had returned to England where he lived a quiet life.

Automobiles soon displaced bicycles as a means of transportation. Crowds still went to watch bicycle races, particularly in the Northeast, where racing remained part of the popular culture through the 1930s. Few people rode bicycles anymore for fitness or the pleasure of taking to the roads in nice weather.

During World War II, when gasoline was rationed, interest in bicycles revived, but after the war bicycles again lost out to cars. One of the few cycling proponents in the postwar years was cardiologist Dr. Paul Dudley White, physician to President Eisenhower in the 1950s. White observed, "The American public is a slave to the automobile."

Not until the early 1970s did any significant number of people heed Dr. White's observation. Fitness-conscious adults took up sports like tennis, running, swimming, and cycling. And when the 1973 oil crisis hit, bicycle sales surged. Men and women began buying bicycles in record numbers.

Another significant development in 1973 started modestly in Iowa. John Karras, a writer for the *Des Moines Register*, recommended that colleague Don Kaul, who worked for the newspaper's Washington, DC, bureau, return in August to ride with him across the Hawkeye State and write about what he saw. Before their six-day ride was over, it became a bellwether of recreation cycling and ushered in the modern era of mass rides.

A month before they left, Karras—an avid cyclist—told readers in a Sunday feature about plans for the 485-mile tour over secondary roads from Sioux City in the northwest to Davenport on the state's eastern border. He pointed out that they weren't racing and invited readers to get a bicycle and accompany them. The ride, essentially from the Missouri to the Mississippi, became known as The Great Six-Day Bicycle Ride Across Iowa. About 300 cyclists were with the newspapermen on the Sunday they wheeled out of Sioux City. Numbers varied daily, with a high of 500, and about 115 ped-aled all the way to Davenport.

The ride promptly took on a populist per-sonality. Contributing to its character was eighty-three-year-old Clarence Pickard of Indianola, who rode out of Sioux City on a woman's bicycle with the dropped top tube similar to the one Le Long had ridden from Chicago to San Francisco. Pickard wore a silver pith helmet, long-sleeve shirt, trou-sers, and high-topped basketball shoes. He had only recently bought the bike and was learning to shift the derailleur to change gears.

Both newspaper writers filed stories on Pickard—and others—daily. By the time the entourage reached Davenport, *Register* readers, especially those who missed taking part, demanded that it be repeated so they could participate in the next one.

The following August, about 1,800 people went to Council Bluffs, in the western part of the state, for what became known as SAGBRAI, the Second Annual Great Bicycle Ride Across Iowa. It was a seven-day mean-der over back roads across the state through Atlantic, Guthie Center, Camp Dodge, Mar-shalltown, Waterloo, and Monticello before concluding in Dubuque on the banks of the Mississippi.

By 1975 it was apparent that a tradition was established. The name officially became its present RAGBRAI, the *Register*'s Annual Great Bicycle Ride Across Iowa, and Roman numerals designated the editions. With RAGBRAI X in 1982, the ride was set for the last full week of July, when it has been held ever since. A limit of 7,500 riders has been imposed to keep the ride manageable.

Karras said that the ride probably would not have become an annual event without Pickard "because when he rode all the way on that first one, it gave a lot of people the idea of, 'Well, if he can do it, I probably can, too.' " When Pickard died in early 1983,

RAGBRAI XI was called The Clarence Pick-ard Memorial Ride in his honor.

RAGBRAI went from being a state event to a national one. Bruce Harmon of Ar-lington, Virginia, who commuted on his bicy-cle to Washington, DC, read in early 1984 about RAGBRAI in *Esquire*'s suggestions for fifty great vacations. "That got me to think-ing about it," Harmon recounted. "The *Es-quire* blurb told where to write at the *Register*. Then I began discovering people in Washington who already had done it, or who had a cousin or sister who had done RAG-BRAI."

Harmon, who had never competed in a bi-cycle race or run a marathon, wrote to the *Register*, which has a lottery in April every year to pick 7,500 riders from among 15,000 seeking to make the ride. "RAGBRAI seemed like a challenge, not like climbing Mount Everest, but extraordinary enough, and I felt I was up to it," he said. When he was selected, he prepared by taking long rides on weekends.

"Bruce ate the whole time he was out there in Iowa and still came back home ten pounds lighter," said his wife, Melissa Merson. "He was raving about the trip. He bought me a bike, and the next year I rode RAGBRAI."

What gave Harmon so much enthusiasm to return with his wife was the friendliness of the people he encountered wherever he went and the festival atmosphere that was part of the ride. "On a bike, you can stop and take time to do things you might only think about doing when you drive past in a car," Harmon said. "One time I pedaled past a river where people were swinging on a rope that hung from a tree with branches extending over the water. Everybody was swinging over the river and dropping in. How many times I've driven past and seen people doing something like that, but was too busy to take fifteen minutes out of my life for it. On my bike, it was so easy to stop and go grab the rope and swing out and splash into the river." He laughed at the recollection. "Felt so good, I did it a few more times. Sure was fun."

RAGBRAI is low-budget. Cyclists sleep under the stars or in tents they bring along. Most campers are up shortly before dawn, take down their tents, and load all the equipment they don't carry on their bicycles into duffel bags. Bags are trucked to a city park or high school at that day's destination.

"I cannot describe what it's like early in the morning when everybody gets going at dawn," Merson said. "There is a ribbon of road with thousands of people riding shoulder to shoulder, going on and on as far as the eye can see. It's quiet. The only sounds are gears shifting and the soft whirr of tires on the road. It is spectacular."

RAGBRAI, which typically ranges from 470 to 500 miles over a different route each year, starts with a 40-mile ride, increases daily distance to a maximum of 75 to 85 miles late in the week, and then tapers back to 40 miles on the final day. (On the longest ride, a circuit is added for those who want to go the extra distance to earn a "Century Patch" for 100 miles.) Riders go at their own pace and nearly always have company. They pedal every day, rain or shine.

"You discover ground-level things about Iowa," Harmon said. "There's so much ethnic diversity. There are Amana Church Society communities, German settlements, Dutch towns. You experience that Iowa is flatter in the north and central part. Southwestern Iowa is hilly. It's a huge agriculture state. You pass lots and lots of cornfields, soybean fields. Later when you go back home and hear in the news that Iowa has drought, you understand what it means to the people there."

Local communities get a boost when the riders pass through. Each cyclist spends at least $10 to $15 daily on food and drink, nearly all of it spent in small communities that rarely get such an influx of tourist trade. This generates about $50,000 in each town where riders stop for lunch, and another $150,000 at the final stop of the day. RAGBRAI officials estimate the ride pumps more than $2.1 million into the state's economy.

"In the evenings we ate in church basements," Harmon said. "We spent $4.50 to $5.00 for a spaghetti dinner. Sometimes it was fried chicken or pork, depending on the specialty of the town we were in. We sat on folding chairs and ate at card tables. Our food was on paper plates and we ate with plastic forks and knives. Pretty simple. Easy to clean up, too."

Merson said she gained confidence on her ride that has carried over to other activities. Afterward, she expanded her athletic range to compete in triathlons involving swimming, cycling, and running. In late 1990 she ran her first full marathon.

"Before I did RAGBRAI, I thought that you had to have talent to be an athlete and start training for your event when you were a kid," she said. "RAGBRAI appealed to me because I wanted to do something amazing. Something huge. But still manageable.

"Riding across Iowa changed my concept of athletics. It helped me become much more serious about what I can do. Every day the ride took me farther than I had ever gone before. One particular day stands out for being so tough. It was pouring a cold rain. Bruce had ditched me to ride up ahead with faster riders. I used to keep track of the distance by watching the numbers on the calculator on my handlebars that told speed, distance, and so on. But rain shorted out the calculator. I got through the ride by singing Beatles songs with another rider for three hours.

"Day after day, the whole experience raised my confidence. On the last day, I got to the end of the ride and dipped my front tire into the Mississippi, a RAGBRAI tradition. I felt I really accomplished something and could go on to more goals. RAGBRAI was an epiphany of sorts."

RAGBRAI's popularity and national media attention have spawned other similar week-long rides, such as Colorado's *Denver Post* Ride the Rockies. This 400-mile journey up and down the Rocky Mountains started in 1986 and takes place in mid-June.

"We have to limit the field to 2,000 riders from the 5,000 who apply because it is not safe with more than 2,000," explained Kathleen MacDonald, promotions manager for the newspaper. "Our route is not closed to traffic. We ride mainly on secondary roads. Every year the route changes. A lot of people come back year after year because it's so scenic. We usually take in some snowcapped peaks, depending on available roads."

A survey of cyclists in the *Denver Post* Ride the Rockies shows demographics consistent with those in RAGBRAI surveys:

- About 70 percent of the riders are men
- Average age is 38
- Nearly 50 percent of the riders are 35 to 49 years old
- 78 percent earn at least $30,000 a year
- 40 percent come from out of state.

Texans are known for their flair for largesse, and that extends to organized bicycle rides. The Hotter'n Hell Hundred, a one-day ride of 100 miles in Wichita Falls, in north Texas, draws huge fields, despite the August heat that pushes the mercury up to 100 degrees.

"It's the Woodstock of cycling," said Joe Simnacher of Dallas, referring to the 1969 rock-music festival in upstate New York that transformed a farmer's field into a metropolis for the weekend. "A thousand riders showed up for the first Hotter'n Hell Hundred in 1982, and more came every year. Since 1988 it's been 12,500."

Woodstock had a wide-open field to accommodate the massive audience. Hotter'n Hell Hundred participants are confined to narrow farmer-to-market roads. Cyclists start in Wichita Falls and pedal a counterclockwise loop around Wichita County that takes them back to the city. "It's fairly easy riding because it's flat, but the heat is brutal and it gets windy, with thirty-mile-an-hour winds," said Simnacher, a veteran. "When you get back to Wichita Falls, you feel you've done something."

The original idea behind the Hotter'n Hell Hundred was to celebrate the centennial of Wichita Falls in 1982. Located on the banks of the Wichita River near Oklahoma, Wichita Falls began as a settlement in the 1870s. When the railroad arrived in 1882, it became a shipping point for wheat and cattle from nearby ranches and grew in importance and size. Wichita Falls today has about 100,000 population.

"We were kicking around different ways to celebrate the centennial," said ride director Robie Christie. "Someone said we could get a thousand people to sit on rocking chairs all day and that might get us in the *Guinness Book of World Records*. But cycling is pretty popular. We decided to hold a ride—a 100-miler."

First time out, the ride was a success. Now it requires a year to plan. "We have a steering committee of fifty people who represent 2,500 volunteers," Christie said. "There are rest stops all along the course. Each rest stop has one to three tents that measure twenty feet by forty feet each. Every rest stop resembles a small town. We hand out drinks, cookies, bananas, plums, peaches, and oranges. Keeping the beverages chilled and the fruit cool in scorching heat takes 100,000 pounds of ice, hauled in three tractor trailors."

For signing up and paying the $15 registration fee ($12 per person for a family registration of three or more), riders receive a commemorative T-shirt and a plastic twelve-

Cyclists who converge on Wichita Falls for the Hotter 'n Hell Hundred weekend in late August spend about $1.5 million, according to the city's Chamber of Commerce. (Harry Tonemah photo)

ounce drinking bottle. The Hotter'n Hell Hundred starts at 7:30 A.M. on the Saturday nine days before Labor Day.

"The start is stratified," Christie said. "Everybody sorts themselves out according to what speed they want to ride. Those who plan to go at twenty miles an hour or faster are at the front. It still takes thirty minutes just to get everybody going and clear the starting area. It used to be worse. With that many people, any turns after the start slowed the ones already out there and delayed the rest from going. We have adjusted our starting point so that at least the first mile is on a straight road."

To accommodate cyclists who want to participate but don't feel up to the distance, alternate routes are offered for 62, 50, 25, or 10 miles. Doctors, nurses, and physical therapists are at each rest stop to tend to rider needs. Red Cross staff cruise the course in vans provided by local car dealers.

In 1986 the Hotter'n Hell Hundred started requiring that riders wear helmets, making it among the first organized rides nationwide to make helmets mandatory. "Ironically, the person who was loudest in protesting against wearing a helmet crashed and landed on his head that year," Christie recounted. "He was wearing a hard-shell helmet, which broke in three pieces. That pretty much ended any resistance to wearing a helmet on the ride."

Roads remain open to traffic. But with plenty of advance publicity touting this established annual event, local motorists tend to steer clear of course roads. Moreover, what's good for the cyclists is good for Wichita Falls, which becomes a regional locus. Hotels are booked up. The pasta dinner in the convention center on the Friday evening before the ride features a consumer show with more than fifty manufacturers and vendors.

"The chamber of commerce estimates that people who come to the ride spend $1.5 million that weekend," Christie said. "It's a clean industry—no pollution whatsoever."

One of the country's oldest continuous recreation rides is the two-day Tour of the Scioto River Valley in Ohio, which started in 1962 and since 1967 has been held on Mother's Day weekend. Popularly known as TOSRV, the ride starts in Columbus and goes south 105 miles, following the Scioto River to Portsmouth, on the Ohio River, which separates the Buckeye State from Kentucky. Cyclists camp overnight in school yards, sleep in gymnasiums, fill the hotels and motels, and stay in the homes of local residents. The next morning everybody pedals back for a total of 210 miles.

Like RAGBRAI, TOSRV has a devoted following that has generated other similar rides, such as TOSRV-West, a 220-mile tour based out of Missoula, Montana. TOSRV-West is the Tour of the Swan River Valley, held on the third weekend in May since its founding in 1971. Cyclists go northeast from Missoula and on the second half of the first day's ride follow the Swan River Valley to Swan Lake, 110 miles away. They camp overnight in a park and ride back for a total of 220 miles.

Inspiration for the first TOSRV came from stories about six-day bicycle races that Greg Siple heard from his father, Charles, while growing up in Columbus. Charles Siple grew up in Pittsburgh and was sixteen in 1934 when he saw his first six-day race in Duquesne Garden, a cavernous old trolley barn in Pittsburgh. He watched three dozen racers like Bobby Walthour, Jr. and cousin Jimmy Walthour, Jr. compete in the international race around a steeply banked board track, ten laps to the mile. Riders raced in two-man teams in 144 hours of continuous competition; one rested and ate on the track infield while the other whipped around the boards. Several times daily, racers sprinted for points and cash premiums: they hit speeds faster than forty miles an hour; over the six days they covered more than 2,000 miles.

Young Charles was fascinated with how skillfully the racers handled their bicycles around the wooden saucer. At speed, they strung out wheel to wheel in a long line. When they let up, they bunched like a swarm of bees in bright silk jerseys. Year after year when the sixes came to town, he was at Duquesne Garden. In 1940 he followed the racers to Buffalo, where he worked as a runner for a team, running for extra food and beverages and a variety of errands. The outbreak of World War II, however, ended the best years of the 6-day circuit, which had been going on for half a century in North America. But the legends lived on in the stories Charles told his son. Charley bought his son a multispeed lightweight bicycle with dropped handlebars, ordered from a Sears & Roebuck catalog.

"In 1962, when I was sixteen, my father and I decided to take a long ride together," explained Greg Siple. "We selected 100 miles because that was a milestone in the 1890s—doing the century run was the big thing."

Their century took them from Columbus, along the Scioto River Valley, to Portsmouth, where they stayed overnight in a hotel. "My father was forty-four and started out riding like he was still in his twenties. He

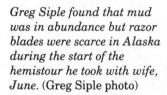

Greg Siple found that mud was in abundance but razor blades were scarce in Alaska during the start of the hemistour he took with wife, June. (Greg Siple photo)

hadn't been on a bike since the war, and at the time he smoked. The ride was a shock to my father. But I liked it a lot."

Greg Siple liked it enough to do it again the next year. His father didn't go, but three friends did. "We couldn't afford the hotel, so we stayed in the Railroad YMCA in Portsmouth," Siple said. "It cost $1.19 a night. The building is no longer there."

More cyclists began to make the ride an annual event. By 1966 it had acquired a regional reputation and drew three cyclists from Chicago. "I thought, 'Wow! Three guys coming from out of the state!' They carried the word back. Then more and more people came every year. Of course a lot of things were happening to cycling over the years. TOSRV kept growing. TOSRV had 1,000

riders in 1970. In 1990 there were 6,500 riders. A couple thousand more were turned away because we couldn't feed them all and give them accommodations."

One of the TOSRV faithful, Dan Burden, moved to Missoula to attend the University of Montana and in 1971 founded TOSRV-West. Siple followed Burden to Missoula in 1972. Together with their wives, Lys Burden and June Siple, they embarked on an intercontinental odyssey to promote recreation cycling. In June 1972 they pedaled out of Anchorage, Alaska, and went south through Canada, the United States, and kept going to Tijuana.

Dan Burden contracted hepatitis in Mexico and had to pull out with his wife. But June and Greg Siple kept pedaling through

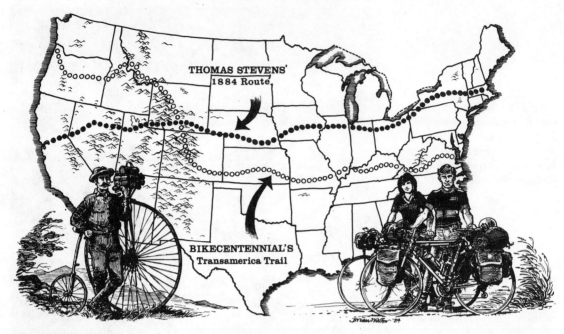

THOMAS STEVENS'
1884 Route

BIKECENTENNIAL'S
Transamerica Trail

More than 4,000 cyclists rode the Bikecentennial route across the country in 1976, intersecting the route of Thomas Stevens nearly a century earlier. (Bikecentennial illustration)

Central America and down the length of South America until they reached Tierra del Fuego, a group of islands on the southern tip of South America.

"We finally arrived in Ushuaia, Argentina, after two years, eight months, nine days," Siple said. "That was 18,272 miles. We did this to promote cycling. Before we left, we had the *National Geographic*'s interest. They gave us about sixty rolls of film to take with us. We published an article in the May 1973 issue on a portion of our ride."

Early in their odyssey, the two couples came up with the idea for celebrating America's bicentennial with a trans-America ride. When the Siples and Burdens met up again in 1975 in Missoula, the Burdens already had their plans for the bicentennial ride well under way. They had an office, paid staff, and a route had been mapped out with overnight locations. "We were working with a staff of forty, all of us paid $250 a month, working out of a hotel in Missoula that we were renting," Siple said.

They mapped out a 4,200-mile route from Astoria, Oregon, on the northwest tip of the state, east across the country to Yorktown, Virginia, a village on eastern Virginia's Chesapeake Bay. "We picked the starting and ending points of the route because of the historical significance," Siple explained. "Astoria is where Meriwether Lewis and William Clark reached the Pacific in their expedition of 1804 to 1806 that led to the Louisiana Purchase and expansion westward for the United States. And Yorktown is where English General Cornwallis surrendered to George Washington's Continental Army in the Revolutionary War."

In the bicentennial summer of 1976, more than 4,000 cyclists rode the Astoria-Yorktown route, with 2,000 pedaling the entire distance, Siple said. "It involved 11 million rider miles. We had indoor and outdoor sleeping accommodations all across the country, styled after the TOSRV, where they slept outside in tents or inside school gymnasiums. Two hundred cyclists came over from Holland for the ride. They were used to more comfortable hostels and thought our conditions in some places were pretty rough."

The bicentennial ride proved so successful that Siple and colleagues remained in business as Bikecentennial. Over the years they have expanded routes to go from:

- San Diego, California, to Ormond Beach, Florida
- Anacortes, Washington, to Bar Harbor, Maine
- Missoula, Montana, to Jasper, Alberta
- Vancouver, British Columbia, to Tijuana, Mexico
- Bar Harbor, Maine, to Fort Myers, Florida

"Most of the people who ride these routes buy maps from us and make the rides on their own," Siple said. "We have expanded beyond routes and maps. We have 25,000 members who support Bikecentennial, which employs a staff of ten to twelve full-time and more part-time. We are the biggest single source for recreational bicycle information in the country. I like to think that all this grew out of enjoyment of recreation cycling from the stories my father used to tell me about what the six-day bike racers did."

The sixth annual Tour de l'Ile in Montréal on June 3, 1990, entered the *Guinness Book of World Records* as the largest recreational ride: 38,000 cyclists rode a forty-mile route through the city's neighborhoods.

"And that was in the *rain*," said Fred Patton of Denver who was there. "People started arriving at 5 A.M., and the ride didn't start

for four hours. The start was staged between Olympic Stadium and the Botanic Gardens. It was a mile long and four lanes wide. As far as you could see, there were cyclists. Parents took kids on bike seats. There were old Italians from Little Italy with fat rolls hanging over their shorts, fit-looking young guys in racing outfits, chicks in halter tops. It was pouring rain and everybody was standing there smiling."

Rain appears to be *de rigueur* in the Tour de l'Ile. Held on the first Sunday in June since 1985, the ride has had precipitation every year. Organizers pass out plastic ponchos and let the good times roll.

The first riders in the 1990 ride began their commute at 9 A.M. Wheels kept on turning over Montréal's neighborhood roads until 8 P.M. Along the way, a regiment of 3,000 volunteers worked on the course. They helped riders fix punctured tires, gave directions, and staffed the five rest stops. Police and fire departments donated their time, keeping the route closed to traffic and redirecting motorists.

"To see all this humanity, riding in the rain, everybody on bicycles, the whole thing successful, was fantastic," Patton said.

STATE LISTING OF MAJOR BICYCLE RECREATION RIDES

Helmets most often are required of all riders. Support crews transport baggage including tents and sleeping bags to the next city, give first aid, and provide mechanical help. For additional ride information, send a business-sized, self-addressed envelope (SASEs reduce the ride organization's volunteer labor force and allow them to devote time to important details).

ARIZONA—Grand Canyon to Mexico
Almost Across Arizona Bicycle Tour

Two tour groups: (a) October 4–13, 1991, goes 580 miles; and (b) October 5–13, 1991, goes 500 miles.

Bus transportation picks up cyclists in Tucson and Phoenix and takes them five hours north to the Grand Canyon National Park where both rides begin. Southbound route to Nogales on the Mexican border takes riders to Tonto National Monument, renowned for the Native American Anasazi cliff dwellings, and Sunset Crater National Monument, a volcanic crater with lava fields, and other national monuments.

"People often remark on the variety of territory and scenery of the ride," said ride director Richard Corbett. "We go through pine forests on the southern rim of the Grand Canyon at 7,000 feet altitude and descend 3,000 feet to the high desert. You can have views of fifty to sixty-five miles."

Bus transportation takes cyclists from Nogales back to their starting points.

The cost for the trip is $250 and covers bus rides, camping, breakfast and dinner daily, support crew, commemorative T-shirt, and maps. Ordinarily, the tour is limited to approximately 100 per group, based on earliest registration. Ride founded in 1981.

Information from:

Richard Corbett
Tucson Chapter, Greater Arizona
   Bicycling Association
P.O. Box 40814
Tucson, AZ 85733
(602) 623-0017

Everybody gets to ride in the Great Western Rally. (AYH photo)

CALIFORNIA—Great San Francisco Bike Adventure

June 9, 1991. More than 14,000 cyclists take over San Francisco's streets which are closed to traffic for this fifteen-mile Sunday tour of the city. Starting at the Marina, riders wend their way along the Embarcadero, through the Broadway tunnel, financial district, market area, and onto the Route 280 freeway for a short distance before turning around and doubling back to the start.

"The emphasis is on having a good time," said Bob Leone of the American Youth Hostel, which sponsors the ride. "We put the experienced riders together, the families together. It's strictly a recreation ride. A picnic is provided afterward."

The $12 cost covers refreshments and T-shirt. Founded in 1986.

Information from:

Great San Francisco Bike Adventure
American Youth Hostel
425 Divisadero, No. 307
San Francisco, CA 94117
(415) 863-1444

CALIFORNIA—Great Western Rally

May 24–27, 1991. Twenty-five different rides from three to 100 miles, plus a wine and cheese party, a swap meet, and a beauty contest for different bicycle classifications (including mountain bicycles, tandems, and road bicycles) draw 2,300 people to this four-day rally over Memorial Day weekend in Paso Robles, in central California. Rides take cyclists past vineyards, horse ranches, avocado and walnut tree groves.

Founded in 1963 in La Jolla in Southern California, the Great Western Rally has changed venue over the years from San Luis Obispo, Solvang, and Santa Maria before settling in Paso Robles where it has been since 1977, said ride director Laverne Boethling. Riders come from ten states.

The cost is $10 per person for the weekend,

covering all activities, rally patch, and century patch for those who ride 100 miles. Camping is another $6 per night.

Information from:

Laverne Boethling
625 Esplanade
Apt. 62
Redondo Beach, CA 90277
(213) 540-0521

COLORADO—Denver Post Ride the Rockies

June 16–22, 1991. There's a limit of 2,000 cyclists for this 400-mile ride over the Rocky Mountains with scenic views. Cyclists are drawn from a lottery of 3,500 applicants. Registration is available beginning February 10 at *The Denver Post*.

The cost is $120. This covers support crew and camp sites. Route varies every year. Founded 1986.

Information from:

Denver Post Ride the Rockies
The Denver Post
1560 Broadway
Denver, CO 80202
(303) 820-1338

CONNECTICUT—Two Ferry Metric Century

September 29, 1991. This metric century of 100 kilometers (62.5 miles) covers hilly central Connecticut, but the ride is broken up with two ferry rides across the Connecticut River and lunch on the grounds of a castle.

Middlesex Bicycle Club President Andre Raymond said the ride his club sponsors starts in the Palmer Athletic Field parking lot in Middletown on the last Sunday in September and goes clockwise around the Nutmeg State. "The first part of the ride is very, very hilly," Raymond said. "It's on narrow, winding country roads, including a dirt-road stretch seven-tenths of a mile that the local residents don't want paved. With the hills, dirt road, and two ferry crossings, there is a little bit of everything on the ride."

The first ferry crossing is in East Haddam. "It's the oldest ferry still operating in the country," Raymond said. "It takes only about thirty cyclists at a time, and it's pulled by a tugboat."

Cyclists then pedal to Hadlyme, where they have lunch at Gillette castle, which actor William Gillette had constructed early in the century. Gillette (1855–1937) introduced American audiences to Sherlock Holmes plays and was one of the most successful actors of his day. His acting made him a millionaire. He indulged in spending a fortune to build a castle in Hadlyme, and his estate is now a state park. After lunch, cyclists take a large ferry back across the river to finish where they started. In 1990 about seventy riders participated.

Cost is $10. Provides a lunch of sandwiches and fruit at Gillette castle. Founded in 1988. Information from:

Andre Raymond
P.O. Box 2325
Middletown, CT 06457
(203) 347-0798

DISTRICT OF COLUMBIA—Capitol City Bike Festival

September 15, 1991. More than 4,000 cyclists pedal twenty-five miles through sections of Rock Creek Park and take in a loop that includes the Thomas Jefferson and Abraham Lincoln Memorials. The ride starts and finishes at Carter Barron Park. The festivities conclude with a live band performance, workshops, and exhibits.

The $9 registration fee provides T-shirt, safety vest, and snacks. The sponsor is the Washington-area American Youth Hostel. Founded 1985.

Information from:

Potomac Youth Hostel
1017 K St., N.W.
Washington, DC 20001
(202) 783-0717

FLORIDA—Cross Florida Ride

May 5, 1991. Not a race, but a demanding 170-mile grind from Cocoa Beach on the Atlantic coast southwest across the state to Pine Island Beach. For the hard-core. Ride director Irvin Hayes said the dropout rate is as high as 40 percent.

"We created the ride in 1975 out of pure insanity, just because it was there," he explained. "First year, it was a more direct route, 130 miles. We encountered fierce headwinds, thunderstorms, searing heat. Eleven started and seven completed it. None of us felt we could do it again. We did, though, and the ride keeps getting bigger. Now there's 500 who start, but only sixty percent complete the whole thing.

"It's a point-to-point ride that has great Florida crosswinds coming at you at twenty to thirty miles an hour, and the sun bears down to heat the temperature into the high nineties. Makes for some pretty interesting bicycle riding."

The cost is $20 and organizers provide support crew, aid stations every twenty miles, food, beverages, water bottle, and patch upon completion. Held on the first Sunday in May.

Information from:

Irvin Hayes
Cross Florida Ride
166 N. Atlantic Ave.
Cocoa Beach, FL 32931
(407) 783-1196

FLORIDA—Mount Dora Bicycling Festival

October 18–20, 1991. Three days of rides from 10 to 100 miles daily draw 1,700 cyclists to Mount Dora, 25 miles north of Orlando. One day features a ride to the Ocala National

Forest. Another ride goes up Thrill Hill, one of the Sunshine State's few hills, located in Mount Dora. A variety of other scenic routes are offered as well.

"We're real family oriented," said Amy Baker, executive director of the Florida Council of the American Youth Hostel. "We have a lot of couples riding tandems who come to the festival. Parents bring their children with them."

The festival cost is $75. Meals and snacks are provided. Held on the third weekend of October. Founded 1985.

Information from:

Florida American Youth Hostel
P.O. Box 533097
Orlando, FL 32853-3097
(407) 649-8761

GEORGIA—Bicycle Ride Across Georgia (BRAG)

June 16–22, 1991. The route varies each year and is known for pastoral countryside, cotton fields, peach orchards, cornfields, pine forests, and peanut fields. Itinerary in 1991 starts in Stone Mountain Park east of Atlanta and meanders southeast over secondary roads for 400 miles to Savannah on the Atlantic coast.

Sponsored by *The Atlanta Journal-Constitution* and Southern Bicycle League.

The cost is $25 for senior citizens and children; $40 for everybody else. It covers camping fees and support crew. Founded 1979.

Information from:

Jerry Colley
3675 Crestwood Parkway
Suite 340
Duluth, GA 30136-5045
(404) 564-3336

ILLINOIS—Harmon Hundred

September 8, 1991. In 1990 more than eighteen hundred cyclists rode this hundred-miler through suburban and rural Illinois northwest of Chicago. Held on the first Sunday after Labor Day, the ride is named after the late Willard Harmon, who cofounded the Wheeling Wheelmen Bicycle Club with his wife, Phyllis, in 1970, the year the ride began. Phyllis Harmon has long been active in the League of American Wheelmen and currently serves as honorary director of LAW.

"Only a handful of riders made the first hundred-miler," said club member Hans Predel. "Every year more people rode it. Broke the thousand mark around 1984 as cycling's popularity increased and mass rides started to become commonplace. Now the ride's start and finish has moved to the Wauconda Apple Orchards in Wauconda to accommodate the crowd."

The cost is $7 for pre-registration; $10 on the day of the ride. The Wheelmen provide commemorative patch, support crew, food, and beverages.

Information from:

Hans Predel
Wheeling Wheelmen
P. O. Box 581-D
Wheeling, IL 60090
(708) 748-7288

INDIANA—The Ride in Rural Indiana (TRIRI)

June 23–29, 1991. Forget Hoosier flatlands. TRIRI's route varies year to year, but it's hilly, especially in southern Indiana, where the 1979 Academy Award–winning movie *Breaking Away* was filmed.

"The movie was set in Bloomington, much of it on the Indiana University campus, and it made people think about riding in the area," said Barbara Anderson of the Bloomington Bicycle Club.

In 1991 TRIRI will start in Indianapolis, which is a level playing field, then head south for the hills all the way to the Ohio

River before turning back to conclude in Indianapolis. Total distance is approximately 500 miles. At least 225 cyclists are expected to go the distance.

The ride is sponsored by the Bloomington Bicycle Club and Indiana State Park Service.

The cost is $125 and covers camping each night in state parks, dinner and breakfast daily, support crew, T-shirt, souvenir patch, and maps. Founded 1982.

Information from:

Joe and Barbara Anderson
c/o Bloomington Bicycle Club
P.O. Box 463
Bloomington, IN 47204
(812) 332-6028

INDIANA—Hoosier Hills

June 8–9, 1991. More than 750 riders participate in this two-day event with rides out of Bloomington, ranging from fifteen to sixty-five miles on Saturday and Sunday, taking different directions each day. It's sponsored by the Bloomington Bicycle Club.

The cost is $10.50. The sponsors provide lunch daily, fanny flag, support crew, and souvenir patch. Founded 1977.

Information from:

Joe and Barbara Anderson
Same as above.

INDIANA—Ride Across Indiana (RAIN)

July 20, 1991. A 160-mile ride that begins in Terre Haute, on the Wabash River on the western border of the state and goes 160 miles east to Richmond on the eastern border abutting Ohio.

"The challenge is to cover the state in a one-day crossing," said ride director Al Abbott of the Bloomington Bicycle Club, RAIN's sponsor.

RAGBRAI 1990 poster. (Des Moines Register)

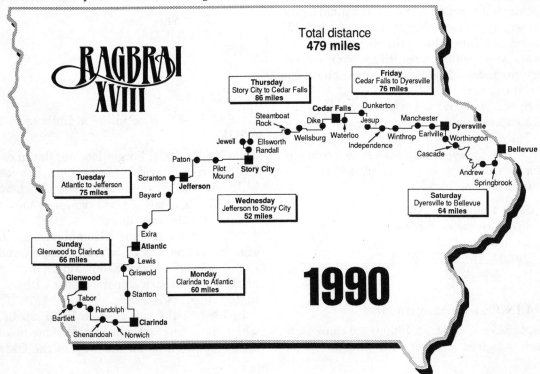

Nine people rode RAIN in 1987 when it was founded, and it has grown steadily every year. Ironically, in 1990 rain fell all day during RAIN, yet nearly all the 180 starters completed the ride, Abbott said.

The cost is $20 and covers food and drink at three stops on the route, a RAIN T-shirt, and an official RAIN coffee mug.

Information from:

Al Abbott
1153 Buckingham East
Bloomington, IN 47401
(812) 331-0708

IOWA—Register's Annual Great Bicycle Ride Across Iowa (RAGBRAI)

July 20–26, 1991. Call it The Original. This weeklong journey from the western part of the Hawkeye State to the eastern border was the first cross-state recreation ride in 1973, and has gone on to become the model for many others. But in Midwestern modesty, ride organizers issue this wry warning: "Not only could you end up with sore arms, legs, knees, and buttocks, but you may also have this strange desire to ride RAGBRAI year after year. Yes, RAGBRAI can be addictive. There is documented proof that people have been driven to use a week of their hard-earned vacation to torture themselves on a bike ride across the great state of Iowa. And in the most severe cases, people plan their entire year around RAGBRAI. Please consider these health risks before you decide to ride."

Only 7,500 of the more than 15,000 applicants are selected by lottery in April for the ride, the third week of July. As many as 2,500 more join to boost the total to 10,000 cyclists.

RAGBRAI is sponsored by *The Des Moines Register*. The $40 cost covers support crew, camping facilities, and commemorative patch.

Information from:
RAGBRAI
The Des Moines Register
P. O. Box 622
Des Moines, IA 50303
(515) 284-8282 (ask for Lois)

KENTUCKY—Old Kentucky Home Tour

September 21–22, 1991. Three routes offer 40-, 62-, and 100-mile rides from Louisville south to Bardstown, a city popular for its wide, tree-lined streets and numerous nineteenth-century houses. One is the manor house called Federal Hill, once owned by John Rowan, whose cousin Stephen Foster wrote "My Old Kentucky Home" while visiting in 1853. Cyclists pass the site on their way to camp overnight on the grounds of the Nelson County High School in Bardstown. Everybody rides the same 50-mile route back to Louisville the next morning.

More than 500 cyclists make the ride over rolling hills and farmland.

The cost is $10 and covers crew support and camping. Founded 1976. Held on the third weekend in September.

Information from:

Jim and Barbara Tretter
9004 Willowwood Way
Louisville, KY 40299
(502) 491-7120

LOUISIANA—Gator 110, Veteran's Day Bicycling Festival

November 9–10, 1991. Two days of riding from thirty to 120 miles daily in circuits from Lake Charles to the Gulf of Mexico. Five circuits offer daily rides of 30, 50, 62.5, 110, and 120 miles. Circuits take in the Gulf of Mexico shoreline and pass through a wildlife refuge replete with muskrats, opossum, raccoons, and game birds such as pheasant and quail.

"More than likely, the cyclists will see alligators in the water or sunning themselves on a riverbank," said Debbie Babaz of the marketing department of the Calcasieu Marine

Kentucky has lovely back roads that lead to Stephen Foster's Old Kentucky Home in Bardstown. (Greg Siple photo)

National Bank, ride sponsor. "That's why we call the ride the Gator 110, after the distance most popular with the cyclists."

The cost is $18 for one day, $24 for the weekend. Sponsor provides T-shirt, water bottle, and directory of events in southwest Louisiana where the ride takes place.

Information from:

Gator 110
Calcasieu Marine National Bank
P.O. Box 3402
One Lakeshore Dr.
Lake Charles, LA 70602
(318) 494-3342

MARYLAND—Cycle Across Maryland (CAM-Tour)

August 4–10, 1991. Seven days of touring from Havre de Grace in northeastern Maryland over rolling country roads in the Piedmont area south to St. Mary's City on the Chesapeake Bay. Itinerary designed for family riding, with daily mileage ranging from forty-five to sixty-two miles, including an optional spur for those who want to make it an even century on Friday, the penultimate day of the tour. Pedal past dairy farms, state parks, horse paddocks, and tobacco and cornfields. Route varies every year.

The cost is $110. It covers support crew, CAM-Tour T-shirt, nightly entertainment at each site, and camping facilities. Sponsored by the First National Bank of Maryland. Limited to 1,500 cyclists; acceptance by postmark with check and application. Founded 1989.

Information from:

CAM-Tour
P.O. Box 11299
Baltimore, MD 21239
1-800-842-BANK

MICHIGAN—Pedal Across Lower Michigan (PALM)

June 22–28, 1991. Two tours, both approximately 250 miles: One starts in Pentwater, the other in Grand Haven, both on the shore of Lake Michigan, and go east to conclude in Pinconning, the dairy town known for its yellow Pinconning cheese.

"Our tours are designed for beginners," said Doris West, the seventy-four-year-old ride director who does the cross-Michigan trip on a tricycle. "A goal is to get people to know the state and enjoy the ride. Our rides are thirty to fifty-five miles daily. The route changes year to year. This year we're finishing in Pinconning, on the shore of Saginaw Bay of Lake Huron."

The cost of $60 provides support crew, PALM T-shirt, and camping facilities. Tours are limited to 500 cyclists each. Founded 1982.

Information from:

Doris West
P.O. Box 7161
Ann Arbor, MI 48107
(313) 665-6327

MICHIGAN—Shoreline Bicycle Tour (SBT)

August 3–10, 1991. Two rides, both along the shoreline of Lake Michigan: One starts in Au Gres, near the thumb of the mitten-shape of Michigan, and the other starts in New Buffalo, at the opposite end of the state, in the northwestern corner, and both conclude with a parade in Traverse City, on Traverse Bay in northwest Michigan. Both routes are 350 miles.

"The two rides meet up in Traverse City for a parade that is like Noah's Ark—two by two," said Richard Klecka, SBT chairman. "We tie up the town for at least a half-hour. The goal of the ride is to stay as close to the shore as possible and still have a safe ride."

More than 750 cyclists did the two SBT rides in 1990. The organizer is the League of Michigan Bicyclists.

The cost is $170 and includes breakfast and dinner daily, camping facilities, support crew, and SBT T-shirt. Founded 1987.

Information from:

Richard Klecka,
SBT Chairman
P.O. Box 16201
Lansing, MI 48901
(616) 755-7335

MICHIGAN—The Dick Allen Lansing-to-Mackinac Tour (DALMAC)

Two rides: (a) August 28–September 1, 1991; and (b) August 29–September 1, 1991. Both start in Lansing and take a northbound route to the Mackinac Straits Bridge. Both groups meet to pedal together on September 1 across the bridge—listed in the *Guinness Book of World Records* as the world's longest suspension bridge, with an overall length of 3.63 miles—to St. Ignace. The bridge connects Lower Michigan to Upper Michigan.

"DALMAC started on a dare," said Doug Powell of the North Tri-County Bicycle Association, which organizes the ride. "In 1971 Dick Allen was a senator in the Michigan government and suggested that there were alternate forms of transportation that didn't use gas. Back then, riding a bicycle was for kids until they turned sixteen and got their driver's license. His colleagues were skeptical, so he responded with a dare. He said he could take riders from the state capitol in Lansing to the bridge.

"Dick Allen and a small group of others took a more direct route, 225 miles. Now the route meanders. Dick Allen is no longer in the state congress, but he comes back every year to ride DALMAC, which starts on the Wednesday before Labor Day weekend."

The cost is $100 for the five-day ride of 400 miles, $85 for the four-day ride of 350 miles. Included are support crew, breakfast and dinner daily, and camping facilities. More than 1,600 cyclists rode DALMAC in 1990.

Information from:

DALMAC
P.O. Box 17088
Lansing, MI 48901
(517) 484-3778

MICHIGAN—Ride Up Michigan (RUM)

July 6–13, 1991. Starts in Manchester, in the southeastern part of the Wolverine State, and goes north to the Mackinac Straits Bridge for a total distance of 525 miles. Ride organizer is the North Tri-County Bicycle Association.

The cost is $130 and covers support crew, breakfast and dinner for seven days. Three hundred cyclists rode the inaugural RUM ride in 1990.

Information from:

RUM
P.O. Box 17088
Lansing, MI 48901
(517) 484-3778

MINNESOTA—Minnesota Ironman

April 28, 1991. Choose either a ride of 100 miles or 100 kilometers (62.5 miles). Starts in the northwestern Minneapolis suburb of Buffalo and makes a counterclockwise loop through Wright County to return to the start. Gently rolling landscape takes cyclists through a county preserve.

"We pass close enough to Lake Woebegone that you can hear the waves lapping on the shore," said ride director Chris Gilchrist. "That's as close as we get."

The cost is $15 and it covers support crew, map, two rest stops with food and drinks. Limited to 4,000 riders. Founded in 1971 and always held on the last Sunday in April.

Information from:

Rachael & Chris Gilchrist
c/o Minnesota Council of the American
    Youth Hostels
2395 University Ave.
Suite 302
St. Paul, MN 55114
(612) 731-8714

MISSOURI—Show Me Tour

June 20–23, 1991. Four days of riding, from Kansas City northeast for 300 miles to Keokuk, Iowa, on the Mississippi. About 200 people rode the SMT in 1990. The sponsor is the Jackson County Department of Parks and Recreation.

The cost is $100. The sponsor provides crew support, camping sites, SMT T-shirts, and air-conditioned bus ride back to Kansas City. Founded 1987.

Information from:

Chris Claxton
Jackson County Parks and Recreation
22807 Woodschapel Rd.
Blue Springs, MO 64015
(816) 795-8200

MISSOURI—Midnight Ramble

2 A.M. August 11, 1991. For twenty-six years, thousands of cyclists have been taking to the streets of St. Louis for this organized ride of 10 to 20 miles through downtown streets, beginning at 2 A.M. Sunday. Ride starts at Forest Park, moves downtown, then back to the start. At dawn, everybody goes back home.

"We're the best known nighttime bike ride

in the country," proclaimed Sheri House, executive director of the Ozark Area Council of the American Youth Hostels of St. Louis which organizes the ride. "We're limiting the ride to 12,000 cyclists now. In 1989 there were 21,000 and that was too much."

The $5 fee provides T-shirt and support crew. Founded 1964.

Information from:

Sheri House,
Executive Director
Ozark Council of AYH
7187 Manchester Rd.
St. Louis, MO 63143
(314) 644-4660

MONTANA—Tour of the Swan River Valley (TOSRV-West)

May 18–19, 1991. Seven hundred cyclists pedal 110 miles from Missoula northeast in a loop that includes the Swan and Mission ranges to Swan Lake, where the population triples when they camp overnight. The next morning, the cyclists pedal back to Missoula.

TOSRV-West was founded in 1971 after the original TOSRV in Ohio. The Missoula Bicycle Club puts on TOSRV-West, held the third weekend in May.

The cost is $45 and covers eight meals, snacks, TOSRV-West T-shirt, and support crew.

Information from:

Lech Szumera
c/o MBC
P.O. Box 8903
Missoula, MT 59807
(406) 543-4889

NEBRASKA—Bicycle Ride Across Nebraska (BRAN)

June 9–15, 1991. Route varies year to year, but always goes east across the state, approximately 500 miles.

"We are limited to 500 cyclists and had to turn down 2,000 applicants in 1990," said Raymond Weinberg of the Rotary Club of Northwest Omaha, which sponsors the ride. "Application deadline is January 15."

The cost is $50. It includes support crew, BRAN T-shirt, souvenir water bottle, and BRAN guide with maps. Founded 1980.

Information from:

BRAN
c/o Rotary Club of Northwest Omaha
10730 Pacific St., No. 227
Omaha, NB 68114
(402) 397-9705

NEW HAMPSHIRE—Tri-State Seacoast Century Weekend

September 14–15, 1991. Starting in Hampton Beach State Park on the New Hampshire coast, this weekend ride offers four circuits of twenty-five to 100 miles along coastal roads, most of which are flat.

"We don't tell people what direction to go because of what the wind directions are from the ocean on a given day and the whim of the people," said Dave Topham, of the Granite State Wheelmen, who organize the ride. "It's not a race. We take in coastlines of New Hampshire, southern Maine, and a little of northern Massachusetts. That takes us past lighthouses, rocky shorelines, pine forests."

The cost is $10 daily and includes admission to the state park, League of American Wheelmen century patch, food, water bottle, and maps. Founded in 1974 and held the weekend after Labor Day.

Information from:

Dave Topham
2 Townsend Ave.
Salem, NH 03079
(603) 898-9926

NEW JERSEY—Jersey Devil Century

September 28, 1991. This ride, held on the last Saturday in September, is named after southern New Jersey's mythical devil, believed to live in the pine barrens. "The devil is supposed to have done some nefarious tricks," explained Arthur Schalick, treasurer of the South Jersey Wheelmen, the club that puts on the ride. "But southern New Jersey is a good place to ride. Lots of flat farmland, scenic, and the weather for the ride is usually always good."

The ride starts in Parvins State Park in Centerton, in the southwest part of the Garden State, and makes a figure eight. It goes fifty miles in a southern route that takes riders back to Parvins State Park for lunch. Then it's northwest for another fifty-mile route to round out an even century. More than 350 cyclists rode it in 1990.

The cost is $10 and covers a route map, marked roads at every corner, lunch, and a souvenir patch. Founded in 1977.

Information from:

South Jersey Wheelmen
c/o Arthur Schalick
P.O. Box 2705
Vineland, NJ 08360
(609) 327-1336

NEW MEXICO—The Santa Fe Century

May 19, 1991. This ride is over roads that follow the Turquoise Trail where Pueblo Indians for centuries mined the green-blue mineral. The Santa Fe Century Committee, which organizes the ride, also offers shorter routes of 25 and 50 miles, and 9 miles of dirt paths for mountain bikes.

Since the Santa Fe Century was founded in 1985, ridership has grown 30 percent a year. More than 1,000 cyclists are expected in 1991, according to ride director Willard Chilcott of the Santa Fe Century Committee.

The cost is $12 for early registration or $15 on day of ride; tandem teams are $15. The fee includes Santa Fe Century T-shirt, water bottle, route map, four rest stops with food and drink, and an extra water stop.

Information from:

Willard Chilcott
c/o Santa Fe Century Committee
885 Camino Del Este
Santa Fe, NM 87501
(505) 982-1282

NEW MEXICO—Santa Fe Trail Bicycle Trek

September 21–October 12, 1991. Follow the historic Santa Fe Trail, from Santa Fe northeast to Independence, Missouri. The original 1820s route of 780 miles, which went in the reverse direction and took 40 to 60 days by horse, is now a recreation bicycle ride of 1,040 miles in 22 days, including three off for rest and day-long sightseeing.

Daily rides range from 45 to 80 miles, with 20 miles on the final day. The route includes Las Vegas and Dodge City, passes farms and ranches, goes over prairies and mountain passes. Itinerary is laid out to leave time for walking tours and sightseeing to appreciate the trail's history.

The cost is $150 per week. It covers camping in national parks and support crew. Twenty-eight people made the inaugural ride in 1990.

Information from:

Willard Chilcott
c/o Santa Fe Trail Committee
885 Camino Del Este
Santa Fe, NM 87501
(505) 982-1282

NEW YORK—New York Ride Across the State (NYRATS)

July 27–August 4, 1991. Cyclists travel 600 miles from Buffalo southeast down the Empire State to New York City.

"It's not a hard ride," said Lawrence Van Heusen of the Mid-Hudson Bicycle Group in Poughkeepsie, which founded the ride in 1986. "The longest day is 100 miles. There are some demanding hills in the Catskill Mountains, but on the ride there are some flat sections. We ride to the American Youth Hostel office on Amsterdam Avenue in Manhattan, near Central Park."

The cost is $350. The sponsor provides accommodations in state college dormitories, fresh linen every night, support crew, RATS T-shirt, and banquet dinner the night before arriving in Manhattan. Limited to seventy-five riders.

Information from:

NYRATS
c/o AYH, Niagara Frontier Council
P.O. Box 1110
Ellicott Station
Buffalo, NY 14205
(716) 648-6272

NEW YORK—Five Borough Bike Tour

May 5, 1991. The granddaddy of the major one-day recreation rides. Back in 1982, the American Youth Hostel Five Borough Tour of New York City made the *Guinness Book of World Records* for having 17,344 riders make the thirty-six-mile route. The record for cyclists has been passed on to Montreal's Tour de l'Ile, but 20,000 still ride the Five Borough Bike Tour. It's always held on the first Sunday in May, which is International Hostel Day.

New York's ride attracts locals who take advantage of a chance to pedal on streets closed to cars. The course takes cyclists through Manhattan, Brooklyn, the Bronx,

Rain or shine, every year some 20,000 cyclists head out to pedal through New York City's five boroughs the first Sunday in May. (AYH photo)

Queens, and Staten Island, where everybody catches a ferry back to Manhattan.

"We have to limit the ride to 20,000 because we can get the streets closed to traffic for only a limited amount of time," explained Boyd Masten, deputy director for AYH of Metropolitan New York City.

The cost is $10 and includes souvenir T-shirt and reflective vest. Ride founded in 1976.

Information from:

AYH/Metropolitan New York City
891 Amsterdam Ave.
New York, NY 10025
(212) 932-2300

OHIO—Tour of the Scioto River Valley (TOSRV)

May 11–12, 1991. One of the oldest continuous recreation rides in the country, dating back to 1962. More than 6,500 cyclists pedal 105 miles from Columbus, south along the Scioto River Valley to Portsmouth on the Ohio River separating Ohio from Kentucky. Cyclists camp overnight in Portsmouth and pedal back to Columbus for a total of 210 miles. TOSRV is chiefly flat riding, with 25 miles of hills between Chillicothe and Waverly.

In 1986 TOSRV was the subject of a book, *The Mighty TOSRV*, celebrating the ride's quarter-century, by Greg Siple, who founded TOSRV with his father, Charles. The book was published by the Columbus Council of the American Youth Hostel, which organizes the ride. Greg Siple credits Charlie Pace with keeping the ride going. "Charlie has directed the event without pay since 1967 and contributed thousands of hours to it," Siple said.

The cost is $25 and includes support crew, one dinner, two lunches, five snacks, TOSRV patch, and camping in Portsmouth.

Information from:

TOSRV
Columbus Council of AYH
P.O. Box 14384
Columbus, OH 43214
(614) 447-1006

OHIO—The Great Ohio Bicycle Adventure (GOBA)

June 16–22, 1991. Seven days of riding around Ohio, averaging fifty miles a day for a total of 350 miles. The course changes from year to year.

"This is designed to be a vacation ride to visit state parks," said ride director Tom Barlow. "The 1991 ride includes an evening outdoor drama based on the life of Tecumseh, the chief of the Shawnee Indians. We also have a visit to the Serpent Indian Mound in south-central Ohio, where the Adina Indians had a 300-foot ceremonial mound shaped like a serpent."

Right from the start of the first GOBA in 1989, the ride has been popular: 1,200 rode the inaugural edition, and 2,300 rode it in 1990, Barlow said. "Some days are hilly, other days are flat," he said. "We tried to create something for everybody to hate."

The cost is $60. That pays for camp sites, crew support, entertainment in the evenings, maps, and souvenir magazine.

Information from:

Tom Barlow
GOBA director
P.O. Box 14384
Columbus, OH 43214
(614) 447-0888, or 1-800-BUCKEYE

OHIO—Tour Along the Shore of Lake Erie (TASSLE)

September 21–22, 1991. More than 2,000 cyclists participate in a variety of rides from fifty to 138 miles, starting out from Cleveland and Toledo on northern Ohio's Lake Erie shoreline.

"We take in the lakefront, which is part of the state's natural beauty," said Jim Gilford of Cleveland. "The route is rolling on the eastern end, flat on the western end. Our rides go past local wineries and include Sandusky, which is a major recreation area on Sandusky Bay."

Organizing the rides are the Lake Erie Wheelers of Cleveland, Fremont Wheelers of Fremont, Sandusky Bicycle Club, and the Toledo Bicycling Touring Society.

The $30 cost covers overnight camping, three meals, and snacks. Founded 1977.

Information from:

Jim Gilford
P.O. Box 10236
Cleveland, OH 44111
1-800-423-7447

OKLAHOMA—FreeWheel

June 9–15, 1991. Second oldest mass cross-state ride, after RAGBRAI. Has been held the second full week of June since 1978 and draws more than 2,500 cyclists.

"We change the route from year to year, but try to make it from south to north, border to border," said Libby Stalter, promotions director for *The Tulsa World Newspaper*, chief sponsor. "The people who make our ride are from eight months old to eighty-six. At least 20 percent of the people in FreeWheel are over fifty years old."

Distance usually ranges from 425 to 500 miles. "A lot of people think Oklahoma is flat and dusty, but we have some pretty good hills," Stalter said. "We have the Ouachita Mountains, a range extending from southeast Oklahoma to western Arkansas. On the flat days, the wind will get you."

A co-sponsor is Phillips Petroleum, with help from the Tulsa Wheelmen, Tulsa Bicycle Club, and Bartlesville Pedalers.

The cost is a $2 mailing fee. "That's it," Stalter said. "People pay for their meals. We provide the baggage truck, support crew, massage team."

Information from:

Libby Stalter
The Tulsa World Newspaper
P.O. Box 1770
Tulsa, OK 74102
(918) 581-8385

OREGON—The Oregon Bicycle Ride

August 16–24, 1991. When Sandy Green of Bend began cycling in 1975, she started hearing stories about RAGBRAI. "I said, 'Gee, Oregon needs something like that, and we have such good roads.'" Over the years, she learned more about cycling and made plans for an Oregon cross-state ride, which she helped introduce in 1986. She developed routes to alternate every two years.

The 1991 edition starts in Denio, Nevada, on the border with Oregon, and goes about 500 miles northwest across Oregon to Bandon, on the Pacific coast.

"There are challenges every day on the ride," Green said. "Winds are in your face, and there are two days of major climbs in the Cascade Mountain Range. You need to be pretty well trained to make this ride."

The cost is $235 and includes breakfast and dinner daily, support crew, shower system, and Oregon Bicycle Ride jersey. Limit of 250 riders.

Information from:

Sandy Green
1324 N.W. Vicksburg
Bend, OR 97701
(503) 382-0740

OREGON—Cycle Oregon

September 8–14, 1991. More than 2,000 riders pedal 350 miles on a north-to-south tour of Oregon, over a new course every year. Susan Bladholm of the State Tourism Division in Salem said the itinerary has a variety of landscape from desert to mountains, past mint fields, dairy farms, nickel mines, apple and cherry orchards, and fields of boysenberries and blackberries.

Cycle Oregon has a reputation for unusual touches. In the 1990 edition, which went 420 miles, riders came from forty states. They put up with temperatures that rose to more than 100 degrees in the desert, and fell to 28 degrees while crossing the Cascades. On the final day, the sky opened up and poured rain.

But everyone had a grand time by then. Small towns on the route made the ride special. In Fossil, which has 500 residents, police closed two streets to traffic for a beer garden and street dance. The town of Sisters opened a llama ranch for camping. In the town of Antelope, formerly Rashneesh Puram, the forty-seven residents cut up thousands of vegetables and greeted riders with sandwiches for a lunch break when they reached town. Riders woke up in the city of Corvallis to belly dancers who got the show on the road with a whole lot of shaking at 5:45 A.M.

The cost is $250 and includes twenty-one meals, camp sites, support crew, and Cycle Oregon IV T-shirt. Founded 1988.

Information from:

Susan Bladholm
Public Relations & Special Events
   Coordinator
Oregon Tourism Division, Economic
   Department
775 Summer St., N.E.
Salem, OR 97310
1-800-547-7842

RHODE ISLAND—The Flatest Century in the East

September 15, 1991. Some 1,750 cyclists pedal 25, 50, or 100 miles on flat roads along the coast of Rhode Island and Massachusetts. Organizing the ride out of Tiverton, in southeastern Rhode Island, is the Narragansett Bay Wheelmen.

"We go on secondary roads through black pine forests, past cranberry bogs, and marshlands," said ride director Clark Richardson. "We usually have 1,500 who ride the century, another 250 riding twenty-five or fifty miles."

The cost is $20 and covers crew support, food, and T-shirt. Founded 1972.

Information from:

Clark Richardson
NBW-TFCE
P.O. Box 428
Tiverton, RI 02878
(401) 434-2385

TENNESSEE—Bicycle Ride Across Tennessee (BRAT)

September 22–28, 1991. This six-day recreation ride sponsored by the Tennessee State Parks averages sixty miles a day. Each year the ride covers a new route. The 1991 edition will start in the Reelfoot Lake State Park in Tiptonville—in the northwest corner of the state, on the Mississippi near the border of Missouri and Kentucky—and go east about 440 miles to the middle of the Volunteer State. BRAT finishes in Standing Stone Park, north of Cookeville.

"The first five days cover gently rolling secondary roads," said BRAT coordinator Jim Hammontree. "But the last two days are hillier and demanding. The route takes in a lot of the state's backroads. We go past corn and soybean fields, a Mennonite community, and a lot of dairy farms."

The cost is $50. It covers camping in state parks, support crew, and BRAT T-shirt. Limited to 500, although Hammontree says, "We've never turned anyone away." Founded in 1986.

Information from:

BRAT
c/o Tennessee State Parks
Program Services Section
Division of Parks & Recreation
701 Broadway
Nashville, TN 37243-0046
(615) 742-6675

TEXAS—Hotter'n Hell Texas Hundred

August 24, 1991. Held on the Saturday nine days before Labor Day, this ride was founded in 1982 to commemorate the centenary of Wichita Falls. More than just a ride, the Hotter'n Hell Hundred turns Wichita Falls into a 1960s-style "happening," prompting its nickname "Woodstock on Wheels."

It all starts on the Thursday evening before the ride, when the Wichita Falls Activities Center opens with a consumer show that draws more than sixty exhibitors. The show is steps away from where cyclists pick up their ride packets or squeeze in a late registration. Friday night features a spaghetti feed in the Activities Center where thousands devour acres of complex carbohydrates. On Saturday morning at 7:30, some 12,000 cyclists roll out for the annual ride. They start in the center of town and pedal counterclockwise over Wichita Falls county roads to finish in Memorial Stadium.

Being Texas in August, it's always hot—in the upper 90s—with winds up to thirty miles an hour. That's part of the challenge. For cyclists not up to going the whole distance, there are four alternative routes from six to sixty-two miles.

Some cyclists want more than just a challenge. For them, the Wichita Falls Bicycling Club introduced a program of races in 1989. Seven categories of U.S. Cycling Federation competition for men and women offer a total purse of $10,000. Six races are held over a flat downtown circuit, around a course eight-tenths of a mile long that is T-shaped and features eight ninety-degree turns every lap. Professionals and top amateurs also compete in the 100-mile route. They start on the century course fifteen minutes before the recreation riders.

Wichita Falls offers something for every cyclist. A regiment of 2,500 volunteers help make it happen. Afterward, a television broadcast of the day's events reaches 20 million households, according to ride organizers.

Cyclists from forty states and at least five countries regularly make the ride.

Registration is $15 for individuals, $12 each for a family discount of three or more living in the same household. Registration provides a ride number, souvenir T-shirt, and cycling entertainment all day.

Information from:

Hotter'n Hell Hundred
Wichita Falls Bicycling Club
P.O. Box 2099
Wichita Falls, TX 76307
Hotline (817) 692-2925

UTAH—Tour of Southern Utah's National Parks

September 8–14, 1991. Starts in Cedar City, in southwestern Utah, and makes a 230-mile loop to take in Bryce Canyon National Park, Zion National Park, and Cedar Breaks National Monument by the time riders return to Cedar City.

"We take time to explore the national parks," said ride organizer Carl Ehrman. "That's the main purpose of the ride."

The cost is $85 and covers park entry fees, camping sites, meals, and crew support. Limited to forty-five cyclists.

Information from:

Carl Ehrman
3247 Bon View Dr.
Salt Lake City, UT 84109
(801) 278-9386

VIRGINIA—Bike Virginia, Shenandoah Valley Odyssey

June 21–26, 1991. Virginia, the Old Dominion State, has a statewide fun ride, averaging fifty miles daily, with extensions for those who want to add miles. See Virginia by the seat of your pants.

Bike Virginia features routes over winding backroads with scenery and considerable history. The 1990 route went through the George Washington National Forest where old oaks gave leafy shade from the sun.

Ride coordinator Martha Edwards said the 1991 ride is scheduled for about 1,000 cyclists. "We had a limit of 500 in 1990, and we had to turn away about 100," she said. "We organized a bigger ride for 1991."

The 1990 ride assembled in Berryville, the end of the route, where a shuttle bus took riders south to the start in Lexington, a town famous for the graves of Civil War Generals Robert E. Lee and Stonewall Jackson. From Lexington, the course went north fifty miles to Staunton, birthplace of President Woodrow Wilson and home of the country singers the Statler Brothers. The route kept going north through Winchester, hometown of Patsy Cline. Her recordings of "I Fall to Pieces," "Crazy," and "She's Got You," are standards.

The cost is $95 and includes campsites, support, maps, guides, souvenir T-shirt, and water bottle. Founded 1988.

Information from:

Martha Edwards
P.O. Box 203
Williamsburg, VA 23185
(804) 229-0507

WASHINGTON—Mount Rainier Tour

October 4–6, 1991. This three-day tour, held annually on the first weekend in October, makes a 165-mile circuit around Mount Rainier, the 14,408-foot peak in western Washington's Cascade Range, one of the highest summits in the United States.

"It's probably one of the nicest scenery rides in the country," said Peter Maas, of the Northwest Touring Society, which organizes the tour. "You're cycling through Mount Rainier National Park, which has a wealth of Douglas fir trees, and you ride up roads that give such a spectacular view. You feel you've got the mountain in your lap."

Starting in Enumclaw, at an altitude of 800 feet, cyclists pedal 65 miles the first day, up to 5,700 feet to Paradise, appropriately named for its wealth of fir and maple trees. On the first night, the group of riders splits to sleep in either Alexander's Inn or Mount Haven Cabins. The second day features more climbing. Riders spend much of the fifty miles that day toiling in their lowest gear, but enjoy occasional downhills and miles of winding roads that meander past waterfalls, trees with trunks that measure fifteen feet in circumference, and spectacular views overlooking valleys. Their second night is spent camping on the Ohanapecosh campground.

On the final day, riders roll over undulating roads that lead to Cayuse Pass, at 5,300 feet. All that climbing has been like depositing gravity in a bank: From Cayuse it's downhill for forty-five miles as cyclists withdraw their investment all the way back to Enumclaw.

The cost for the tour is $90. It includes accommodations (tent required for second night), two breakfasts and two catered dinners, support crew, park-entry fees, and maps. Tour limit is seventy. Founded 1974.

Information from:

Peter or Hannelore Maas
18249 SE 147th Place
Renton, WA 98059
(206) 255-4192

WASHINGTON—Seattle-to-Portland

June 29–30, 1991. Best known by its acronym, STP, this 205-mile ride from Seattle south to Portland draws 10,000 people on the weekend with the longest daylight of the year.

Most of the ride is flat and follows valley floors through rural farmland. "On a nice day, there is a constant view of the mountains," said one of the ride's founders, Josh Lehman. "From the start there is Mount Rainier. Then there is Mount St. Helens, Mount Adams, and Mount Hood. They are like towering sentinels."

About one-third of the 10,000 riders take advantage of the flatness of the route to make the ride in one day, said Dave Shaw of Seattle. "For a double century," he said, "it doesn't get much easier."

The other 7,000 or so camp in towns along the midpoint. Centralia, Cehalis, and Winlock are overrun with tents and people, Shaw said.

Lehman, who afterward moved across the country to the Boston suburb of Beverly, helped found the event in 1979 when he worked for the City of Portland's Department of Transportation. "I thought of the American Youth Hostel bike trains I used to participate in when I lived in New York in the early 1960s," he said. "A group of us took a bike train from New York City out to the end of Long Island. We rode our bikes around back roads, then took the train back. It seemed like the sort of fun group-ride that would work in the Northwest."

After Lehman suggested the ride to friends, the idea grew. About 100 people made the first ride in 1979. When Mount Helens erupted May 18, 1980, and threw volcanic ash for many miles, the ride was canceled and its future questioned. But in 1981 STP resumed and gained stature. It kept growing until STP was capped in the late 1980s at 10,000.

The Cascade Bicycle Club organizes STP. Registration opens the third week of February and stays open until May 1 or the ride limit is reached.

Cost is $35 for club members; $40 for non-members. The cost includes bus transportation for riders and bikes from the finish in Portland back to Seattle.

Information from:

Cascade Bicycle Club
P.O. Box 31299
Seattle, WA 98103
(206) 298-8222

WISCONSIN—Great Annual Bicycle Adventure Along the Wisconsin River (GRABAR)

June 29–July 6, 1991. Cyclists meet on June 29th in Prairie du Chien, in southwest Wisconsin on the bank of the Mississippi, near Iowa, and take a seven-hour bus ride north to Land O'Lakes at the opposite end of the state, next to Michigan's Upper Peninsula. The next day cyclists begin pedaling 500 miles south to Prairie du Chien.

"The course is rolling in the north, where we go through a lot of pine forests," said ride director Bill Hauda. "Central Wisconsin is flat and sandy. We ride past a lot of crop farms. Southern Wisconsin gets rolling again, and the ride goes past a lot of dairy farms."

The cost is $125 and covers bus transportation to Land O'Lakes, support crew during the ride, and camping facilities. Limited to 750 cyclists. Founded 1986.

Information from:

Bill Hauda
16 N. Carroll St.
Suite 310
Madison, WI 53703
(608) 256-2686

WISCONSIN—Hidden Valley Ride

July 8–13, 1991. Hidden Valley in southwest Wisconsin got its name from the Blackhawk Indians who sought refuge there in the 1830s when the Illinois militia drove them out. "Young Abraham Lincoln was a captain in the Illinois militia that went up into Hidden Valley, but he said he never saw any Indians in the seven months he spent there," explained ride director Mel Welch. "There's a lot of hills and valleys and rivers in southwestern Wisconsin, which was still a territory after Illinois became a state in 1818."

The peace pipe was smoked between the Indians and settlers by the time Wisconsin

Cyclists ride forty miles around Montréal in the Tour de l'Ile to celebrate the start of summer weather the first Sunday in June every year. (Jean-François Béreubé photo/ Tour de l'Ile de Montréal)

was granted statehood in 1848. Today cyclists enjoy a peaceful ride through Hidden Valley. They start at the University of Wisconsin campus in White Water in the southeastern corner of the Badger State and pedal west across the state to Dubuque, Iowa. The route takes a swing through Galena, Illinois, returns to Wisconsin, and goes back to White Water for a round trip of 360 miles.

The cost is $160 and includes all meals and accommodations in college dorms. Ride founded in 1986 as a weekend trip. In 1990 it was expanded into a weeklong ride and drew seventy cyclists.

Information from:

Mel Welch
3632 West Maple St.
Milwaukee, WI 53215
(414) 383-5563

CANADA

MONTREAL—Tour de l'Ile

June 9, 1991. TOSRV may be the oldest continuous annual recreation ride in the United

States, RAGBRAI may be the largest cross-state event, but the Tour de l'Ile is the biggest recreation ride of them all: it draws three times TOSRV and RAGBRAI combined. In 1990, 38,000 cyclists rode forty miles around Montréal to make the Tour de l'Ile the record holder for largest mass recreation ride, topping the tour's previous record of 36,000 in 1989. That is more than double the 17,344 participants in the 36-mile Citibank-AYH Five Borough Tour (Manhattan, Brooklyn, Staten Island, the Bronx, and Queens) of New York City in April 1982, which went into the *Guinness Book of World Records* as the largest bicycle ride.

The Tour de l'Ile derives its name from Montréal's position as a city on an island in the St. Lawrence. Montréal is the largest city in Canada, with about 1.5 million population. It is also the second-largest French-speaking city in the world, although most of its people speak English as well. The city lies at the foot of Mount Royal and has a harbor on the St. Lawrence Seaway. Cyclists ride a serpentine route around the city to explore the diversity of its neighborhoods.

The cost is $15 and includes an official rider's bib, support crew, and a snack of milk and cheese. Held on the first Sunday in June to celebrate the start of summer weather, which means a lot that far north. Founded in 1985.

Information from:

Tour de l'Ile
Suite 310
Montréal, Quebec
H2X 2T7
Canada
(514) 847-8687

TOUR COMPANIES

For a little more money, and considerably greater comfort, private cycling tour companies have been proliferating. Companies that provide tours offer a wide variety of venues over traffic-free back roads and through towns and cities that are tourist attractions. These tours typically range from weekends to ten days each. They feature challenging yet satisfying rides, allow enough time daily to enjoy the sights, and at the end of the day's ride reward riders with fine restaurants. All this helps make for convivial company around the dining table.

For those who seek a cycling vacation yet don't have a bicycle, or don't want to travel with theirs, touring companies often either provide bicycles or have ones to rent. During the rides, mechanics and support crew accompany the cyclists. Many touring companies have catalogs and brochures that are compelling enough to inspire a reader to plan a vacation early to have something to look forward to.

More information is available from:

Vermont Bicycle Touring (The
   Original)
Box 711-JG
Bristol, VT 05433
(802) 453-4811

Bike Wisconsin Ltd.
P.O. Box 3461
Madison, WI 53704
(608) 249-4490

Backroads Bicycle Touring
1516 Fifth St.
Suite S1
Berkeley, CA 94710-1713
(415) 527-1555

Classic Bicycle Tours
P.O. Box 668
Clarkson, NY 14430
(716) 637-5970

Breakaway Vacations
164 E. 90th St. #2Y
New York, NY 10128
(212) 722-4221

Euro-Bike Tours
P.O. Box 40-L
De Kalb, IL 60115
(815) 758-8851

Gerhard's Bicycle Odysseys
P.O. Box 756
Portland, OR 97207
(503) 223-2402

Pocono White-Water Adventures
Route 903-L
Jim Thorpe, PA 18229
(717) 325-3656

Bicycle Adventures
Dept. L
P.O. Box 7875
Olympia, WA 98507
(206) 786-0989

CANUSA Cycle Tours
9932 Maplecreek Dr., S.E.
Calgary, Alberta T2J 1T6
Canada
(403) 560-5859

Cycle Portugal
Box 877
San Antonio, FL 34266
1-800-245-4226

Cycle Swiss Alpine
P.O. Box 2216
Winchester, VA 22601
1-800-326-2728 daytime, (703)
    662-3255 evenings

Island Bicycle Adventures
Dept. C
569 Kapahulu
Honolulu, HI 96815
1-800-734-0700

CHAPTER 3

BICYCLE RACING: AN AMERICAN TRADITION

ON THE final day of the 1989 Tour de France, Greg LeMond raced the perfect ride up the Champs-Elysées in Paris to the finish by the Arc de Triomphe. He raced faster than anyone ever in the eighty-six-year-old event to overcome a fifty-second deficit behind French rival Laurent Fignon and win the 2,025-mile race by eight seconds (about 100 yards).

LeMond, already a superstar in Europe for his previous Le Tour victory in 1986 and the world road-racing championship in 1983, was featured on page one of newspapers across the United States. ABC Television, which broadcast coverage of the three-week July event, named him "Person of the Week" and televised a five-minute documentary on the athlete, who lives in the Minneapolis suburb of Wayzata, during a prime-time evening newscast. He became a household name and catapulted bicycle racing to prominence.

LeMond concluded the season by cap-turing his second world championship, in Chambéry, France. President George Bush invited him to lunch at the White House. *Sports Illustrated*, which had already featured him on the cover for his Le Tour triumph, now concluded the year with LeMond again on the cover as "Sportsman of the Year."

Americans were being inundated with LeMond, the celebrity cyclist, but bicycle racing, second only to soccer internationally in popularity, was still considered a minor sport in the United States. A San Francisco newspaper columnist complained in print that nobody had ever heard of bicycle racing.

Yet the sport is one of the country's oldest, with annual national amateur championships dating back to 1882, a decade before basketball was invented. In the 1890s, cycling enjoyed tremendous popularity and led the way in professional sports. Top racing cyclists were headliners for decades. People

Greg LeMond guts it out on a climb up Luz Ardiden in the 1990 Tour de France. (Beth Schneider photo)

dressed up to watch track events. Champions were treated like heroes. Until Babe Ruth began hitting his peak years in the early 1920s, the best-paid athletes in the country were bicycle racers. LeMond won his third Tour de France in 1990 to generate a new round of media exposure. His success and celebrity status have a dimension of *déjà vu*.

When major-league baseball legends like Christy Mathewson and Ty Cobb were earning $5,000 a year, their counterparts in cycling such as Major Taylor, Bobby Walthour, Sr., and Frank Kramer each were getting more than four times the money. Most Americans today think of Jackie Robinson as the

first black athlete to cross the color line in professional sports when he integrated the Brooklyn Dodgers in 1947. But nearly a half-century earlier, Major Taylor won the world professional sprint championship as well as the U.S. title. Promoters in France and Australia were paying him $5,000 in appearance fees to visit their country and compete. Race purses were generous. Winners were amply rewarded.

Taylor came from Indianapolis, where his father worked as a coachman for a wealthy family who had a son Taylor's age. His early years were spent as a playmate to the privileged son. They wore identical tailored clothes and shared a live-in tutor. Taylor grew up accustomed to expressing his views, eating with silver cutlery on damask table linen, and being treated as an equal in an aristocratic white household.

When he took up bicycle racing in the early 1890s, Taylor showed promise. He was winning races around the Midwest, as far away as Peoria and St. Louis. Then the sport exploded in popularity. Bicycle races were not just athletic events but big entertainment in those days before mass communications.

Taylor went east for the big events where he caught the attention of the swaggering promoter Billy Brady. When Taylor was a rising amateur in the Midwest, Brady was managing world champion boxer Jim Corbett. Brady had powerful connections in the sports world and lobbied on Taylor's behalf to get him a license to turn professional in late 1896. Brady became Taylor's manager and negotiated shrewdly on his behalf.

At the 1899 world cycling championships in Montreal, Taylor beat an international field to win the prestigious one-mile world professional sprint championship. The following year he triumphed in race after race and captured the U.S. national title. Promoters overseas made him offers he couldn't refuse. Taylor left the United States and

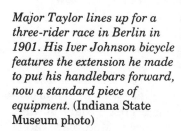

Major Taylor lines up for a three-rider race in Berlin in 1901. His Iver Johnson bicycle features the extension he made to put his handlebars forward, now a standard piece of equipment. (Indiana State Museum photo)

wound up spending most of the decade abroad—in France, Belgium, Italy, Germany, England, and Australia—until he retired at thirty-two in 1910. Brady left cycling to become one of Broadway's biggest producers.

Taylor's worst adversary was racial prejudice, a factor that contributed to his overseas campaigns and his relatively early retirement. In Europe and Australia he was treated with adulation and enjoyed first-class accommodations. But American society was racially segregated; few hotels and restaurants even let him in the lobby. As Taylor's career progressed, the strain of being a black man in white America affected him more every year until he retired.

His impressive record at top international cycling, his world championship, and world records make Taylor arguably one of America's greatest cyclists. Two of his rivals who won world championships, set world records, and competed successfully in the United States and Europe also merit consideration for being among America's greatest cyclists, leaving wheelmarks for LeMond to follow: Bobby Walthour, Sr. and Frank Kramer.

* * *

Then, as now, top cyclists were making more for capturing a single big event than a typical worker earned in a year. At the turn of the century, the average salary was $500. Walthour, with his partner, Archie McEachern, made that much in the opening hours of the December 1901 six-day race in New York's Madison Square Garden. They beat a sterling international field, which helped increase the bonuses that product sponsors paid Walthour for riding a particular brand of wheels, saddle, and make of bicycle. Walthour and McEachern won the six-day after riding 2,555 miles—420 miles farther than the 1990 Tour de France that LeMond rode in 21 days.

"All told," *The New York Times* related in tabulating total race winnings, "Walthour will make $4,000." Converted to today's purchasing power, that prize money amounts to more than $52,000.

Walthour, not quite twenty-three years old in 1901, was still on his way up. He had a devoted following. Legend has it that his elopement on a tandem bicycle with Daisy Bailey inspired the song "Daisy, Daisy," sometimes called "A Bicycle Built for Two."

The cyclist came from a genteel Georgian

family near Savannah, where the town itself was named after the family: Walthourville (population today is about 30,000). Cycling ran in the family. His brother, Palmer, founded a distributorship of bicycles and parts shortly after the turn of the century. Walthour-Hood, Inc., remained one of the country's oldest cycling distributorships until it went out of business in 1986. Bobby Walthour's identical twin brother, Jim, lacked his competitive zip, but was a highly skilled stunt rider who made a comfortable living on the vaudeville circuit.

Cycling drew young Bobby to Atlanta, where he worked as a bicycle messenger. In

Bobby Walthour, Sr. and Greg LeMond are the only U.S. cyclists ever to win two world professional championships in the glamorous but dangerous motorpace event. (Continental Tire Company photo)

an Atlanta meet in 1893, the fourteen-year-old cheerfully entered the boys' event and the five men's events. He won them all. By age eighteen he had turned professional and followed the sport's migratory flow to the Northeast, where promoters like Brady organized races that paid the best money.

Walthour was a versatile rider. He teamed with Bennie Munroe of Memphis in 1903 to win the Madison Square Garden six-day. His most impressive riding was in motorpace racing, in which a cyclist pedals at high speed behind a motorcycle. Motorpace racers dazzled audiences, although it was dangerous riding, especially in those days before helmets or even gloves for protection in a crash.

A French promoter invited him to race there for the 1904 season. Taylor had turned down the invitation after he returned from competing in Australia for the winter season and stayed at his home in Worcester, Massachusetts. Walthour showed he was a worthy alternate. He won sixteen straight motorpace races and attracted an enthusiastic following. At the world championships late in the summer in London, he sped ahead of a field of riders from seventeen countries in the 62.5-mile motorpace event to win his first world championship.

The next year, at the world's in Antwerp, Belgium, he won his second world motorpace title. Over the next twelve years, he enjoyed tremendous popularity all across Europe, where he dominated motorpace racing. In the winter months, he returned to the United States to compete in the indoor six-day circuit.

His career at the top of the sport ended in a spectacular crash in Paris in the summer of 1917. During a motorpace race, the front tire blew on his bicycle, throwing him to the cement track where other riders and motorcycles ran over him. His head, legs, and arms looked as though he had been blasted by an artillery shell.

Bobby Walthour, Jr., followed his father's wheelmarks and became national champion. Here he rides a Dayton bicycle with a Major Taylor extension. (Russell Mamone collection)

Newspaper stories in this country and across Europe were as grim as obituaries as they carried updates on Walthour's recovery. It was nearly Thanksgiving before he was released from the hospital and boarded a steamship to take him back to his family in Newark.

Walthour was an iron man. He recovered sufficiently enough for promoters to induce him back to cash in on his name at the Madison Square Garden six-day that December. He was beaten by younger riders, and it was apparent that he was past his prime. The Garden's crowds, who had joyously cheered

victories of his youth, were jeering him. He didn't finish.

In the audience that day was fourteen-year-old Bobby Walthour, Jr. He turned to his mother and vowed to become a champion and beat the riders lapping his father. And he did just that. In 1921 he won the national amateur championship. Young Walthour, known as "Creampuff" for his straw-blond hair, promptly turned professional to follow his father's career.

When Walthour, Jr., was national amateur champion, Frank Kramer reigned as professional champion for the eighteenth time. Kramer, forty-one, had compiled a career that puts him in the same pantheon as the elder Walthour, and he is arguably a fair rival for the title of America's greatest-ever cyclist.

Kramer was a native of Evansville, Indiana, and grew up in Newark. He took up cycling in 1896 as a skinny teenager. He filled out to a deep-chested power sprinter, five feet eleven inches tall, the same height as Walthour, Sr., but weighed 180 pounds, twenty pounds more than Walthour. In 1898 and 1899 Kramer won the national amateur championship. He was content to remain an amateur until after a Philadelphia meet in late 1899. Taylor brandished a roll of money he had won and told Kramer that he was silly to ride amateur when he was fast enough to make it in the cash ranks. Taylor was right. The next year the two Hoosiers were rivals for the professional title, which Taylor won.

Kramer improved, and in 1901 Taylor shipped out to compete in Europe. That year Kramer won the national title and started his remarkable string of American national professional championships. Foreign riders challenged him for the title year after year. They took reports of his speed and tactical savvy across the Atlantic. Kramer was offered a lucrative contract to compete in France for the early portion of the 1905 season.

One of the premier European track events was—and remains today—the Grand Prix de Paris, a program of May races on the Parc des Princes in Paris that culminated in a one-mile sprint final. It was considered as important as the world championships held later in the summer. At the Grand Prix, Kramer reached the final against two Frenchmen, Gabriel Poulain and Emile Friol, both world champions. More than 30,000 spectators paid to watch the American champion against the French champions.

It was a dynamic race with a close finish, and Kramer edged out his opponents at the line. The French celebrated his triumph with gusto. They fêted him at a state dinner that night and made him the guest of honor. When called upon to make the first speech of his life, one he was to deliver through an interpreter, he lost his composure. A quiet, modest man, Kramer was thrust into the spotlight without his bicycle and discovered that speechmaking, even when it involved only a few gracious remarks about his hosts and his opponents, required a tremendous effort. He was still recovering three days later when he lost his next race. Nevertheless, Kramer eventually recovered his composure and concluded his European trip with fourteen victories in twenty-three starts.

In 1906 Kramer returned to Paris and again captured the Grand Prix de Paris. He enjoyed another successful trip to France and Belgium, and returned to win another national U.S. title.

Year after year, Kramer was perennial national champion. Those titles, however, were not always determined in a clear-cut manner. Often they were held in the best vaudeville custom of playing to the house. National championships were determined over a series of events during the season. Points were awarded to the top four finishers in five designated events from the quarter-mile to five miles. When the crown was closely contested and spectators flocked to the tracks in large numbers to pay admission and watch, promoters took advantage and arbitrarily declared the championship series would be repeated—once or twice more, depending on ticket sales.

National professional championships grew out of the mid-1890s when enthusiasm for cycling bordered on making it a national pastime. Way back when basketball was just starting to catch on, cyclists were competing for a number of professional titles. Some were held on dirt horse-tracks, others on cycling tracks made of asphalt, cement, or wood. Promoters held races on tracks to conveniently charge admission, and crowds liked watching the races in which they could follow the action from their seats.

In winter months there was the national indoor championship on short tracks with steep banking, usually ten to twelve laps to the mile. Jay Eaton of Newark was dubbed "King of the Indoor Tracks" for winning indoor titles regularly in the late 1890s. When the weather improved and the venue moved outdoors, there was the national handicap championship. This was the province of a tall Californian named Floyd MacFarland. He became a hero for the way he thrilled audiences by catching all competitors who had head starts and then outsprinting them to the line. Most prestigious of all was the national sprint championship, especially the national professional title, which became the emblem of the sport.

Eddie Bald of Buffalo reigned among the pros as national sprint champion from 1895 to 1897. He retired at age thirty with enough capital to open a car distributorship in Pittsburgh. Tom Cooper of Detroit won the title in 1899 and funded Henry Ford.

These titles were as much for the marquee value to entice spectators and enhance the gate as they were to reward the riders. Bicycle races were exciting entertainment, with a program of twenty to thirty amateur and professional events. Audiences would roar their lungs out to cheer their favorites in close contests.

Most outdoor tracks were six elliptical laps to the mile, with steep banks and gently sloped straights. They featured a band in the infield that played popular tunes between heats. We get a feeling for the atmosphere from John Held, Jr., who later became an illustrator and a leading interpreter of the jazz age. He grew up in Salt Lake City, where races were held on Tuesday and Friday evenings before packed houses. Held was the bandleader's son and got into the races in return for lugging the concert sheets for the fifty-piece orchestra in a large leather portmanteau.

"The parts for a full band for an evening's concert in most cases weighed more than I did at the time," Held wrote in his memoir, "but my custodianship of the sheet music always admitted me to the races. The 'Echo Quartet' was a feature of these concerts. Dad was also very fond of a composition called 'My Creole Sue,' and he would beat the living bejesus out of it on his coronet."

Races remained a big draw, especially in the Northeast, where Kramer emerged as a consistent winner. He liked being a champion and was careful not to squander his talent.

Kramer's consistency made him a headliner. His fans formed long lines to buy tickets at tracks where he was scheduled to race in Newark, Boston, New York City, Providence, Philadelphia, and other cities. He was making at least $20,000 a year, which made him the best-paid athlete in the country when Taylor retired.

American racing got a real boost at the end of the first decade of the twentieth century when Floyd MacFarland retired from competition and took over as the country's foremost promoter. He was innovative and pumped vitality into race programs. When he wanted to infuse enthusiasm among spectators in

cities where he put on races, he announced a national championship event was coming. He promised the press that Frank Kramer would be there.

Championship races were the quarter-mile, half-mile, one-mile, two-mile, and five-mile, with points of 5, 3, 2, and 1 for the top four finishers. Consistent with track events everywhere, there were qualifier heats, semifinals, and the final. Depending on how the athletes were doing and what the audiences were like, MacFarland would have finals with four riders, sometimes three, even just two. These were bicycle races, but they also were show biz.

And business was good. First prize at the races started out at $50 when Kramer turned professional, then doubled to $100 by the end of the decade. This was when a nickel beer entitled a patron to a free lunch in any saloon.

In the spirit of show business as well as a reflection of America's standing among cycling nations, the world championships were held in September 1912 in Newark. Early in the spring, Kramer went to Europe and had a good campaign. He came back to win the national championship and the world professional championship; he remains the last U.S. rider to win that title.

The next year he returned a fourth time to France, where he won all ten races he entered. In Paris he enjoyed his biggest one-day stakes: $2,250. Kramer returned to the United States to win his thirteenth consecutive national championship.

But the timing of when the championship races would be held was left to MacFarland, who used them as a trump card. Championship races were not events around which riders could plan their season.

In 1914, for example, Alf Goullet was leading Kramer in points. This was the first time that Kramer's hold on the national title was threatened. Goullet was a native of Australia who had emigrated at age nineteen in

Frank Kramer is all grins after winning the world professional sprint championship in 1912 in Newark. He remains the last U.S. rider to win the title. (U.S. Bicycling Hall of Fame photo)

1910 to race professionally in America. Mac-Farland was fond of Goullet. They had traveled together to compete around Europe during the winter of 1912–13, and MacFarland had managed Goullet. But MacFarland wanted to protect Kramer's streak. MacFarland arranged for Goullet to travel from Newark to Boston on the train to compete in a Saturday-night card.

"The next morning, MacFarland announced two championship events were on for Newark that afternoon," recalls Goullet, who lives in Red Bank, New Jersey. "When I got on the track, I was so worn out from the previous day's travel and racing, I couldn't get out of my own way."

Kramer won both events and leapfrogged in points over Goullet. MacFarland announced that they were the final championship races of the season, which closed with Kramer's fourteenth straight title.

If MacFarland was manipulative, he was also temperamental. The next spring he was fatally stabbed in a trivial argument.

His successor was John M. Chapman, who came from Georgia and had a vastly different managerial style. Where MacFarland was imaginative, Chapman was cautious but autocratic. But they agreed on the value of featuring Kramer, America's national champion.

"Kramer was a very big draw, no question about that," Goullet points out. "He looked good on the bike, could sprint well, was a true champion in every sense of the word. He could do a full quarter-mile at top speed. Easily. He was awfully hard to beat."

For the national championship, Kramer was even harder to beat, as Chapman sought to protect him. Chapman manipulated the races that scored for the title. When Kramer broke ahead in points, the championship races were cut off; when he trailed, the championship series was repeated, with more frequent races that suited Kramer against particular rivals.

Yet there was no complaining among the riders. Kramer was the people's choice. His presence filled the stands. Steady attendance meant steady prize money.

But in 1917 Kramer faltered and finally was defeated by Arthur Spencer, the burly sprinter from Toronto. "Kramer took the defeat pretty well," recalls Goullet, who finished second to Spencer. "Arthur was strictly a short-distance sprinter. He could put in a good eighth-mile."

Kramer, much to the delight of his fans, came back to win the 1918 title. When he got ahead on points, Chapman declared the championship series was over, although there still was a lot of other racing in the season.

Ray Eaton, whose father had ruled indoor racing in the late 1890s, came of age and won the national title in 1919. Kramer was still packing the stands, and first prize doubled that year to $200.

Kramer won his last title in 1921, having garnered eighteen national professional championships. He retired midway through the next season at forty-two, with earnings of more than $400,000—megabucks for athletes at the time.

National championships were never the same after Kramer. Eleven riders succeeded him before World War II dealt professional cycling a serious blow, but none replaced him. No national champion has played to the house like Kramer.

Bobby Walthour, Jr. stayed in his father's wheelmarks. He trounced the pros who had beaten his dad. On the way, he became a champion six-day racer. Walthour and his partner, Fred Spencer of Rahway, New Jersey, were so popular that President Calvin

Alf Goullet, left, Ray Eaton, and Frank Kramer line up for a quarter-mile race on the Newark Velodrome in 1920. (U.S. Bicycling Hall of Fame photo)

Coolidge invited them to the White House following the early December 1925 six-day in Madison Square Garden.

The day after meeting with President Coolidge, Walthour and his fiancée, Margaret Murray, drove to Georgia and eloped, as his parents had.

In 1929, however, the stock market crashed. The following year, the country plunged into the Depression. Bicycle racing had thrived for five decades, but professional cycling was in a downward spiral in the 1930s.

Over the ensuing years, the achievements and heroics of the Walthours, Kramer, and Taylor faded. Even legends are evanescent. But now that LeMond is leading a new generation of U.S. cyclists in international competition, renewed interest in American cycling is reviving the hard-earned reputations of champions past. They finally can take their places with today's champions, who are keeping up a rich American tradition.

In American bicycle racing, four families stand out for having garnered twenty-one national championships over four generations—and counting.

Two of the sport's early greats rode as teammates in the December 1899 six-day in Madison Square Garden when that was the highlight of the racing season. Jay Eaton was the national indoor champion and teamed with Bobby Walthour, Sr., who was then a rising star. Walthour went on to win two national championships in the daring and glamorous motorpace event in 1902 and 1903.

Both riders were succeeded by their sons. Eaton's son, Ray, won the national professional championship in 1919, defeating the legendary Frank Kramer. Two years later, Bobby Walthour, Jr. won the national amateur championship.

Yet another Walthour went one better by winning both the national road and track championships in the same season. Jimmy Walthour, Jr., son of Bobby Senior's twin brother, won the amateur national title in 1927, based on points accrued during the season. He then went to Louisville for the amateur road-racing championship. There he won the national road title to become the first of only two cyclists who won both titles in the same year.

Willie Fenn, Sr., started a family legacy when he won the national amateur sprint championship in 1900. His son, Willie Fenn, Jr., regained the same title for the family in 1923. From this family came Bobby Fenn, who in 1960 became the third-generation Fenn to win the national championship. Bobby Fenn won the 1960 junior nationals (ages fourteen to sixteen) in Milwaukee.

Bobby Fenn, left, a third-generation racer, shares a victory lap with Perry Metzler after they won a one-hour team race in New York City in June 1964. Metzler was the first black to be national-cycling champion after Major Taylor. (Jack Simes III photo)

Jack Simes III succeeded his father as national champion in 1964 and went on to win more than fifteen national titles. (Jack Simes III photo)

In 1936, at the national amateur championships in St. Louis, John Weston Simes, Jr., a second-generation rider from New Jersey, won the national crown. Simes taught his son, Jack Simes III, about bicycle racing at an early age. Simes III won the junior nationals in 1959 in Kenosha, Wisconsin. Five years later, Simes III succeeded his dad as national men's amateur champion by capturing three of the four events that composed the omnium that determined the national champion. Simes followed that up by winning three more national amateur titles—he was senior sprint champion in 1965 and 1967 and won the national ten-mile title in 1969.

After turning professional, Simes III won the national professional championship in 1973 and 1974. He was reinstated as an ama-

teur in 1988 and won three more gold medals in the forty-to-forty-four age-group division.

The Eatons, Walthours, Fenns, and Simes families make up the dynasties of American cycling. In recent years, a fourth-generation Bobby Walthour has emerged in the wheel sport to keep up the family tradition. Jack Simes IV was born in 1988 and could very well follow his family's wheelmarks into the next century.

When Jack Dempsey was a teenager growing up in Utah, he used to hang around the Salt Palace Velodrome, an outdoor board track eight laps to the mile in Salt Lake City. Bike racers were local heroes. Crowds of 5,000 filled the stands for races on Tuesday and Friday evenings from May through Labor Day.

"Dempsey used to polish shoes and run errands for the bike racers," recalled Alf Goullet, who raced there during the summer of 1912, when Dempsey turned seventeen. Dempsey's favorite racers were a bearded Russian named Teddy Denesovitch and San Jose native Hardy Downing.

Young Dempsey, born William Harrison Dempsey, was called Harry. He was a tall, swarthy youth with raw physical power. Goullet recalled seeing him train and occasionally enter amateur races on the track. Dempsey, in his 1940 autobiography, *Round by Round* (Whittlesey House), written with Myron M. Stearns, recounts competing in a race from Provo to Salt Lake City, about forty miles: "I decided I'd rather win bicycle races than shine shoes."

He didn't win, and subsequently followed his older brother, Bernie, into copper, silver, and gold mines around Utah and Colorado. Bernie Dempsey boxed and used the ring name of Jack Dempsey, after the Irish middleweight champion called Jack Dempsey the Nonpareil. But Bernie had a glass jaw and didn't earn money fighting. Harry felt he could succeed in the ring.

Jack Dempsey, far left, gets ready to fire the starting pistol of the March 1922 six-day race in Madison Square Garden. Ten years earlier he had been polishing shoes for racers including Alf Goullet, second rider from the right. (Russell Mamone collection)

Harry Dempsey served an apprenticeship in mining-camp bars. Money—usually nickels, dimes, and quarters—was tossed into a hat for a purse as little as a dollar. By 1916 Dempsey turned twenty-one and decided it was time to get serious about boxing. He hopped a freight train to Salt Lake City, where Downing had retired from bicycle racing and ran a boxing gym.

Dempsey tried to cash in on his dark features by calling himself Kid Blackie. He asked Downing for the chance to break into professional boxing. It was a night when Downing's matchmaker had a pair of Hancock brothers matched on the card. Downing disapproved of the match and sent Kid Blackie in to fight the one called Kid Hancock. The prize was $5 to the winner.

Loud hissing and razzing greeted Kid Blackie when he made his professional debut. He was so pumped up that when the bell rang he knocked Kid Hancock out cold in twelve seconds.

Downing, who had raced bicycles professionally around the United States and Australia against riders like Major Taylor and Bobby Walthour, Sr., paid Kid Blackie only $2.50. When the boxer protested, Downing explained he hadn't put on a show for his paying customers.

But Downing, who liked Dempsey's rough-and-tumble style, told him, "Stick around. Maybe I can use you again on the card."

Kid Hancock's brother wanted to fight Kid Blackie. At the end of the evening they squared off and Kid Blackie won his second fight to claim the other $2.50. Downing invited him to stick around for more fights later.

Dempsey did. He also appropriated Bernie's ring name, Jack Dempsey, from the previous champion, whose real name was John Kelly and had died in 1895, the year William Harrison Dempsey was born. The new Jack Dempsey started to make a name for himself and soon was bound for New York City.

Downing wrote a letter to Willie Ratner, an influential sportswriter on *The Newark Evening News*: "There's a big kid named Jack Dempsey headed for New York. Look him up and introduce yourself. He's going to make it someday."

Dempsey made it all the way to heavyweight champion of the world, reigning from 1919 to 1926. *Ring Magazine* rates him as the fourth-greatest all-time heavyweight champion.

He never forgot bicycle racing. He was a regular at six-day events, particularly in Madison Square Garden. At the March 1922 six-day, as the official starter he fired the pistol to get the event rolling. One of the riders lined up shoulder to shoulder on the starting line was Goullet.

CHAPTER 4

THE BICYCLE FOR YOU

WHETHER YOU WANT to ride a bicycle to lose a few pounds and improve your fitness, commute to work, or go for rides in the countryside on a day too nice to spend indoors, it helps to have a bicycle that fits your particular needs. Racing bicycles, like those top professionals ride, retail for more than $3,000 and may be a trophy to own, but a racing bicycle doesn't fit recreation riding needs. A $3,000 bicycle is not necessarily six times better than a $500 machine. Take an existential view: buy your bicycle to fit your needs.

A helpful general publication is *Bicycle Guide's Buyers' Annual*, which comes out every May. (Copies are available at newsstands and bicycle shops, or send $3.95 to *Bicycle Guide's Buyers' Annual*, 711 Boylston St., Boston, MA 02115.) Some of the specifications can be overwhelming, but the introductory articles to the different sections take the novice patiently by the hand.

Bicycling also publishes a buyer's guide issue in March that surveys more than 900 new bicycles. The editors of *Bicycling* select twenty-five bicycles as their pick of best buys. (Copies are available on newsstands and bicycle shops for $2.95, or order a copy from *Bicycling*, 33 E. Minor St., Emmaus, PA 18098.)

MODELS TO CONSIDER ARE:

Sport Touring. This is a good all-around bicycle. Adapts well to commuter travel as well as long recreation rides. Lightweight—typically twenty to twenty-two pounds—and equipped with a derailleur that has twelve to eighteen speeds. Price range is $350 to $1,200.

Touring. Consider the touring bicycle the Clydesdale of the species: hardy draft horses, built for carrying heavy loads. Touring bicycles are designed to carry the rider and forty pounds of tent, sleeping bag, and other camping gear. Eighteen speeds cover a wide gear-range to pedal all that baggage up extended grades in the Rocky Mountains. Touring frames often have extra water-bottle mounts for treks on long, hot days.

Touring bicycles are the Clydesdale horses of the species—built for carrying loads and a comfortable ride over long distances. Robert Hammersmith at seventy-nine pedaled across the United States in seventy-eight days, camping all but nine nights. (Bikecentennial photo by Greg Siple)

These bicycles have long wheelbases (distance from front hub to rear hub) to give a more cushioned ride, and a front fork that slopes more to take road shock. Built for comfort and durability. Price range is similar to the touring bicycle.

Mountain Bike. Sometimes called ATBs for All Terrain Bikes, these are the fastest-growing models in bicycle sales. They feature a smaller, more compact frame than sport touring or touring bicycles, straight handlebars, wide tires, a comfortable upright position, and eighteen speeds.

In the mid-1970s, a hardy coterie of cyclists in Marin County, north of San Francisco, began riding one-speed, balloon-tire bicycles up and down nearby Mount Tamalpais. Innovations led to borrowing motorcycle handlebars for extra strength, and knobby tires for better traction. From racing bicycles, the riders took derailleurs, which gave them eighteen speeds. Stronger brakes were added. These prototypes were rugged,

but weighed up to forty-five pounds, the equivalent of ships on wheels.

Craftsmen began designing lighter frames and lighter but stronger components. Lighter alloys decreased the weight to twenty-four to twenty-eight pound range, which contributed to increased popularity. The new bikes were designed to put the rider's weight over the rear wheel for better traction. Derailleur shift levers were set on the handlebar to work with a flick of the thumb. *Voilà!* The modern mountain bicycle was cruising dirt trails in northern California and was headed east.

Commercial mountain bicycles were introduced in 1981. Sales were modest at first, but began picking up every year at a steadily increasing rate. "In 1990, mountain bicycles made up 65 percent of all bicycle sales," said Tim Blumenthal, managing editor of *Mountain Bike Magazine.*

The Bicycle Institute of America estimates that 14 million Americans are riding moun-

Criterium racing bicycles are made for riding at speed around courses with sharp turns. The bicycles have stiff frames that are highly responsive. (Seth Golzer photo)

Road-racing bicycles look similar to criterium bicycles, but they have a longer wheelbase and slightly more rake in the fork to absorb more shock. Andy Hampsten rides his road bike, which has served him well in winning the Tour of Switzerland twice and the Tour of Italy, the only U.S. rider to win the tours. (Beth Schneider photo)

Track bicycles such as the one that Connie Young is riding are pure bike—no brakes or extra gears. They are meant for riding on a smooth-surface track. (Rich Cruse photo)

tain bicycles. A good mountain bicycle costs in the range of $300 to $800.

Racing. There are four main racing models. The most popular is the *criterium racer*, built for competing around street circuits, often less than a mile a lap, called criterium racing. Criteriums are the bread and butter of American bicycle racing. Typically, criteriums are about fifty miles in the men's open division, which takes less than two hours to race; women's races usually are twenty-five miles, and require less than an hour of competition. Criterium racing bikes have a high bottom bracket (the bottom of the frame, where the pedal axle goes through the frame) to let the cyclist pedal through the turn, a fork that has little rake, and a short wheelbase to get the bicycle through the turn as quickly as possible.

The second racing model is the *road bicycle*, like the one Greg LeMond rides in Europe, where races often go from city to city, over rough roads, in five to six hours of racing daily, rain or shine. Road bicycles have a longer wheelbase and lower bottom bracket than criterium bicycles for a responsive yet

cushioned ride. Depending on the event, such as the premier spring classic in northern France, Paris-Roubaix, which covers 160 miles over roads that include many sections of cobbles the size of bread loaves, racers may fit their frames with a touring fork.

Criterium and road-racing bicycles weigh eighteen to twenty pounds. As the races get longer, such as the three-week Tour de France, riders tend to favor comfort over any possible weight they may save.

The third racing model is the *track bike*, a pure bicycle whose basic design has remained essentially the same for a century. Riders compete on a closed track, approximately five laps to the mile, with a glassy-smooth surface. Their bicycle is basically the frame, wheels, saddle, and handlebars. They ride with a fixed gear that rolls the pedals around constantly—no coasting. Many coaches feel that riding a fixed gear makes a cyclist a smoother pedaler, although riding a fixed gear takes getting used to. Track bikes usually weigh sixteen pounds. Not meant for city streets or city traffic.

The fourth model is a hybrid—the *time-*

trial bike, designed specifically for competing against the clock. It is aerodynamically designed for hard solo efforts.

Once you've decided on the bicycle that fits your needs, buy the bicycle that fits you.

Look for a frame with a top tube (the top of the frame parallel with the ground) that you can straddle with clearance of three-quarters of an inch to an inch-and-a-half on a touring bicycle, or two to four inches on a mountain bike. Your frame also should allow for three to five inches of seatpost to show, although this is optional and is difficult to get for people under five feet four inches.

When shopping for a bicycle, take the one you're interested in buying out for a test ride. Have the mechanic adjust the seat and handlebars so that you sit comfortably, and take the bike out for a short spin. The proprietor wants you to see what a fine product you've selected, and wants you to be satisfied with your purchase. Try the brakes and run through the gears on your test ride. They should work smoothly and quietly. If something doesn't work right, take it back and tell the mechanic. Often it's just a matter of a minor adjustment. Then continue your test ride.

After you make your purchase, a standard procedure among bike shops is to take your bicycle back thirty days later for an overall check. New brake cables tend to stretch, spokes need tightening, and other parts need a routine going-over.

Many runners and some tennis players are converting to cycling because it is exercise that is easier on the knees, but turning over too big a gear, or bad saddle position, can give a cyclist knee pain. That's easily avoided, though.

Pedal with moderate gears: use a gear that you can spin at seventy to ninety revolutions a minute. This cadence is easier on the knees. It's also an aerobically efficient cadence, and the spin momentum helps carry you uphill. Keep pedaling smoothly and regularly, like a metronome, even up hills and into the wind. A jerky stroke can strain knee tendons. Let your legs do the pedaling; keep your torso steady.

Saddle position is very important. A saddle that is up too high overextends the legs and puts extra stress on the tendons and ligaments behind the knee. Conversely, a saddle that is too low forces the knees to bend too much at the top of the pedal stroke, leading to inflamation of the tendon over the kneecap.

The general rule in determining correct saddle height is to sit on the saddle, wearing the shoes you will ride in (cycling shoes have thin soles and a minimal heel). Lean against a wall while doing this (or have someone hold you up) and pedal backwards with your heels on the pedals. Your knees should straighten without your rocking on the downstroke. When riding with the balls of your feet on the pedals, your knees should be bent at about 20 degrees at the bottom of the stroke.

Next in importance is the position of your handlebars. They usually fit in a line that would make the top of the handlebars parallel with the bottom of the saddle. The handlebars should be located so that when you pedal comfortably with your hands on the handlebars (or brake-lever hoods if your handlebars are dropped), your handlebars should block sight of your front-wheel hub. If the hub is behind the bar, you may be stretched too far forward.

Finally, your seat can slide forward or backward several inches. Position alignment is best determined by holding the crank arms horizontal with the ground. While you are on the bicycle with your leg in its powerful, downward pedal stroke, have a friend drop a plumb line to the middle of your forward kneecap so that the string aligns with the pedal axle. If your plumb line needs correction, loosen the seatpost clamp and slide the saddle back or forth to get the right align-

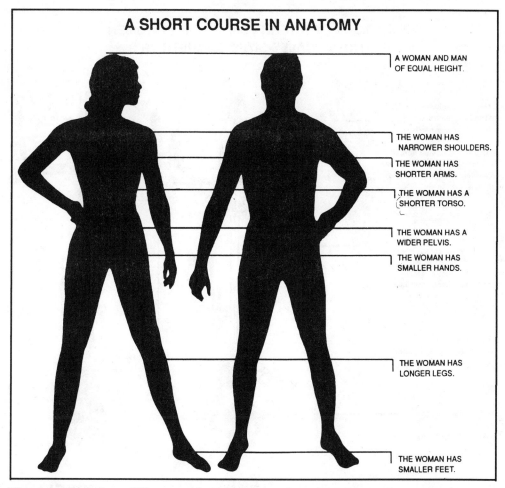

A SHORT COURSE IN ANATOMY

A WOMAN AND MAN OF EQUAL HEIGHT.

THE WOMAN HAS NARROWER SHOULDERS.

THE WOMAN HAS SHORTER ARMS.

THE WOMAN HAS A SHORTER TORSO.

THE WOMAN HAS A WIDER PELVIS.

THE WOMAN HAS SMALLER HANDS.

THE WOMAN HAS LONGER LEGS.

THE WOMAN HAS SMALLER FEET.

Women and men have different needs in bicycles and components. A woman and man the same height have different proportions in the arms, legs, torso, and hands. (Georgena Terry illustration)

ment. Having the right plumb line improves efficiency of the pedal stroke and reduces the likelihood of knee strain.

Women and men have different needs in a bicycle and components. A woman and man of the same height have different proportions: the woman has narrower shoulders, shorter arms, shorter torso, a wider pelvis, smaller hands, and longer legs. Nearly all the bicycles sold, however, are built for men.

Women have to be careful when purchasing a bicycle to make sure that the bicycle and components fit them.

"Riding a man's bike is like wearing a man's suit," observed Wil Bradford, an advertising copywriter. "It just doesn't fit."

One of the few makers of bicycles for women is Georgena Terry, who started making custom frames in 1981 in upstate New York. Four years and many dozens of frames later, she did an analysis of female and male

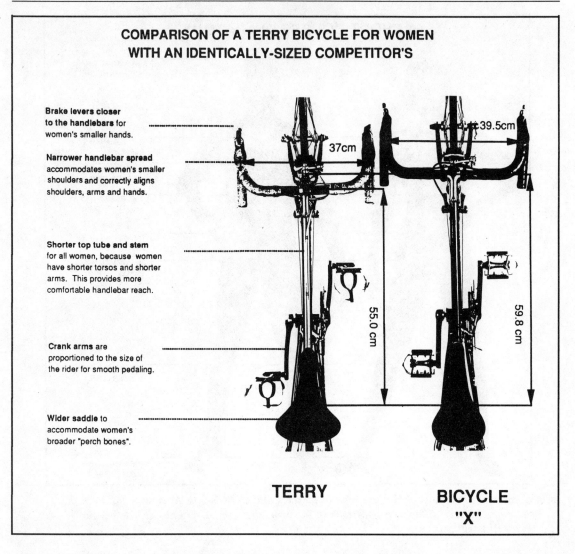

COMPARISON OF A TERRY BICYCLE FOR WOMEN WITH AN IDENTICALLY-SIZED COMPETITOR'S

Brake levers closer to the handlebars for women's smaller hands.

Narrower handlebar spread accommodates women's smaller shoulders and correctly aligns shoulders, arms and hands.

Shorter top tube and stem for all women, because women have shorter torsos and shorter arms. This provides more comfortable handlebar reach.

Crank arms are proportioned to the size of the rider for smooth pedaling.

Wider saddle to accommodate women's broader "perch bones".

37cm

39.5cm

55.0 cm

59.8 cm

TERRY

BICYCLE "X"

body structures. She discovered that problems women cyclists traditionally experienced were not an indication of their lack of fitness or tone but rather the fit of the bicycles, which were made for men's proportions.

"To me, the fit of a bicycle is crucial to the enjoyment of riding, which I think should be a mystical experience," Terry said. "The bicycle should be invisible to what you are doing physically and mentally and metaphysically. Even if you are riding around a familiar circuit, one you've ridden for years

and know intimately, the ride should be a mystical experience."

Terry rides a bicycle more easily than she walks. As a child growing up in Montgomery, Alabama, in the 1950s she contracted polio, which left her with a weakness in her left leg. "It's a neurological failure," she explained. "It doesn't get worse, but it doesn't get better."

During the gas shortage of the mid-1970s, Terry was among many who looked to the bicycle as an alternate form of transportation. "It was something different, something fun to do, and I like being physically active."

As a woman five feet three inches tall, she found that getting a bicycle the right size was tricky. "My most difficult part was that I could ride the bike all right, but I couldn't straddle the frame. I have a long torso. I'm built more like a gorilla—long arms, short legs. I put up with a bike that didn't fit particularly well. I just had to be careful when I stopped in traffic or got off the bike."

She was spending most of the 1970s in a variety of careers that didn't fit particularly well, either. Terry was methodically and studiously preparing for one vocation, stopping, and then trying another.

In 1972 she graduated from Chatham College in Pittsburgh with a degree in drama, specializing in stage management and lighting. Then she went to the University of Pennsylvania for a Master of Business Administration in finance from the Wharton School of Business. That led to a job as financial analyst and stockbroker.

"Later I went to Carnegie-Mellon University, where I got a degree in mechanical engineering," she said. "Which is probably what I should have done in the first place."

By 1980 she had moved to Rochester, New York, where she worked as a project engineer at Xerox. She started looking at bicycle frames metallurgically, to learn more about how the top tube, seat tube, and down tube were joined by brass lugs in the diamond frame.

"Brazing is soldering at a very high temperature," she explained. "For brass brazing, which is what is used in building a bicycle frame, the temperature is about 5,000 degrees Fahrenheit."

Terry read books, wielded an oxyacetylene torch and a hacksaw, and in her basement in 1981 made a frame—an exact copy of the one she rode. "I just wanted to learn. That frame is still hanging in my basement."

Her experiences led to making frames for

Georgena Terry makes bicycles designed to fit women. "To me, the fit of a bicycle is crucial to the enjoyment of riding." (George S. Morgan photo)

friends. "I was trying to listen to what people wanted," she said. "What they liked and what they didn't like."

A perfectionist by nature and an engineer by training, Terry's work in making custom bicycles was highly appreciated. Her frames for women featured a shorter top tube— usually an inch or an inch and a half shorter than a comparable man's frame. That made it more convenient for women to reach their handbrakes. She fitted her bicycles with smaller handbrakes to correspond to a woman's smaller hand, handlebars that were narrower, seats that were wider. For women under five feet three inches, she introduced a model with a smaller front wheel, twenty-four inches (compared to the standard twenty-seven inches).

Her bicycles fit her growing clientele, and in the process she discovered a vocation that fit her as well. Demand grew, production increased, and she went full-time in 1985 with Terry Precision Bicycles for Women, Inc. She was the first bicycle maker to acknowledge what other manufacturers had long overlooked: that women need different bicycles than men.

"I really enjoy cycling. I want others to enjoy it too," she said in an interview. Photos consistently make her look relaxed, but they don't convey the calmness she radiates. Her presence makes the metaphysical properties she attributes to good riding seem natural.

"To me, the nearest experience to cycling is surfing," she continued. "There is always the perfect ride that comes up. You're eating right. Feel just right. It all clicks. And it is like that in surfing. There's the draw of the perfect ride—enough to keep you up day after day."

Sales of Terry Precision Bicycles have kept up, and press attention followed. *The Wall Street Journal* puckishly noted that her success has prompted some Japanese manufacturers to follow her example, which dealers have dubbed "Terry-yakis." *Sports Illustrated, Newsweek, Inc.,* and newspapers from Phoenix to Boston have published features on the maverick bicycle builder.

Each year her sales have increased a steady 20 percent, up to 3,000 bicycles in 1990, she said. Her product line has expanded to eight touring and racing models and two mountain bicycles. They are made for women from four feet ten inches to five feet ten inches, and cost from $450 to $1,500.

"My perspective is that the women's market has been potentially very large since 1985, but it is difficult to pin down what works," she said. "When I pick up a magazine, or watch television, the ads I see have macho images. They're aimed at men. And women and men don't respond to the same stimuli in the ads."

Yet women are increasingly getting into cycling, Terry points out. "But I don't know what is drawing more women into cycling. It's not any one thing. Runners who get injured are taking up cycling. Women work out in aerobic classes, then want to get outside the gym and take up cycling. Maybe it's cases of women going out on a ride with friends and discovering that it isn't just riding around the block, but really getting out into the countryside.

"And there are social aspects to cycling. One of the nice things about cycling is that it satisfies so many needs. If you're in a gregarious mood, you can go out with a group. Or you can go alone—solo. If you're in an aggressive mood, you can go fast, or if you're tired and want to unwind you can go slow. A bicycle doesn't discriminate in age, either. You can be ten or eighty-five. It doesn't matter."

She smiled to herself. "You can do it with your family, or to get away from your family."

About the time Terry was starting to make custom frames in the early 1980s, Lillian Miller's two teenage sons returned from an afternoon of whizzing on their bicycles through streets around their home in the Washington, DC, suburb of Bethesda, Maryland. "The kids said, 'Gee, Mom, it's too bad you can't come out and ride with us,'" she recounted. "I never had a bicycle, never learned to ride one."

But husband Jay, an active runner and recreational cyclist, spotted a magazine ad for an ingenious rear-wheel kit from England that converted a bicycle into a tricycle. They mailed away for the kit, which added only seven pounds, including the extra wheel, to Jay's lightweight bicycle.

"I started riding the tricycle and enjoyed it," said Lillian, a high-school science teacher. "I was gliding along and having a nice time."

That led to her purchasing a custom-made tricycle in a Georgetown bicycle shop. She went on rides through Washington's Rock Creek Park and other venues with her husband, who kept the conversion kit on his vehicle until he decided to follow suit and buy a tricycle, too.

"When you think of a tricycle," Jay Miller said, "what usually comes to mind is a big, seventy-pound, three-speed trike that you see in retirement communities in Florida. Or pedicabs that college kids ride with freezers on the back in the summer to sell ice cream along the Atlantic City boardwalk. Our tricycles weigh less than thirty pounds and have twelve speeds."

Riding a tricycle is not as easy as it looks. "It took me a couple of weeks to get used to riding," Jay admitted. "The problem is that the trike follows the slope of the surface you're on. A bicycle is always perpendicular to the road, but a trike has a different center of gravity. That can be unnerving and make a trike difficult to ride."

Around turns, centrifugal force takes over body and machine. "I shift my weight, sometimes by getting off the saddle and moving my whole body sideways," he continued.

"He's more daring than me," Lillian Miller said. "But I go the way I feel. It's automatic. You have to get rid of that feeling that you are going to fall." She smiled slyly. "A lot of people have tried my tricycle and they think it's going to be like riding a bicycle. Then they get going and find it impossible to control. People get embarrassed."

Yet there are advantages over a bicycle, particularly in traffic as the Millers pointed out. "You can come to a complete stop at a red light and sit comfortably with both feet on the pedals," Lillian said. "When the light changes, you are ready to go." Her husband Jay added "Some car drivers give you a wider berth because a tricycle takes up more space."

The Millers ride as much for exercise and transportation as they do for recreation. Jay has ridden sixty-five miles in a day and regularly pedals 1.5 miles each way to and from the National Institutes of Health, where he works as a scientist.

Although cycling industry officials estimate there are 90 million cyclists in the country, the number of tricyclists could pass through a single light change. Tricycling is popular in England, where the Tricycle Association in Gillingham, Kent, publishes a quarterly news magazine circulated on both sides of the Atlantic. The Millers joined the Tricycle Association about the time Jay bought a tricycle from England.

But the couple doesn't have to worry about their sons taking their wheels out for a spin when they're not around. Eldest son Geoffrey, twenty-five, said he doesn't like the feel of riding a tricycle. "Ironically, I still use Dad's old bike with the original tricycle converter, down in the basement, for workouts on the wind trainer," he said.

With several years of experience riding on three wheels, has Lillian felt the urge to master riding on two?

"When I grew up in New Brunswick, New Jersey, my mother was very protective. I didn't even roller-skate. Learning to ride a tricycle was an adjustment, but it wasn't as hard for me as it was for Jay, who already rode a bicycle and had different habits to overcome. I like tricycling because it is interesting and different. But I don't feel like trying a bicycle."

When Barbara and Randy Swart of Arlington, Virginia, go cycling, she has no difficulty keeping up with her husband—even up hills and into the wind. She sits directly behind him on their navy-blue tandem.

"Riding together on a tandem is a great equalizer of our riding styles," Barbara observed. "This way we exercise together and we're still close enough that we can talk."

"It's a wonderful way to go out into the

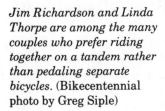

Jim Richardson and Linda Thorpe are among the many couples who prefer riding together on a tandem rather than pedaling separate bicycles. (Bikecentennial photo by Greg Siple)

countryside and be together," Randy said. "It's more fun than when we had solo bicycles. I always wanted to go faster and farther. We got a tandem and solved that problem."

Another couple, Helen and Harvey Geller of Greenbelt, Maryland, found riding a tandem together was a solution not just to their physical disparity but also got Helen cycling even though she had never learned to ride a bicycle.

"About five years ago we were down in Florida on vacation in a campground that had a bike rental shop with a tandem," Harvey said. "I talked my wife into trying the tandem, ensuring her that I would do all the work and keep it balanced."

After practicing starts and stops, then right and left turns, the Gellers were off for the open road. When they returned home, they bought a green five-speed tandem for recreation rides around Greenbelt and nearby College Park. They took their tandem on other trips for rides together through Yellowstone National Park in Montana, along the Pacific Coast Highway in Southern

California, and through the vistas of the northern Rockies in British Columbia.

The Swarts and Gellers are part of a growing number of couples riding tandems. Jack Goertz of Birmingham, Alabama, president of the Tandem Clubs of America, said that nationwide sales of quality tandems in 1989 doubled to around 5,000, and went up even more in 1990.

"In the cycling industry, the only two areas that increased in sales in 1989 and 1990 were mountain bikes and tandems," Goertz said. Quality tandems usually start at $1,000 and go up to $4,000.

TCA has approximately 3,000 members around the United States, Canada, and some members in Europe. They keep in touch through a bimonthly newsletter, aptly named *Doubletalk*.

Club secretary Laura Mappin of Palo Alto, California, said that the club recently surveyed members to see who was riding tandems. "About 95 percent of our members are couples—husbands and wives, or significant others," Mappin said. "Some members have triples—that is, a third seat, handlebars, and set of pedals—for their kids to ride with them. Some members take blind people out for rides on their tandem."

Barbara and Randy Swart, both forty-seven, are members of TCA as well as members of the metropolitan-Washington Potomac Pedalers Touring Club. On a typical weekend between March and December, when the weather permits, they go on rides of thirty-five to sixty miles.

During the summer they also participate in tandem rallies, usually made up of 150 tandem teams, all riding matching jerseys and shorts. Some tandem groups in the Midwest are known by acronyms for farm animals. In Wisconsin there are COWS, (Couples on Wheels) and they attend tandem rallies wearing black-and-white outfits; Michigan has MUTTS, or Michigan Units Tandem Touring Society; CATS are the Chicago Area Tandem Society. The twin cities of Minneapolis–St. Paul chose the tandem grouping of letters to form TCTC, for Twin Cities Tandem Club.

"The tandem rallies are quite friendly," Randy said. "They can last two or three days each, usually riding fifty or so miles a day. We have gone to them around the Finger Lakes of upstate New York, or around the Berkshires of western Massachusetts." They even ventured overseas to ride in China, Ireland, and Bermuda. "And the people at rallies are really sociable. Otherwise, the various teams wouldn't be together," Randy added.

The rider who sits in front is called the captain. The captain does the steering, applies the brakes, and shifts the gears. The rear-seat rider, called the stoker, adds extra pedaling power.

Helen Geller, sixty-eight, said she enjoys sitting on the backseat where she doesn't have to pay much attention to the road while she takes in the scenery.

"She does give me assistance in going up some hills," said Harvey, sixty-nine, who has won several medals at the National Senior Olympics in St. Louis and in his age-group division in state championships in running and race-walking.

Barbara and Randy Swart are among the most avid tandem cyclists in the Potomac area. Their lightweight twenty-one-speed tandem is equipped with four water bottles on the frame and a small tool bag on the front handlebars.

"We like going out together on rides," Randy said. "Besides, you can really get rolling on a tandem. It's not unusual to go faster than fifty miles an hour down hills. Tandems are especially good to ride into a headwind. When a tandem team rides alongside a couple of regular bicycle riders and everyone is exerting the same effort, the tandem team will pull right away."

Mention the word tandem and what comes to mind is the nostalgic song "Daisy, Daisy," sometimes referred to as "Bicycle Built for Two." Although a few generations of cycling afficionados attribute inspiration of the song to the elopement on a tandem bicycle by Bobby Walthour, Sr., and Blanche "Daisy" Bailey in 1898, the copyright date indicates another likely origin.

According to *The Book of World-Famous Music: Classical, Popular, and Folk,* by James J. Fuld (Crown Publishers, 1971), the song grew out of sarcasm for a tariff levied on an Englishman who wanted to take his new bicycle home after visiting the United States.

The Englishman, Frank Dean, was a professional songwriter and was miffed at the customs duty he had to pay in New York City. He had purchased a new safety bicycle, with the chain drive that had begun to supplant the highwheelers a century ago. A friend joked that he was fortunate the bicycle had not been built for two—or the duty would have been twice as much.

Dean may have used that inspiration for the song. He apparently was of two minds about the experience by the time his ship docked in England. In late 1892, when "Daisy, Daisy" was published, and enthusiastically received, he took out copyrights at the British Museum in London and the Library of Congress in Washington under the pseudonym of Harry Dacre.

Apparently he liked dabbling in doubles. Dean also wrote songs under the pen name of Henry Decker. He died in London in 1922.

Information on Terry Precision Bicycles for Women, Inc., is available from a local dealer or from:

Terry Precision Bicycles
   for Women, Inc.
1704 Waynesport Road
Macedon, NY 14502
(315) 986-2103

Information on the Tricycle Association is available from:

Tricycle Association
D. Heighway, National Secretary
23 Kingswood Rd.
Gillingham, Kent, England
ME7 1DZ

Numerous clubs are available for tandem riders. They include:

Tandem Clubs of America
Jack Goertz, President
2220 Vanessa Dr.
Birmingham, AL 35242
(205) 991-5519, or

Tandem Clubs of America
Laura Mappin, Secretary
P.O. Box 83
Palo Alto, CA 94302
(408) 562-5601

Twin Cities Tandem Club
c/o Sara and Doug Laird
5232 Edenmoor St.
Edina, MN 55436
(612) 925-5185

Tandem riding for Illinois, Kentucky, and Indiana:

c/o Dave & Valerie Northcutt
109 East Madison St.
Villa Park, IL 60181
(708) 279-3753

Tandem riding for Iowa, Nebraska, South Dakota, North Dakota, and Minnesota:

c/o Bruce Perry
2652 West 34th St.
Davenport, IA 52806
(319) 386-2919

Mountain-Bike Organizations include:

WOMBATS (Women's Mountain Bike
   and Tea Society)
Box 757
Fairfax, CA 94930

Mountain Bicycle Resource Group
University of Oregon Outdoor Program
Erb Memorial Union
University of Oregon
Eugene, OR 94703
(503) 346-4362

International Mountain Bicycling
   Association
Route 2, Box 303
Bishop, CA 93514
(619) 387-2757

Responsible Organized Mountain
   Pedalers (ROMP)
Ken Detrick, President
15064 Kennedy Rd.
Los Gatos, CA 95032
(408) 356-8230

Concerned Off-Road Bicycle
   Association (COBRA)
15236 Victory Blvd., Box 149
Van Nuys, CA 91411
(818) 991-6626

CHAPTER 5

YOUR BICYCLE, EQUIPMENT, AND DIET

"ACTUALLY, BICYCLES are sort of silly-looking things, but they like to stay right side up and go," mused Phil Wood of San Jose, renowned for his high-quality hubs and other components. "A bicycle stays up because it wants to." Mischief flickered in his eyes. "It has nothing to do with science."

Wood sat for an interview behind a small metal lathe. A stainless steel ruler protruded from his shirt pocket with calibrations in millimeters and centimeters. To one side was a workbench with hubs, chain rings, cranks, and other bicycle-transmission-related components he has designed and manufactured. He is a mechanical engineer and machinist, as much in his element with tools as Neptune, chest deep in water, is with a trident in his hand.

"You take a bicycle, with nobody on it, and just plain push it and it will go," Wood said. "Bicycles are stable. You can ride a bicycle

through impossible conditions, and it will go through them all right."

He is asked, What keeps a bicycle up? Gyroscopic action?

Wood nodded. "There is gyroscopic action involved in maintaining equilibrium, but a bicycle will stay up without it. For example, you go through a turn at speed and keep pedaling. Then go back and ride through the same turn at the same speed but without pedaling. When you coast around the turn, the bike will handle a little more squirrelly, because pedaling contributes to the stability of the bicycle through the turn. But you can get through the turn with or without pedaling. The bicycle just wants to go."

Often the bicycle we have is better at going than we are. Athletic coaches of all disciplines are fond of telling their charges that muscles work on the principle of use 'em or

Getting enough to drink while exercising helps keep the juices flowing. (AYH photo)

lose 'em. Layoffs mean the athlete must work to regain the muscle tone he (or she) had before the break. Nature has no truck with seniority.

Dr. David Costill, director of the Human Performance Laboratory at Ball State University in Muncie, Indiana, has published dozens of studies on athletes. One study looked into the effects of layoffs on the heart. The study showed that college-scholarship athletes who retired from sports after graduation had the same hearts that sedentary nonathletes had by the time both groups reached their middle years. When both groups began exercising in their middle years, however, the former athletes tended to improve at a faster rate than their sedentary colleagues.

Regardless of your age when you take up cycling, the three areas of the body that most noticeably feel the effects of the first time out are the legs, upper back, and the butt. Almost always, the first three days are the hardest. Stick with it, for improvements will come. It helps to start your training ride into the wind so you can finish with a tailwind. Another help, when pedaling up a hill, is to shift into a bigger gear before the top; this gives added momentum over the crest to speed the rate of descent.

Think of your muscles as a sponge. Set out on the sink to dry, the kitchen sponge becomes hard and solid. If you grip it and twist, the sponge will tear. But just add water and the sponge becomes extremely flexible. Where a sponge takes water, muscles take blood, which works into the muscles during the warm-up. Allow yourself at least fifteen minutes of easy riding to warm up and get blood flowing into your muscles—not just your legs but also your heart and other areas. A trained athlete can have up to an extra quart of blood in his (or her) body as a result of conditioning.

If Gertrude Stein were part of today's Me Generation instead of the Lost Generation of the 1920s, she likely would be an avid recreation cyclist. She might be associated with her phrase, "Conditioning is conditioning is conditioning." There is no shortcut to getting into shape. When rider and bicycle are matched for a good fit, cycling becomes a matter of fitness. The body is willing to negotiate. All negotiations involve give and take: allow rest days between hard efforts. Rest days mean lighter workouts, chiefly to get the circulation flowing to flush out dead cells and promote muscle growth.

Try to exercise at the same time daily, so that your body gets into a rhythm, at least four days a week. Sometimes a feeling of drowsiness after exercise is a sign of dehydration. Drink plenty of fluids.

Increase your distance gradually, usually 10 to 15 percent a week, depending on your mood and how your body is feeling. Meeting a challenge is always a good confidence builder. Many of the recreation rides make for good challenges, but they require some preparation. Be realistic in setting goals. But don't get consumed in training so that the rides are no longer recreation. Take time to smell the flowers. Remember something else Gertrude Stein said: "A rose is a rose is a rose."

Nobody goes out for a ride with the intention of falling. But with the amount of car traffic on the roads, a light rain that may mix with oil on the pavement to make a turn slicker than usual, or a pothole you didn't see in the road ahead, crashes are inevitable.

"There are 5,280 ways to crash every mile," said Randy Swart, the tandem rider who also is in charge of the Bicycle Helmet Safety Institute, a helmet testing and advocacy program of the Washington Area Bicyclist Association. "There is no question about *if* you are going to crash, but *when* you are going to crash."

Since hard-shell helmets were introduced in the mid-1970s, their use has proliferated. A newer type without the shell is lighter and has taken up much of the market. Industry officials said that 2.5 million helmets were sold in the United States in 1990, and another 1.5 million were sold overseas.

Hard-shell helmets likely have an advantage over the no-shell helmets as the best protection for a cyclist's head. Helmets cost from $20 to $110, and should be looked upon as an investment. Their cost is less than a trip to the emergency room. Today's helmets contain expanded polystyrene, a stiffer version of the white picnic-cooler foam used to keep your lemonade cool in the summer. The expanded polystyrene spreads out the length of impact.

The helmet should fit—it is, after all, a piece of clothing. (Bell Sports photo)

"The delay softens the peak blow," explained Swart. "In other words, instead of a blow lasting one millisecond, it would last six or seven milliseconds. It makes a big difference. The expanded polystyrene spreads the shock. That translates to saving lives."

In shopping for a helmet, look for the following:

Performance standard sticker, either Snell or ANSI, inside the helmet. Snell refers to the Snell Memorial Foundation, named after race-car driver Pete Snell, who was killed in a car crash in the 1950s while wearing a helmet that was more decorative than functional. The foundation established in his name has headquarters in St. James, New York. The foundation's standards for helmets made for race-car drivers, motorcyclists, and bicyclists are high. Snell stickers are green or blue and have a serial number.

ANSI refers to the American National Standards Institute, based in New York. ANSI's standard is regarded as easier to meet than the Snell standard.

Fit. Try on the helmet to make sure it is comfortable. It is, after all, a piece of apparel, and should be something you'll wear for extended periods. The helmet should sit level on your head and cover as much as possible. Look at the chin buckle for long-term durability.

"The critical part is to buckle up and then try to tear the helmet off your head or have a friend try to tear it off," counseled Swart. "If it doesn't come off your head in the store, it very likely won't come off in a crash. Bear in mind that the worst crashes are with a car. Then you've got a double hit.

"First, you hit the car. It is not uncommon to get knocked through the air like a sack of potatoes. Then you hit the pavement—and street pavement is so hard. People have no idea how hard the impact is when they hit the street. The helmet you buy has to be able to stay on your head to take these hits."

Ventilation and weight. These are up to the

Cycling shorts and jerseys cut wind resistance, are comfortable, and make riding a picnic. (John Kelly photo/Pearl Izumi)

rider. Bald cyclists should avoid helmets with large vents on top unless they don't mind odd tan lines.

Bright colors to show up in traffic. Every preventive measure helps.

To take care of a helmet, wash with mild soap and water. Replace any helmet after you fall and hit the helmet hard. Because a helmet softens the impact, you may not be aware of how hard your head was struck. Damage may not be visible on the outside, but the helmet may be weakened.

Manufacturers recommend replacement after five years.

Cycling shorts and jerseys make riding

easier. Cycling shorts, made out of Lycra, a lightweight synthetic fabric that dries quickly, don't bunch up on the saddle the way cotton running shorts are likely to. Ten years ago Lycra shorts started replacing wool shorts, which also are comfortable, although they are fading out of circulation. Cycling shorts cost from $25 to $60.

Jerseys come in a variety of vibrant colors and exotic patterns. They fit snugly yet comfortably and don't drag in the wind. Many styles have two or three deep pockets in the back to carry a map, extra water bottle, or food, or all three. Also made of Lycra, or sometimes wool, jerseys cost $25 to $70.

Racers usually wear an undershirt beneath their jerseys as a second skin in case of a spill.

For driving to Iowa to start RAGBRAI, or just to get out of the city on a weekend, it's a good idea to have a rack on your car. Car racks are easy to install and are fitted so they won't scratch the paint.

Rear racks hold two bicycles and cost $50 to $150.

Roof racks usually start at $50 and go to $350. They can accommodate up to four bicycles.

A good lock is a must, especially in the city. Fastening a lock on your bicycle doesn't guarantee that it won't be stolen, but it is a deterrent. Price range is $12 to $60.

Computers are wonderful devices, and these gadgets which sit inconspicuously on your handlebars will tell you all you want to know about your ride: what your peak speed was, distance covered, average speed, how many revolutions per minute your feet are spinning, and what time it is. They weigh nearly nothing, yet do everything except squeeze orange juice. Their prices range from as little as $30 to as much as $70.

Rear racks fit over the trunk and can hold one or two bicycles for driving to a new cycling venue. (Rhode Gear photo)

Bike locks, such as this one seen in action, are most effective when securing the bicycle to something fixed, like a steel pole. (Kryptonite photo)

Cycling gloves—cut off at the first joints—look like an upscale article of clothing from a nineteenth-century English vegetable vendor in Covent Garden. But they have padding to absorb the shock of bumps on the road. Even on the hottest days, they are a welcome piece of cycling accoutrement. And if you fall, the gloves protect the skin on your paws. Usually under $15.

The bicycle travel bag, suitable for transporting your bike for an airline trip, is a convenient way to free you when you travel. When a bicycle is taken apart and packed to ship, it resembles a piece of Picasso sculpture, but it fits neatly into a travel bag. Cost is around $200 without caster wheels, which are another $20.

Why stay at home with your child? Put a helmet on the little critter and strap her or him into a child's seat made of high-density plastic, which fits behind the seat and over the rear wheel, and off you two go. There are safety concerns, however, such as the tendency of children to turn the bike over while sitting at a stoplight. When you have a babysitter, the child's seat can be used to carry a

bag. Child weight is best limited to forty pounds. Cost of a child's seat is around $80.

Water bottles fit conveniently on the frame in neat cages and are worth their weight, even when the sun is behind the clouds. They also make for good promotion spots.

Cycling shoes for recreation riders have been introduced in recent years with the upswing in cycling, which makes it easy to buy good ones. A cycling shoe should have a stiff forefoot area to help you pedal, and a modified cleat (in the form of a groove across the width near the ball of the foot) to lock the shoe on the pedal and prevent slippage. That saves you muscle exertion from keeping your feet in position on the pedals. Most models cost between $30 and $100.

These products are carried in the approximately 5,000 bicycle shops nationwide. Dealers have a variety of price ranges of equipment to choose from and are glad to service what they sell to members of their community. Dealers who are members of the National Bicycle Dealers Association—based in Costa Mesa, California—attend annual expositions where the bicycle industry

Tony Pranses introduces grandson Tyler to riding the TOSRV with the help of a child's seat. (TOSRV photo by Greg Siple)

displays its new wares for the upcoming season. Both NBDA expositions are in the early fall, one in Anaheim, California, the other on the East Coast, in Atlantic City. These shows, however, are not open to the public.

If you don't have the opportunity to shop at a bicycle store near your home, four major mail-order houses publish four-color catalogs every three months. These mail-order houses carry an entire line of products, like any bike shop, guarantee their products, and give prompt service, including overnight weekday delivery for a nominal fee.

One mail-order house is Performance Bicycle Shop, based in Chapel Hill, North Carolina. Performance has thirteen shops in California, Colorado, Maryland, North Carolina, and Virginia. More information is available twenty-four hours a day, seven days a week, from:

Performance Bicycle Shop
P.O. Box 2741
Chapel Hill, NC 27514
1-800-727-2453

Another is Bike Nashbar of Youngstown,

Bicycle computers sit on the handlebar inconspicuously and tell you all about your ride: peak speed, distance covered, average speed, and more. (Avocet photo)

Ohio. Bike Nashbar has two outlet stores in Ohio, one in Massachusetts, and a fourth in Virginia. More information is available from:

Bike Nashbar
4111 Simon Rd.
Youngstown, OH 44512-1343
(216) 782-2244

A third mail-order shop is Colorado Cyclist, Inc., of Colorado Springs. Information is available from:

The Colorado Cyclist, Inc.
2455 Executive Circle
Colorado Springs, CO 80906
1-800-688-8600

A fourth mail-order shop is Cyclesource, which Bikecentennial of Missoula, Montana, runs. While the other mail-order houses are stocked with a wide variety of parts and equipment, Cyclesource specializes chiefly in clothing for cyclists and stocks the biggest supply of maps and cycling-related literature of any shop or mail-order outlet in the country. More information is available from:

Bill Wiles, Sales Coordinator
Bikecentennial
P.O. Box 8308
Missoula, MT 59807
1-800-835-2246, ext. 158

What about diet? A recreation cyclist who looks to world-class cyclists for a guide of what to eat will likely be amused at how eclectic habits are. What is amazing is the quantity of food they consume. But what a world-class athlete eats depends on the athlete.

Greg LeMond, the only American to win the Tour de France and the world professional road racing championship, said he prefers to start off the day with a two-part breakfast. "I usually eat a regular breakfast, with cereal, toast, and juice. Then I have a plate of pasta, usually spaghetti."

When Bob Mionske of Madison, Wisconsin, winner of the national amateur road race in 1990 and fourth in the Seoul Olympics road race in 1988, heard LeMond describe his breakfast, he shook his head. "Spaghetti for breakfast," Mionske sighed. "I guess I'll never be a professional cyclist."

They made their dietary observations in May 1989, before the start of the ten-day Tour de Trump in Albany, New York. The race covered 800 miles of five Northeast and Middle Atlantic states, going south as far as Richmond, Virginia, before concluding on the Atlantic City boardwalk. LeMond used the race as part of his buildup for his second Tour de France victory, followed soon after by his second world championship. Mionske pulled out of the Tour de Trump.

Within the spectrum of athletes, cyclists are among the most fit. Food and fluids are fuel that keep their legs churning. In a 150-mile road race, their legs pedal 32,000 revolutions. They burn up 10,000 calories—equivalent to walking 100 miles.

For a recreation rider pedaling fifty miles a day or so in RAGBRAI across Iowa or Free-Wheel in Oklahoma, the cyclist is pedaling nearly 11,000 revolutions daily to burn up more than 3,000 calories—the same as walking thirty miles.

When Bruce Harmon and Melissa Merson rode RAGBRAI, they ate a lot of chocolate chip cookies for snacks, and dinners of spaghetti and other pasta. Elaine Mariolle of San Francisco, by contrast, set a record when she won the 1986 Race Across America (RAAM)—3,107 miles in 10 days, 2 hours, 4 minutes—without eating spaghetti or any pasta.

"The only solid food I ate in the RAAM was rice crackers or fruit," Mariolle said. "Mostly what I consumed was a liquid diet. It is much more efficient for prolonged endurance events. A liquid diet with complex carbohydrates, amino acids, and vitamins is easier to digest and hits the bloodstream more quickly. I experienced no big mood swings. In a race like RAAM, you have to be able to maintain your speed all the time."

Mariolle explained that when she competed in the 1984 transcontinental race, from San Francisco to Atlantic City, she ate conventional food, including a veritable harvest of potatoes, which she ate baked.

"I'm five feet two inches and 113 pounds," she said. "Riding that hard, I was burning up 8,000 calories a day. The solid food I ate was taking time to break down in my system. In 1985 I rode RAAM when Jonathan Boyer won. He told me about the liquid diet he was using. I used it the next year and really recommend it."

Boyer, best known as the first American, in 1980, to ride in the Tour de France, is careful in his approach to diet. He avoids all red meat and alcohol. For his RAAM assault, he had an 80 percent liquid diet, supplemented by vegetarian platters, mineral supplements, cheese, raisins, and cookies. After his triumph he told reporters, "I think junk food, bananas, and riders who eat them and try to do well in RAAM are history."

Obviously cyclists vary on their approaches to diet, but what they agree on overall is that what works for one person doesn't always work for someone else. When Roy Knickman, one of the country's top talents, discusses food, he sounds like a member of a hospital staff. A listener expects to see him wearing a white lab smock rather than his blue-and-white Coors Light Racing Team jersey.

At six feet and 160 pounds, Knickman learned when he turned professional and rode in 1987 for the French team Toshiba-Look that one of the bigger adjustments he had to make in European professional ranks was the food he ate. At races, he was one of 200 or so sitting down to meals where the standard fare was white bread and overcooked vegetables. The top athletes in major-league bicycle racing, some of whom were the subjects of posters adorning bedroom walls on both sides of the Atlantic, were eating food Knickman felt was devoid of nutrition.

"Americans who go to Europe to race have a lot of adjustments to make," he said. "That is part of what makes it so hard to race there."

He found it difficult to hold up a hand for attention at the mass meals and tell his colleagues that white bread and overcooked vegetables were not the best fuel. Particularly not for *Les Grands* of the sport.

"People start asking questions about whether you're better than they are to deserve special food," Knickman said. "You can't just say that white bread and mushy vegetables wreck your system. Besides, there's a language problem you have to deal with. Not everything you say translates well."

Knickman, from Boulder, Colorado, had to resort to carrying his own wheat germ and almonds in a bag for sprinkling on his overcooked food.

"I found that I have to eat well and rest well to perform well in races," said Knickman, twenty-five. "There are certain things I just can't do at all. I can't go out with the guys and drink a lot and expect to race well. It's a pretty strict life."

Even the sprinters—who burn up fewer calories than road racers like Knickman, LeMond, Mariolle, and Mionske—differ on what they eat.

"At times I've used special diets," admitted 1984 Olympic gold medalist Mark Gorski of Newport Beach, California. "Like a vegetarian diet with lots of vitamins. Then I'd go to a major international meet and see the East Germans at the next table, gorging themselves on greasy French fries and Wiener schnitzel. The East Germans would go out on the track and set world records. It does make you wonder sometimes about diet."

Riding behind other cyclists substantially reduces wind resistance to save energy. (TOSRV photo by Greg Siple)

During the Los Angeles Olympics, Gorski was so nervous that he couldn't eat much. "The meet would start at 10 A.M., and I would get up at 6 A.M., but I had such a case of butterflies in my stomach that I couldn't eat. I wound up existing on fruit juice and fruit. This lasted over four days."

Gorski, a hardy six feet two inches and 200 pounds, tends to lose five or six pounds in international track cycling meets.

"They usually last two to four days," he said. "Although my main event is the 1,000-meter (two-thirds of a mile) matched sprint, we usually wind up riding twenty-five to thirty miles a day in warm-ups, qualifying heats, and warm-downs. Usually the only meal we can eat all day is from one to two o'clock in the afternoon. You need four hours to digest food before a competition. In the mornings, we have qualifying heats. Then there's the main competition in the evening.

That schedule doesn't allow for much regular eating."

At the 1988 Seoul Olympics, the only U.S. cyclist to capture a medal was Connie Young of Indianapolis. She maneuvered around an irregular meal schedule by supplementing her food with sports nutrition capsules that contain amino acids. She called the capsules "a lifesaver."

Young, twenty-eight, won an Olympic bronze medal in the women's 1,000-meter matched sprints. In 1990 she won that event at the world's in Maebashi, Japan.

Thirty-one-year-old Gorski has eighteen years of racing experience. He is a two-time Olympian and former national champion. He said that after trying various diets over his career, he has settled on eating from a basic balance of the major food groups. "I eat red meat once or twice a week, and put more emphasis on complex carbohydrates, like pasta," he said. "That may not sound exciting, but that's what I've found through the years that works for me."

Runners who helped make that sport boom in the 1970s are taking up cycling in unprecedented numbers in the 1990s. They find cycling an alternative sport that is, as President Bush would phrase it, kinder and gentler.

Riding a bicycle takes the weight off the legs, doesn't pound muscles and joints, and gives the cyclist a variety of gears that are unavailable to a runner. The choice of gears gives the cyclist a chance to enhance leg speed.

Cyclists have another distinct advantage over runners. A rider pedaling directly behind another can exert 25 percent less energy to stay tucked behind at the same speed. In a pack of riders, all the cyclists except those at the front are protected in a shell of reduced wind resistance, which helps those in the pack conserve energy.

The generic term for riding in reduced wind resistance is *drafting*. Some cyclists call it *sitting in*. When riders feel they are being taken advantage of by having to tow a rider, they call it *wheel sucking*. Drafting, sitting in, and wheel sucking all figure inherently in cycling, whether it's fast recreation riding or racing.

Runners stepping along at a five-minute pace are moving at 12 miles an hour. There is some advantage to drafting at 12 miles an hour, but not nearly to the same degree as a comparable pace on a bicycle, which would be 27 miles an hour.

Moreover, it is not unusual for cyclists descending a long hill to exceed 50 miles an hour—more than double what the peak speed would be for an Olympic 100-meter champion. No distance runner could suddenly speed up to match the pace that sprinters hit without going into oxygen debt.

Cycling can help some runners who suffer

chronic knee problems stemming from a muscle imbalance between the hamstrings, at the back of the thigh, and the quadriceps, on the front of the thigh. Sometimes a break from running to ride a bicycle and strengthen the quadriceps is needed.

One of the most important developments in the advancement of the bicycle this century has been the derailleur, which the cyclist uses to change gears while riding. Hardly anyone for at least the last quarter-century has considered buying a bicycle without one. Most people deliberate whether they want a derailleur that will give them twelve, fourteen, or eighteen speeds.

Yet when Paul de Vivie introduced gears early in the century in his home in southern France, Gallic pride was insulted. Vivie was from an aristocratic family whose fortune came from manufacturing silk. In the late 1880s, he sold his silk business, founded a magazine, *Le Cycliste*, and opened a shop to import English bicycles. Vivie was thirty-six in 1889 when he produced the first bicycle made in France, La Gauloise, one of the early chain-driven bicycles with a diamond frame. He pondered how to create variable gearing while riding up and down the hilly landscape where he lived.

In 1901 he created a *dérailleur*, a device causing the chain to shift. His prototype fitted his La Gauloise. It consisted of two concentric chain rings, which required manually lifting the chain from one ring to another. He progressed to a three-speed derailleur, and extolled the virtues of gear shifting before a reluctant public.

Vivie became known through *Le Cycliste* for his dark, bushy mustache and for his pen name, "Vélocio." As Vélocio, he regularly wrote articles about the derailleur, and he answered letters by the mailbag. He was a determined nonconformist, riding his bicycle more than 100 miles a day well into advanced age, at a time when physicians believed that rigorous exercise was dangerous, even unhealthy.

"Every cyclist between twenty and sixty in good health," he wrote, "can ride 130 miles a day with 600 feet of climbing, provided he eats properly and has the proper bicycle."

Controversy over gears prompted Vélocio to suggest in 1902 that the Touring Club of France organize a 150-mile test over climbs that totaled 12,000 feet. French champion Edouard Fischer rode a single-speed bicycle against Marthe Hess, who was equipped with one of Vélocio's Gauloise bikes equipped with a 3-speed derailleur.

Of no surprise to today's cyclists accustomed to the advantage of multiple gears, Hess won convincingly. Newspapers hailed his victory because "the winner never set foot on the ground over the entire course."

Traditionalists remained unconvinced, however, including Henri Desgrange, who founded the Tour de France the following year.

"I applaud this test," Desgrange wrote in the newspaper he published, *L'Auto* (predecessor to today's *L'Equipe*, the largest-circulation sports daily newspaper). "But I still feel that variable gears are only for people over forty-five. Isn't it better to triumph by the strength of your muscles rather than by the artifice of a derailleur? We are getting soft. Come on, fellows. Let's say that the test was a fine demonstration—for our grandparents! As for me, give me a fixed gear!"

Decades passed before road racers used derailleurs. Only tourists who had time to fuss over equipment used them. Racers preferred riding with rear wheels that had a fixed sprocket on one side of the rear hub and a freewheel on the other side. Standard practice required everyone to stop at the base of an arduous hill, remove the rear wheel, turn it around for the smaller gear which would let the rider pedal up the grade, and freewheel down the other side. Later the riders would stop again to revert to the fixed gear.

Derailleurs were still experimental until 1932, when Alfredo Binda of Italy won the world professional road-racing championship in Rome by a wide margin on a bicycle equipped with a derailleur. The result was the same as the race thirty years earlier that Vélocio arranged between Fischer and Hess. But this time a champion like Binda gave derailleurs credibility. A new era was begun.

Improvements were made in derailleurs in Italy and France. Derailleurs became common all over the continent.

Americans, however, were slow to accept them, and it was the early 1960s before they gained the acceptance here that they acquired in Europe thirty years earlier.

Vélocio, meanwhile, continued to ride well into his seventies, when, tragically, he was struck by a streetcar while crossing a street in St. Etienne. He died clutching his bicycle.

Vélocio remains one of the legends in French cycling. Each year at Easter, cyclists gather outside St. Etienne to follow an eight-mile route up to the Col du Grand Bois at 3,000 feet. It was his favorite ride, one he did most mornings before breakfast, often accompanied by friends and local cyclists. At the top of the pass there is a stone monument to the derailleur's strongest proponent. Each year on "Vélocio Day," riders take a moment to reflect that they couldn't have made it without him.

Just who designed and wore the first cycling helmet is a matter of debate among some experts. But the June 1, 1938, issue of England's *Cycling Weekly* attributes the first crash helmet—made of leather and known as the hairnet—to Hans Ohrt, the burly sprinter from Beverly Hills, California. In 1915 Ohrt won the national amateur championship and embarked on a successful professional career as a sprinter on the board tracks, called velodromes, in the United States and Europe.

In 1920 Ohrt competed in the world cham-

Derailleurs, which shift the chain from sprocket to sprocket over the rear-wheel hub and on the chain rings over the pedals, are standard equipment on most bicycles today. (TOSRV photo by Greg Siple)

pionships in Antwerp, Belgium. He advanced to the semifinal where he was defeated in a match race by Bob Spears of Australia, who won the title that year.

Earlier in the season, Ohrt had suffered a nasty fall on the Sempione Velodrome in Milan, Italy. A couple weeks after the world's, he crashed in a race and landed on his face. Infection lingered through 1921, and it flared up when he was in Nice, France, where he underwent emergency surgery. He was in the hospital for two weeks. When released, his physician cautioned that he wear something to protect his head.

"Thusly, I hied myself to an understandable bootmaker located opposite the old Velodrome Pont-Magnan in Nice," he said in the 1938 *Cycling Weekly* story. For a nominal fee, the bootmaker made two simply designed helmets: they had a thick band of leather around the head, and two strips of leather crossing over the top of the head.

Ohrt introduced the first helmet on Christmas Day 1921 in the Grand Prix Noël at the Vélodrome d'Hiver in Paris.

"The press hardly even noted the use of a sprint helmet for the first time," Ohrt recalled. "But considerable mention was made by the British press when, on Good Friday (April 14) of 1922, at Herne Hill in the Southern Counties Cycle Union meeting, a sprint helmet was worn in my futile attempt to beat William J. Bailey (the winner) and Pete Moeskops in the international match race."

(Losing to Bailey and Moeskops was no disgrace: between them they won nine world championships.)

The following spring, Ohrt returned to the United States, where he was racing at the velodrome in Newark, New Jersey, where his helmet was the subject of mockery. Reporters teased, "Why the big fear?"

The only athletes in the country wearing helmets at the time were football players, who wore pigskin helmets designed, remarkably, by basketball's creator, James Naismith, and motorpace cyclists, who wore leather helmets that resembled football helmets.

Helmets for cyclists began to accrue respect in 1924. Italian star sprinter Mario Bergamini suffered a serious fall at speed during a race on the velodrome in New York City. He was a favorite among the New Yorkers, who filled the 20,000-seat grandstand and bleachers. Everyone waited anxiously for Bergamini's recovery that afternoon. When he finally returned to the track, the Italian donned a leather helmet like the one Ohrt had been wearing.

One by one, other riders began to join Ohrt and Bergamini in wearing helmets on the track.

Helmets remained optional in races until 1946, when the Amateur Bicycle League of America (predecessor to today's U.S. Cycling Federation), started to make helmets mandatory in sanctioned races. The helmet requirement took effect beginning with the ABL national championships that August in Franklin Park in Columbus, Ohio. Ironically, a cyclist died of a head injury in one of the races.

Eighteen-year-old Louis C. Brill, Jr., of Buffalo, New York, was crowded to the edge of the park road within yards of the finish in the one-mile final. He smashed headfirst, going at least 40 miles an hour, into a 350-pound Fox Movietone newsreel camera mounted on a tripod at the road edge. It was the first fatal accident at the nationals.

Hans Ohrt went on to retire from racing in the early 1930s and returned to the West Coast. He opened a bicycle shop in Beverly Hills, where many of his customers were actors and actresses who exercised to keep trim. Ohrt was in such demand as an exercise consultant in the film industry that he regularly conducted bicycle academies in Beverly Hills and North Hollywood. He became known as "The Bicycle Salesman to the Stars." Among his customers were Clark Gable and Carole Lombard.

Ohrt never sought to profit from introducing the cycling helmet. In a letter to a friend, he wrote: "The regret is that I so carelessly gave the two pioneer helmets away."

The following hard-shell helmet models have Snell approval:

All American Products: 5010 Kiddie Kap, 5020, 5026, 5030 Fiero, 5048 Corsica, 5050

Bell: Brava, Cool Cap, Li'l Bell Shell II, Little Bell, Ovation, Premier, Quest, Spectrum, Street Rider, Tiny Top, Tourlite, V-1 Pro

Davies Craig: Hartop

Denrich Sporting Goods: Model 824960 (Spalding, GSX, L.L. Bean, Raleigh Microlite), Model 612

Giro Sport Design: Hammerhead, LeMond, Prolight

Helmtec Industries: 2001-HL (Simpson)

Innova-Dex Sports: Leader (Avantil), Gara (Leader)

Life Technology (LT): Enduro, LT700, LT1100, Master Lite, Matrix, Matrix Microshell, Sabre 500/Aero

MPA: Vetta Corsa Lite 2, Vetta Corsa Lite 3, Schwinn Microshell, Schwinn Team

Osaka Grip (OGK): Avenir

Pro-Tec: Mirage, Pro X
Rhode Gear: Ultralight
Shoei: RC 2
Specialized Bicycle Components: Specialized, Air Force, Ultralight, Ground Force
Wolf and Associates: Wolf Pro
—Compiled by the Bicycle Helmet Safety Institute

More information on helmets is available from:

The Snell Memorial Foundation
P.O. Box 493
St. James, NY 11780
(516) 862-6440

American National Standards Institute (ANSI)
Safety & Health Department
1430 Broadway
New York, NY 10018
(212) 354-3300

The Bicycle Helmet Safety Institute
Randy Swart, Director
4611 Seventh Street South
Arlington, VA 22204-1419
(703) 521-2080

CHAPTER 6

ORGANIZATIONS AND WHAT THEY OFFER

OF ALL the bicycling organizations that have come and gone since cycling was the sport of the nineties a century ago, the League of American Wheelmen has endured. Founded in 1880, LAW blossomed in the 1890s: Membership in 1898 topped 102,000. Four years later, interest in cycling dissipated and LAW membership plummeted below 9,000. LAW sputtered out and was revived, sputtered out again and once more was revived, most recently in 1964. It keeps growing with the recent revival in cycling. Membership in 1990 was 20,000 nationwide, representing an 11 percent increase over the previous year.

In 1990 LAW celebrated its 110th anniversary. Its continuity may have been broken, but its spirit has remained the same—a cycling advocacy organization to serve as a nationwide network of affiliated cycling clubs and organizations, and organize rides.

A trait that characterized LAW was the quality of people it attracted. LAW's founder was Kirk Munroe, who became a celebrated author of children's books. Munroe was thirty when he organized and founded LAW in Newport, Rhode Island. He had knocked around the West when it was wild and knew General George Armstrong Custer, Wild Bill Hickok, Buffalo Bill Cody, and Kit Carson. When Sioux warriors killed Custer and his 264 troops in 1876 at the Battle of the Little Big Horn in Montana, *The New York Sun* hired Munroe to write background articles on Custer, Indians, and the West. That became his entry into journalism and prompted his move to New York City, where he was introduced to bicycle riding on highwheelers.

Bicycles were a new toy for upperclass men. (The long skirts that women wore, sweeping to the ground, made it awkward for them to ride the highwheelers.) Bicycles were expensive, especially in those days a

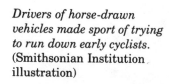

Drivers of horse-drawn vehicles made sport of trying to run down early cyclists. (Smithsonian Institution illustration)

generation before the concept of installment payments. Bicycles cost about $150, the equivalent of more than $2,000 today. Men who rode them called themselves Wheelmen. They wore short Norfolk jackets, knickers and long socks, and round hats with a short bill. Club riders wore uniforms that had military styling, with brass buttons.

Highwheelers boasted new technology: ball bearings in the hubs, wire wheels, and hard-rubber tires. The chief liability of high-wheelers was that they set the rider directly over the bicycle's center. On the dirt roads of the day, a stone or wagon-wheel rut would pitch the rider headfirst over the handlebars. Falls, aptly called headers, were frequent, and injuries were common.

Drivers of horse-drawn vehicles made sport of trying to run down cyclists. Children were tempted to jam a stick between the spokes of a cycle passing by. Dogs preyed on cyclists. These hazards made Wheelmen reluctant to ride alone. Clubs came into vogue as protective organizations as well as for their sociability.

Munroe sported a handlebar mustache and approached whatever he did with panache.

He quit his newspaper job after three years to become a free-lance journalist and author. In early 1880 he helped form the New York Bicycle Club. That year also marked the establishment of the first bicycle-riding school in New York as Wheelmen proliferated.

Many of America's gentry spent their summers in Newport, Rhode Island, to take advantage of the ocean breeze. Munroe wrote a letter to Newport Mayor J. Truman Burdick to offer a parade of cyclists in uniform on Decoration Day (now called Memorial Day), which apparently struck His Honor as a quaint novelty, for he granted permission for a parade on Main Street. Munroe issued invitations to forty bicycle clubs in Connecticut, New Jersey, New York, Massachusetts, Pennsylvania, and Rhode Island to come to the resort town for the Decoration Day weekend.

Some 130 Wheelmen convened in Newport. They decided to create a national organization and called it the League of American Wheelmen. Munroe, the charter member, was elected commander. On Decoration Day, the unprecedented parade of cyclists attracted crowds that lined Main

Off to a solid start in 1880, LAW founders posed for a group photo, when cameras and bikes were new.
(Smithsonian Institution photo)

Street and adjacent thoroughfares. People from surrounding towns commuted in on buggies and farm wagons. Excursion trains brought in more spectators from outlying areas. It had become a festive occasion by the time the bugles sounded the League of American Wheelmen to pedal in military formation up Main Street.

Growth was steady in LAW. Membership reached 8,000 in 1890, when safety bicycles began to succeed the highwheelers, and women took to riding bicycles. Women started wearing shorter skirts. A sports outfit called the bloomer—a short skirt and loose trousers gathered and buttoned at the ankle—was scandalous clothing in the 1880s, but by the 1890s had gained acceptability.

Munroe by then was a best-selling author. His 1887 novel, *The Flamingo Feather*, about a sixteenth-century Frenchman who became a member of the Seminole Indian tribe of Florida, made Munroe a household name. He left LAW to devote his time to traveling worldwide and writing.

Vast numbers of men and women were riding bicycles on city streets, on park roads, along country lanes, especially on Sundays and holidays from early spring through late autumn. On weekdays, cyclists who commuted to work and later back home filled the streets.

With such demand for bicycles, the industry was one of the largest in the country. By 1895 there were 300 factories manufacturing bicycles. Women's bicycles were in high demand. Consumers had to wait months for their bicycles.

LAW membership was mushrooming. The press followed club secretary Abbott Bassett's release of figures as the organization headed to 100,000 members. In September 1897, *The New York Times* reported that Robert Buggelyn of Corona, New York, became member No. 100,000. Buggelyn joined LAW's ranks with John D. Rockefeller and Frederic Remington.

In 1898, membership reached a high of 102,636. But soon interest in bicycle riding began to disappear. Electric and cable street-cars were introduced and replaced bicycles as a means of transportation. The cost of bicycles soon declined to less than $100, which diminished their cachet. Soon the adults who had once waited for the bicycle they bought to be delivered were ordering cars instead. LAW's membership diminished to 8,600 in 1902.

After the adult market for bicycles dropped off, the children's market developed. Parents bought inexpensive, durable bicycles for their offspring. The children's market kept the industry in business. Bicycles remained unchanged until the Schwinn Bicycle Company of Chicago brought out bicycles with balloon tires in 1933. They measured two and one-eighths inches wide, five-eighths wider than the prevailing standard.

A few years earlier, the automobile industry had converted cars to balloon tires and mounted a brisk advertising campaign to sell them to consumers eager to buy the latest in personal transportation. When bicycles came out with balloon tires, parents took another look at their kids' bicycles and bought

new ones. Surging sales stimulated other manufacturers to produce balloon-tired bicycles.

Rising demand in bicycles prompted the Cycle Trades of America, the association of bicycle manufacturers, to revive LAW, which had lapsed with the death of Secretary Bassett in 1924. One of those involved in the revival was Phyllis Harmon, then a resident of Evanston, Illinois. In the mid-1930s, she was part of a group of 400 women and men recreation cyclists who took trains to different venues for rides.

"There were baggage cars for bikes and one extra baggage car for square and folk dancing," she said. "It was a lot of fun doing reels on the board floor that bounced as the train went clacking over the rails." Bicycle trains, as they were called, went on excursions within a three-hour radius of Chicago. They went south downstate to Kankakee, north to Wisconsin's Lake Geneva and Union Grove. "We would take the train and square dance on the way," Harmon said. "When we got to where we were going, we took our bikes from the baggage cars and went pedaling forty miles or so. Then we got back on the train and went back to Chicago."

Harmon, twenty-one in 1937, became part of the LAW revival in metropolitan Chicago. "I was a charter member of the Evanston Club. Other chapters were in Oak Park and the Rambler's Club of Chicago. Three clubs formed a council. Then other clubs joined in Indiana and Wisconsin. In 1940 a convention was held in Chicago. It was the first national convention since LAW petered out in 1923."

Clubs joined from other states to boost LAW to twenty-three clubs by the time the Japanese bombed Pearl Harbor in December 1941 and President Roosevelt declared war.

After the war, production of cars went up to all-time levels and took over the roads. "Cars got wider after the war," Harmon said. "The roads remained the same width. That made riding a bicycle more difficult. The fellows returned from the war, gradually settled down, got married and raised families. Our membership went down. Then, in November 1955, LAW just quit."

Harmon and her husband raised six children. She continued to ride a bicycle up to the seventh month of her pregnancies because "I discovered that bicycling is very good for varicose veins." Nearly ten years had elapsed when Harmon joined three others in Keith Kingbay's living room in Chicago to discuss reorganizing LAW. "That was in October 1964," recalled Kingbay, who lives in the suburb of Buffalo Grove. "In Illinois there is a state law that says any bank account that has been untouched for ten years automatically reverts to the state. We discussed this at the meeting. One thing led to another and we decided to hold a dinner in Chicago to reorganize LAW."

Several dozen former LAW members, bicycle dealers, and industry representatives attended. Kingbay, currently on the LAW board of directors, observed that even when the organization went into the doldrums, its tradition continued. "I rode my first century in 1928 in Kenosha, Wisconsin, where I grew up, and that was put on by LAW," he said. "I was fifteen years old and didn't have the thirty-five cents to buy the LAW century pin. It was a little round pin with the winged insignia and two tiny loops. There was always a little nucleus of LAW that survived in the Midwest because there were a lot of bicycle makers there."

Massive road construction in the early 1960s improved roads nationwide, which included making roads substantially wider. Cycling conditions were significantly better in the 1960s than the previous decade. In 1965 LAW held its first convention in several years in Chicago. "It didn't take long to become a national organization," Harmon said.

Organization headquarters was set up in

Bicycle trains in the 1930s took cyclists on commutes from the city, such as this one out of Chicago, so they could ride their bicycles in different venues. (Toivo Kaitila photo, courtesy of Phyllis Harmon)

In the summer of 1990, Phyllis Harmon at seventy-three pedaled 3,300 miles across the country in seven weeks. (Phyllis Harmon photo)

1971 in the Chicago suburb of Palestine. In 1979 LAW's headquarters moved to Baltimore for easier access to Washington's Capitol Hill, a benefit in its work as an advocacy service organization.

LAW publishes a magazine, *Bicycle USA*, eight times a year. Its biggest issue is the December *Almanac*, which has 134 pages offering a wide variety of resources, from maps to books to ride information. The March issue is the forty-eight-page *TourFinder*, which features a comprehensive list of bicycle tours. The other six issues are thirty-two pages each.

Harmon continues to serve LAW as honorary director. "I ride for the camaraderie," she said. "When people get technical and discuss cadence and rpms, that stuff just leaves me cold."

In the summer of 1990 she rode her fifteen-speed bicycle 3,300 miles from Los Angeles to Boston with sixty-five others in seven weeks. "The youngest rider was eighteen, and ages went all the way up to several men in their sixties," she said. "I was the senior rider at seventy-three."

Annual LAW dues are $25 for an individual, $30 for a family.

More information is available from:

The League of American Wheelmen
6707 Whitestone Rd., Suite 209
Baltimore, MD 21207
(301) 944-3399

Region 1, New England: Maine,
    Vermont, New Hampshire,
    Massachusetts, Connecticut, and
    Rhode Island:
John Torosian
P.O. Box 305
Atkinson, NH 03811
(603) 362-4572

Region 2, Middle Atlantic: New York,
    New Jersey:
Beth Silverwater
14 Gould Place, No. 2
Caldwell, NJ 07006
(201) 228-7208

Region 3, Eastern: Pennsylvania,
    Delaware:
Robert Nordvall
303 South Washington
Gettysburg, PA 17325
(717) 334-0742

Region 4, Coastal: Maryland, District
of Columbia, Virginia, West
Virginia, and North Carolina:
Robert Carson
205 E. Joppa Rd., No. 607
Baltimore, MD 21204
(301) 828-8604

Region 5, Southeastern: Alabama,
Florida, Georgia, Mississippi, and
South Carolina:
George Brewton, Sr.
402 W. Broad St.
Louisville, GA 30434
(912) 625-3305

Region 6, East Central: Ohio,
Kentucky, and Tennessee:
Larry Hodapp
4724 Bokay Dr.
Dayton, OH 45440
(513) 435-9366

Region 7, Great Lakes: Michigan and
Indiana:
Steve Gottlieb
2310 Queens Way
Bloomington, IN 47401
(812) 334-4058

Region 8, Central: Illinois:
Keith Kingbay
450 Checker Dr.
Buffalo Grove, IL 60089
(708) 459-8242

Region 9, North Central: Wisconsin,
Minnesota, Iowa, and Missouri:
Steve Clark
Route 1, Box 99
Cushing, WI 45006
(715) 648-5519

Region 10, South Central: Oklahoma,
Arkansas, Louisiana, and Texas:
Marc Weiss
1618 7th South, #E
New Orleans, LA 70115
(504) 899-8575

Region 11, Mid-Continent: North
Dakota, South Dakota, Nebraska,
and Kansas:
Richard Froyd
2512 Seabrook
Topeka, KS 66614
(913) 272-6862

Region 12, Rocky Mountain: Montana,
Wyoming, and Colorado
Debby Phelps
P.O. Box 1306
Gunnison, CO 81230
(303) 641-1273

Region 13, Southwestern: Utah,
Arizona, New Mexico, and Nevada
Yvonne Morrison
8238 E. Rancho Vista
Scottsdale, AZ 85251
(602) 949-1517

Region 14, Far Western: California and
Hawaii
Alan Forkosh
33 Moss Ave., No. 204
Oakland, CA 94610
(415) 655-4221

Region 15, Northwestern: Idaho,
Oregon, Washington, and Alaska
Phil Miller
15670 N.E. 70th Court
Redmond, WA 98052
(206) 885-7924

Honorary Director
Phyllis W. Harmon
356 Robert Ave.
Wheeling, IL 60090
(708) 537-1268

Another group dedicated to recreation riding is the American Youth Hostels, which has more than 100,000 members. AYH is a member of the International Youth Hostel Federation, representing more than 5,000 hosteling organizations in more than sev-

(Greg Siple photo)

enty countries. Observers of cycling such as Greg Siple credit AYH with helping to carry recreation cycling through the lean years of the 1930s through the 1950s.

Two schoolteachers in Northfield, Massachusetts—Isabel and Monroe Smith—founded AYH in 1934. AYH was an outgrowth of the movement that German schoolteacher Richard Schirrmann started in 1909 to make the countryside accessible to schoolchildren of the great industrial centers.

World War I interrupted the hostel movement, but after peace was restored in 1918 hostels spread. They opened up in Switzerland, Poland, Holland, France, England, and Wales. Some hostels were farmhouses, others were schools or camps. They were basically inexpensive places to stay overnight while traveling. Hostels featured separate sleeping and washing facilities for men and women, and a common kitchen and dining room—a custom that remains characteristic of hostels everywhere. A hostel manager or house parents supervised the hostels, another custom that continues. Hostels appealed to people traveling alone or with a companion or two.

In 1932 an international hosteling conference met in Holland. A plan for uniformity was developed to enable members of each youth hostel to travel freely from country to country and stay in hostels on the way.

Isabel and Monroe Smith went to Europe in 1933 to conduct a survey of the youth movements there and discovered the Youth Hostel Movement. Upon returning to their home in western Massachusetts, they embarked on a traveling tour around the United States to speak about the new movement. The Smiths worked to build a national advisory board. They got off to an auspicious start when Mount Holyoke College President Mary E. Wooley was appointed first president.

The Smiths opened the first American hostel on December 27, 1934, in Northfield. The following June, the couple bought a colonial house on Main Street. It became the first official hostel in this country. The hostel movement caught on here as it had in Europe. By 1942 there were more than 200 hos-

Isabel and Munroe Smith founded the AYH in 1934 in Northfield, Massachusetts. (AYH photo)

tels nationwide. World War II forced a decline in hosteling as staff and young men and women left for military duty. Many hostels were converted to military housing. After the war, AYH was reorganized and higher standards were instituted.

Public awareness and use of hostels increased substantially in the 1970s. A more extensive travel program and improved operating policies resulted in membership growth. Now there are more than 200 hostels

across the country. They provide dormitory-like accommodations.

Many are historic buildings developed into hostels. Others are in state and national parks. One is in a lighthouse on the California coast—Pigeon Point Lighthouse in Pescadero, fifty miles south of San Francisco. Another is a World War II battleship, the U.S.S. *Massachusetts*, in Fall River, Massachusetts.

"AYH is an aspect of recreational touring that has received little notice, yet they carried the torch during the lean years," Siple said. "AYH ran a bicycle tour in Europe in 1935 and, with the exception of the World War II years, has been doing it ever since, in addition to domestic tours they run."

Simplicity is the rule of the hostels. Hostelers provide their own personal items, such as bed linens or sheet sleeping sack, towels, and food. Hostelers are expected to clean up after themselves and help with the general chores, which contributes toward keeping overnight fees so low, typically around $10. (The hostel that the Smiths founded costs $7.50 a night. Tel. 413-498-5311, ext. 502.)

All that's needed is to show your AYH membership card and your sheet sleeping sack, pay the overnight fee, and that's it. Reservations are not required, but it's a good idea to book in advance, especially during peak seasons.

AYH membership is $25 for adults, ages 18 to 54; $10 for youths under 18; $15 for senior citizens 55 and up; $35 for families; and $250 for life membership.

Members are entitled to stay in hostels. They also receive a 224-page handbook with detailed listings—including maps—of more than 200 AYH hostels in forty-one states and the District of Columbia. Members receive *Knapsack Magazine*, published twice a year, with entertaining travel features and other information. The *AYH Council Newsletter*, published in each of the forty councils that make up the national, is sent to members.

Information is available from:

American Youth Hostels, Inc.
P. O. Box 37613
Washington, DC 20013-7613
(202) 783-6161

American Youth Hostels also have forty local council offices across the country that offer a wide range of programs, from weekend outings to mass bicycle rallies. Local council offices provide hosteling cards, hostel handbooks, travel brochures, seminars and much more. For details get in touch with the council near you:

EASTERN REGION

Connecticut
Yankee Council
118 Oak St.
Hartford, CT 06106
(203) 247-6356

Riding along a ribbon of road that cuts a swath through the countryside is to commune with nature. (AYH photo by Greg Siple)

(AYH photo)

District of Columbia
Potomac Area Council
P.O. Box 28607
Central Station
Washington, DC 20038-8606
(202) 783-4943

Massachusetts
Greater Boston Council
1020 Commonwealth Ave.
Boston, MA 02215
(617) 731-6692

New York
Hudson-Mohawk Council
P.O. Box 6343
Albany, NY 12206
(518) 449-8261

Metropolitan New York Council
891 Amsterdam Ave.
New York, NY 10025
(212) 932-2300

Niagara Frontier Council
P.O. Box 1110
Ellicott Station, Buffalo, NY 14203
(716) 852-5222

Syracuse Council
535 Oak St.
Syracuse, NY 13203
(315) 472-5788

PENNSYLVANIA

Delaware Valley Council
38 S. Third St.
Philadelphia, PA 19106
(215) 925-6004

Pittsburgh Council
6300 Fifth Ave.
Pittsburgh, PA 15232-2998
(412) 362-8181

SOUTHERN REGION

Florida
Florida Council
P.O. Box 533097
Orlando, FL 32853-3097
(407) 649-8761

Georgia
Georgia Council
P.O. Box 930053
Norcross, GA 30093
(404) 263-6339

North Carolina
Coastal Carolina Council
275 N. May St.
Southern Pines, NC 28387
(919) 692-8108

Piedmont Council
P.O. Box 10766
Winston-Salem, NC 27103

Research Triangle Council
R.R. 7, Box 115
Durham, NC 27707-9602
(919) 968-3531

Texas
Bluebonnet Council
5302 Crawford
Houston, TX 77004
(713) 523-1009

North Texas Council
P.O. Box 781192
Dallas, TX 75378
(214) 350-4294

Southwest Texas Council
2200 South Lakeshore Blvd.
Austin, TX 78741
(512) 444-2294

MIDWEST REGION

Illinois
Metropolitan Chicago Council
3036 N. Ashland Ave.
Chicago, IL 60657
(312) 327-8114

Indiana
Northwest Indiana Council
8231 Lake Shore Drive
Gary, IN 46403-0016

Iowa
Northeast Iowa Council
P.O. Box 10
Postville, IA 52162
(319) 864-3923

Michigan
Michigan Council
3024 Coolidge
Berkley, MI 48072
(313) 545-0511

Minnesota
Minnesota Council
2395 University Ave., West #302
St. Paul, MN 55114
(612) 659-0407

Missouri
Ozark Area Council
7187 Manchester Road
St. Louis, MO 63143
(314) 644-4660

Nebraska
Nebraskaland Council
129 N. 10th St. #413
Lincoln, NE 68508
(402) 472-3265

Ohio
Columbus Council
P.O. Box 14384
Columbus, OH 43223-0111
(614) 447-1006

Lima Council
P.O. Box 173
Lima, OH 45802
(419) 339-4751

Northeast Ohio Council
6093 Stanford Road
Peninsula, OH 44264
(216) 467-8711

Toledo Area Council
6206 Pembridge Drive
Toledo, OH 43615
(419) 841-4510

Tri-state Council
P.O. Box 141015
Cincinnati, OH 45250
(513) 488-3755

Wisconsin
Wisconsin Council
2224 W. Wisconsin
Milwaukee, WI 53233
(414) 933-1155

WESTERN REGION
Alaska
Alaska Council
P.O. Box 24037
Anchorage, AK 99524
(907) 562-7772

Arizona
Arizona-Southern Nevada Council
1046 E. Lemon St.
Tempe, AZ 85218
(602) 894-5128

California
Central California Council
P.O. Box 28148
San Jose, CA 95159
(408) 298-0670

Golden Gate Council
425 Divisadero St. #307
San Francisco, CA 94117
(415) 863-9939

Los Angeles Council
335 W. Seventh St.
San Pedro, CA 90731
(213) 831-8846

San Diego Council
1031 India St.
San Diego, CA 92101
(619) 226-1099

Colorado
Rocky Mountain Council
P.O. Box 2370
Boulder, CO 80306
(303) 442-1166

New Mexico
New Mexico Council
101 N. Cooper St.
Silver City, NM 88061
(505) 388-5485

Oregon
Oregon Council
99 W. Tenth Ave. #205
Eugene, OR 97401
(503) 683-3685

Washington
Washington State Council
419 Queen Anne Ave. N. #108
Seattle, WA 98109
(206) 281-7306

LAW's decline around the turn of the century spawned another organization that is still highly visible in today's cycling. LAW was the sport's governing body when amateur and professional bicycle races flourished from coast to coast. Officials certified records, and its network of clubs put on events, including annual national championships, dating back to 1882. Late in the 1890s, demand started for races on Sunday, corresponding to baseball teams introducing Sunday games. LAW officials adamantly opposed Sunday competitions and dropped their affiliation with racing in 1899. Independent promoters and track owners responded by forming the National Cycling Association as an alternative organization to hold their own races, especially Sunday events.

The NCA, however, existed chiefly to promote professional cycling and reap a profit. By 1920, professional races had consolidated in the Northeast. That year, John M. Chapman, who ruled the NCA absolutely, wielded final approval of the Olympic cycling team going to the Games in Antwerp, Belgium, but he left the funding to the informal Inter-Club Bicycle Road Racing League. About a dozen New York City–area bicycle clubs formed the Inter-Club league in 1914 in response to the neglect of amateur races, which suffered after LAW's withdrawal. Chapman's autocratic handling of the Olympic selection, only to leave the financing of eleven riders, a coach, and a manager to the Inter-Club league, prompted club members to action. They changed their name and formed the Amateur Bicycle League of America to embrace all amateur clubs in the country. The ABL, as it was called, was incorporated in 1921 in New York City.

In 1921 the ABL held its first national championship in Washington, DC. Ed Bieber of Washington was ten years old when he watched the championship—a series of four races from the half-mile to five miles. They were held in West Potomac Park near the Thomas Jefferson Memorial in downtown Washington.

"There were thousands of people out there watching," Bieber recalled. "The races were for senior men only—ages seventeen and up. No juniors. No women. It was the only time they were ever held like that, probably because they were just starting."

The ABL sanctioned amateur races and records. National championships were shifted annually around the country. At the 1922 nationals in Atlantic City, the junior boys' category was introduced for riders 16 and younger. The women's division (called girls' division until 1954) was introduced at the 1937 nationals in Buffalo.

One struggle after another characterized the ABL. When Chapman needed professionals, he unilaterally converted his pick of amateurs to professionals. The ABL relied on volunteer help and donations, which kept the organization hard-pressed to hold races and award decent prizes.

Chapman retired in the late 1930s, when professional cycling was in a downward spiral in the depths of the Depression. The outbreak of World War II in 1940 struck a blow to the colorful 6-day era that kept professional cycling going. "The war," Keith Kingbay sighed, "broke a lot of things."

In the postwar years, the ABL shouldered bicycle racing in the United States. It had more spirit than support through the mid-1970s, when rules governing amateurs internationally began to relax. In 1975 the ABL changed its name to the U.S. Cycling Federation to make it consistent with the name of governing bodies in other nations.

The entire structure of amateur sports in the United States, including cycling, went through a transformation over the next three years. The U.S. Olympic Committee took over an abandoned Air Force base in Colorado Springs, where the USCF opened its office in 1978.

Today the federation employs a staff of twenty-two in its head office. A budget of $3 million comes from corporate contributions, the U.S. Olympic Committee, membership dues, and race-sanctioning fees.

Growth has been steady, and women make up the sharpest rate of increase. Figures show the federation membership has gone up 15 percent a year during the 1980s to 35,000 in 1990. About 3,500, or 10 percent, are women, whose rate of growth over the decade averaged 327 percent. The number of clubs has proliferated to approximately 1,100 in all fifty states. Race permits went up an aver-

Mountain bikes open new areas to exploration on a two-wheeler. (Bikecentennial photo by Michael McCoy)

age of 14 percent during the 1980s, to about 1,700 in 1990.

Primary goals of the federation are to promote development of the athletes in open and interscholastic competition for the Olympics, Pan American Games, and world championships. Clubs function as the grassroots of cycling activities. They promote training rides, clinics, entry-level races, and social activities.

Membership is $35 annually. Members receive the monthly tabloid, *Cycling USA*, and are eligible to compete in USCF races.

More information is available from:

U.S. Cycling Federation
1750 E. Boulder
Colorado Springs, CO 80909
(719) 578-4581

The fastest-growing segment of cycling is in mountain bikes, over which the National Off-Road Bicycle Association serves as the governing organization for competition. NORBA was founded in January 1983 and now has 5,000 members in about 110 clubs. Bicycle industry officials estimate there are approximately 14 million mountain-bike riders nationwide. Beyond the statistics, what has characterized mountain-bike riders is a sense of adventure.

"The people who started mountain bikes, back in the mid-1970s, were counterculture people," observed Tim Blumenthal, managing editor of *Mountain Bike Magazine*. "They were high-spirited, with a touch of zaniness. These were people who came from road racing. They liked bikes and wanted to do something different."

Riders like Gary Fisher, Tom Ritchey, and Joe Breeze pedaled balloon-tired bicycles with one speed over dirt trails that climbed up Mount Tamalpais, a 3,000-foot coastal mountain in Marin County, a short distance from San Francisco's Golden Gate Bridge.

"What makes Marin County so attractive to mountain-bike riding is that so much of the county is unsettled," said Marin resident Owen Mulholland. "There must be fifty miles of dirt trails—single tracks or fire lanes—for every mile of paved roads."

Blumenthal pointed out that the first mountain bicycles were heavy. "But these were creative people," he said. "They made improvements, and the bikes got lighter. In September 1981, Specialized brought out the first mountain bike to hit the market."

National distribution led to a rapid expansion of the new line of bikes. But not everybody was enthusiastic about this new sports craze. Mountain-bike riders shared dirt trails with hikers and equestrians, who complained that the bikes were eroding the trails and that carefree riders were careening down hills at speeds that jeopardized others. Hikers and equestrians mounted a rigorous campaign against the mountain bikers.

In 1983 access to trails was an issue, and the number of people riding mountain bicycles rose that year to 200,000. NORBA was formed to sanction the races and work for trail access. NORBA founders were Fisher, Ritchey, Breeze, Mike Sinyard, Charlie Cunningham, Charles Kelly, Tom Hillard, Jack Ingram, Jacquie Phelan, and Wende Cragg.

The mountain-bike industry made its biggest jump in 1985 to 1989, when sales went from one million to 11 million, Blumenthal said.

Mulholland was a slow convert. "Mountain-bike riding didn't appeal to my imagination the way road riding does," he admitted. "But once I started riding a mountain bike, there was no turning back.

"Most people who ride mountain bikes like riding without the fear of picking up a piece of glass in their tires and getting a flat. The bikes themselves are practically bulletproof, they're so sturdy. After I've been out riding on a muddy trail, I just hose off my bike to clean it. With a road bike, I would have to take Q-tips to get it just right. Besides, riding off the road, you don't have to worry about cars."

In January 1989 NORBA went under the USCF wing to devote itself to sanctioning competition. NORBA's new format shifted it away from working for land access. NORBA put its support behind the new International Mountain Bicycling Association, now the voice for trail access for mountain bicycles. IMBA is based in Bishop, California. It provides land access and educational information for responsible off-road cycling. IMBA is also the umbrella organization for Concerned Off-Road Bicycle Association and Responsible Organized Mountain Pedalers, both based in California.

One measure of NORBA's success was the first internationally sanctioned World Mountain Bike Championships, held in mid-September in 1990 in Purgatory, Colorado. Such an unlikely name fits a tough sport: More than 800 riders from twenty-four nations competed in a grueling but glorious program of men's and women's events composed of hill climbs up Rocky Mountain ski-slope trails, downhill races over twisting dirt paths, and gruesome cross-country grinds up to 32 miles.

Another measure of NORBA's success is that mountain-bike racing has succeeded in going global. In 1991 a World Cup circuit features three races in the United States, one in Canada, and five in western Europe. The 1991 world championships are scheduled for September 29 to October 6 in Lucca, Italy.

"What's remarkable is that the European riders are following the example of Americans in mountain bikes," Blumenthal said.

"The market is expanding really well in America, but in Europe the rate of increase is even greater. It's an interesting switch after seeing our riders, like Greg LeMond, adapt to European-style of racing on roads."

Charles Fischman, NORBA administrative director, said one-third of the organization's members are in California. Another quarter is in Colorado and Utah, and the rest are in the Northeast and Middle Atlantic, he said.

NORBA membership is $25 a year. Members receive a monthly tabloid, *NORBA News*.

Information is available from:

National Off-Road Bicycle Association
1750 E. Boulder
Colorado Springs, CO 80909
(719) 578-4717

Responsible Organized Mountain
   Pedalers (ROMP)
Ken Detrick, President
15064 Kennedy Rd.
Los Gatos, CA 95032
(408) 356-8230

Concerned Off-Road Bicycle
   Association (CORBA)
15236 Victory Blvd., Box 149
Van Nuys, CA 91411
(818) 991-6626

For the ambitious and talented who want to follow in Greg LeMond's wheelmarks, there is the U.S. Professional Cycling Federation, which oversees professional road and track racing in the United States. USPRO, as it is called, has about 100 members, including LeMond.

After John M. Chapman retired from the National Cycling Association in the late 1930s, the NCA floundered. A small number of promoters attempted to revive interest in professional cycling in the postwar years. Once again six-day races were held on wooden velodromes constructed in armories and municipal auditoriums in New York City, Cleveland, Chicago, Buffalo, and other cities. These winter sixes drew top European riders from 1946 to 1951. Switzerland's Adonis of the bike, Hugo Koblet, won a six-day race in New York in 1949 and also triumphed in the 1951 Tour de France.

Six-day races held on velodromes constructed in armories and municipal auditoriums were popular attractions in New York City, Buffalo, Pittsburgh, St. Louis, Chicago, and other cities. Eyeing the starter at the top of the track is Jimmy Walthour, Jr., of the famous Walthour family. (Russell Mamone collection)

More than a dozen U.S. pros competed in the six-day circuit with the visiting Europeans. American six-day riders included Mike Abt, Charley Logan, Ray Bedard, Tino Ribaldi, Jerry Rodman, Bill Anderson, Bill Jacoby, Charley Yaccino, Erwin Pesek, Danny Esposito, Harold Nauwens, and Ted Smith.

The revival fizzled, and America's professional cycling, as well as the NCA, went with it. One of the pros who came over and stayed was Chris Van Gent of Belgium. He settled in Denver and opened a bike shop. In the 1950s and 1960s he saw that American cycling lacked guidance and felt that a strong professional class would give it direction.

In 1968 Van Gent founded the Professional Racing Organization, which he soon incorporated, with former NCA officials serving on PRO's original executive board. But PRO was little known and so small that for several years Van Gent had to pay the organization's dues to the Union Cycliste Internationale—the sport's governing body, headquartered in Geneva, Switzerland—out of his own pocket.

Most of the action in American cycling was in amateur races that the USCF governed. In 1979, three-time Olympian Jack Simes III and his Olympic teammate Dave Chauner formed a business to help competitive cycling expand. They saw a need to develop a professional class. With support from Van Gent and others, Simes and Chauner took over PRO.

PRO's debut in the major leagues was in May 1982 in Baltimore, where the 62.5-mile USPRO championship was held, offering an impressive $100,000 prize list. The championship changed venue in 1985 to Philadelphia, where it continues to be held, on a Sunday in early June. Called the CoreStates USPRO Championship, it is 156 miles long in a circuit that wends through Philadelphia neighborhoods.

President of USPRO is Fred Mengoni, of-

ten referred to as the Godfather of American professional cycling. A native of northern Italy, Mengoni raced bicycles on the roads during the late 1940s and 1950s. At age thirty-three, in 1957, he emigrated to New York City. He applied the same energy and enthusiasm to real estate as he had to cycling, and became one of the most successful real estate entrepreneurs in the Empire State.

In 1981 Mengoni started to help USPRO, which then had only a small number of riders, but one was LeMond, who was on his way to becoming a media event of his own. Mengoni sponsored his own amateur team, which had consistent winners. He personally paid expenses for pros to events such as the world championships in Europe. (Pros are on their own for expenses to the world's because it is the one race of the year where they compete for their own country rather than their trade team.)

"America gave me great opportunity to come here and do well," he explained. "I want to help the sport."

LeMond showed his appreciation in a magnificent manner for what Mengoni has done. During the 1989 Tour de France, Mengoni was traveling with the LeMond entourage and turned sixty-five on the last Friday stage. LeMond told him he would win the stage, seventy-eight miles to Aix-les-Bains, as a birthday present. LeMond's victory set up his dramatic triumph two days later in Paris. When LeMond was invited to the White House September 27th, Mengoni was his guest. President Bush gave USPRO President Mengoni a pair of cuff links with the presidential seal.

Information is available from:

U.S. Professional Racing Organization
Jack Simes III, Executive Director
R.D. No. 1, Box 1650
New Tripoli, PA 18066
(215) 298-3262

John Marino's face shows the strain of his 1978 cross-country record ride, the equivalent of running forty-three consecutive marathons, but he achieved his goal of making the Guinness Book of World Records. *(John Marino photo)*

Mae West once remarked, "Too much of a good thing can be wonderful." For those who like to apply her remark to riding a bicycle, there is the Ultra-Marathon Cycling Association.

It started in 1978 when John Marino of Irvine, California, rode into the *Guinness Book of World Records* for pedaling across the United States in 13 days, 1 hour, and 20 minutes. He kept at it for another two years and shortened his time to 12 days, 3 hours, and 41 minutes. His efforts were the subject of a twenty-three-minute documentary, *Psychling*, which Peter Rosten of Hollywood

produced to emphasize motivation and goal setting. *Psychling* won nine film awards and drew the attention of executives in the American Broadcast Company. (More recently, Rosten was executive producer of the 1989 movie *True Believer*, starring James Wood and Robert Downey, Jr.)

ABC's interest led to establishment of the 3,100-mile Race Across America in 1982, referred to as RAAM, and billed as the longest nonstop bicycle race in the world. ABC's *Wide World of Sports* coverage of the inaugural RAAM created a national event. The race involved four riders—Lon Haldeman, who won; John Howard in second; Michael Shermer third; and Marino in fourth—in a dramatic event. Riders took only short nap breaks of two to four hours daily. They pedaled over the Sierra Nevadas, the Rockies, vast stretches of Midwest farm fields, over the Applachians, through pouring rain and burning sun. ABC's coverage involved a production crew of more than thirty riding in eight vehicles. ABC won an Emmy in sports programming for their coverage.

For Marino it was a successful redemption for a baseball career that was promising until he injured his back, at nineteen, in 1969. "I was doing dead lifts in the gym, attempting 525 pounds, and *boom!* my back went." He never fully recovered. Marino played catcher through graduation at San Diego State and made it to the minor leagues, playing for the Oakland Athletics farm team in Tempe, Arizona, before he was cut in 1974.

"I was a frustrated jock," he recounted. His frustration mounted when he discovered two years later that running aggravated his back injury. His hope of running the Boston Marathon was dashed.

"Then I was thumbing through the *Guinness Book of World Records* and saw the record for the transcontinental ride. I wanted to do something to get my self-esteem back. I saw that in 1973 Paul Cornish had set the record for riding from city hall in Santa Monica, California, to city hall in New York City in 13 days, 5 hours, and 20 minutes. The book said he lived in Costa Mesa, about five miles from where I was living. I called him up and went over to interview him with a tape recorder. I had a hundred questions all prepared, from what kind of bike to ride, to how many people in a support crew, to diet. I was a real nuisance, but he was patient."

Two years and many thousands of miles later, Marino set out to get his name in the *Guinness Book of World Records*. "When I got into cycling, I discovered how good a rider Paul was. I decided if I couldn't break his record, I would try to get close. It turned out that I beat his record by four hours. It was absolute hell. It was most dreadful. What kept me going was my support crew. There were four of them, traveling in a motor home. It was a fantastic experience, but it was tough."

Marino found his niche in ultra-marathon cycling. In 1980 he cofounded the Ultra-Marathon Cycling Association with Shermer of nearby La Canada to sanction long-distance city-to-city bicycle rides. Previous record attempts relied on witness signatures and newspaper clippings to convince the *Guinness* representatives or the bicycle industry. UMCA established a set of standards for certifying records, categorized and maintained lists of past records, formally recognized record-setters, and set up a network of qualified officials around the country.

RAAM attracted national interest when ABC's *Wide World of Sports* broadcast the 1982 event. RAAM has been held annually since then. The number of entrants increased to 26 by 1986, the last year ABC covered the race.

In 1987 RAAM went from San Francisco to Washington, DC. In 1990 and 1991 RAAM was 2,930 miles, from Marino's hometown of Irvine to Savannah, Georgia. The 1991 RAAM is scheduled to start July 27th. The field is limited to fifty.

"My goal with the Ultra-Marathon Cycling Association is to have a record set in every one of the fifty states," Marino said. "There are a lot of riders who want to set records. There's Trans-Texas, Trans-California. A lot of states. There still are a lot of states without records, though. When you look at track and field, there are records for every distance. If we can keep up ratifying records that people set, fifty years from now anyone can look back and see what we were doing."

Membership fees are $27.50 for the first year, $13.50 for annual renewals. Lifetime membership is $250. Members receive *The RAAM Book: The Complete Guide to the Race Across America and Long Distance Cycling*, and a monthly newsletter.

More information is available from:

Ultra-Marathon Cycling Association
John Marino
4790 Irvine Blvd., No. 105-111
Irvine, CA 02720
(714) 544-1701

Bikecentennial was founded in September 1973 in Missoula, Montana, to celebrate the country's 1976 bicentennial with a cross-country route, and it has since become the bicycle travel association. Bikecentennial, which derives its name from a wordplay on the bicentennial, was incorporated in 1974 as an education organization. It is a non-profit, member-supported service organization for recreation bicyclists. A staff of fifteen professionals serves some 20,000 supporting members, plus thousands more cyclists, through a network of more than 150 affiliated clubs around the country.

The bicentennial bicycle birthday party along the route that Bikecentennial mapped out involved 6 federal agencies, 8 regional offices, 10 states, and 90 city governments. The Department of the Interior's Bureau of Outdoor Recreation awarded Bikecentennial the Outdoor Achievement Award. American

Youth Hostels, Inc., presented its External Service Award to Bikecentennial for advancing the concept of hosteling in America. Bikecentennial was rolling.

"Bikecentennial has expanded into areas besides routes and maps," said Greg Siple, the organization's artist-photographer-writer. "We still run group tours—450 people rode in our groups in 1990."

For recreational bicycle information, Bikecentennial is the biggest single source in the country. They publish a variety of maps, all of which give helpful extra information such as a weather chart with high and low temperatures April through September, when rides typically take place, monthly precipitation averages, and narrative explanations of what is indigenous to the area the map covers. All this enhances understanding and appreciation of each locale.

Annual membership is $22. Members receive *BikeReport*, a twenty-four-page magazine published nine times a year. Other Bikecentennial publications are the *Cyclist's Yellow Pages*, an annual comprehensive cycling resource guide with cycling information covering all fifty states, twelve Canadian provinces, and fifty-eight foreign countries. Members also receive *Bicycle Forum*, the journal of bicycle education and advocacy, and *Cyclosource*, a catalog that carries mail-order items close to a cyclist's wheels.

Information is available from:

Bikecentennial
P.O. Box 8308
Missoula, MT 59807
(406) 721-1776

Another educational organization is Pedal for Power, a program of the LAW's Bicyclists' Education and Legal Foundation. Pedal for Power organizes two cross-country rides a year that raise money through pledges. After overhead expenses, half the money raised

Bikecentennial offers forty-two maps covering 17,000 miles of bicycle touring routes in thirty-three states. (Bikecentennial photo by Greg Siple)

goes to the charity of each rider's choice; the other half goes to the LAW Educational and Legal Foundation.

"This is the only fund-raising that goes on to help cycling," said David Eagan, former chief operating officer of Pedal for Power.

Each participant solicits pledges from sponsors. Pledges range from one cent a mile, for a total pledge of $33 for 3,300 miles from Los Angeles to Boston, to a dollar a mile for a total pledge of $3,300. Each rider must get enough pledges to raise a minimum of $5,000 in pledged funds. The Los Angeles-to-Boston ride is scheduled to start May 11, 1991, and conclude forty-seven days later in Boston, on June 27th.

A north-south ride of 1,600 miles is set to start September 21st in Portland, Maine, and end 23 days later on October 12th in Orlando, Florida. Each rider must raise a minimum of $3,000 in pledged funds.

"This is a luxury ride for the cyclists," Egan said. Riders rest in motels recommended by the American Automobile Association. Breakfast and dinner every day is in a restaurant chosen for the quality of its food—and the quantity, to replace the 4,000 calories a day the riders burn up.

A deposit of $150 is required for each ride. Pedal for Power also provides three support vans and a rolling mechanic to take care of bicycle problems.

Pedal for Power offers more than fifty charities around the United States and Canada to receive pledge contributions. Charities range from AIDS Volunteers of Cincinnati to the Literacy Volunteers of Chicago to Women's Way. The LAW's Bicyclists' Educational and Legal Foundation, established in 1981, promotes bicycle safety and education for riders. The foundation furnishes legal assistance where the rights of riders are threatened, and it awards research grants.

According to Pedal for Power, a ride that raises $6,000 in pledges would result in $4,500 (75 percent) divided between the charity of the rider's choice and the LAW foundation ($2,250 each), and $1,500 (25 percent) would go for ride costs.

More information is available from:

Pedal for Power
Box 898
Atkinson, NH 03811
(603) 382-2188

Motorcycles developed when bicycle riders attached motors to their bicycles. An ironic reverse trend grew out of Southern California around 1970 when a group of parents who raced motorcycles saw their children riding bicycles and imitating the way they were speeding laps, called motos, around the track.

"The parents said, 'Why not?' " explained Scott Stevenson, field representative for the National Bicycle League, based in Dublin, Ohio, a suburb of Columbus. "Some of the parents made a short track for their kids to ride around. This was the start of BMX, for bicycle motocross."

Stevenson, a veteran racer, said that BMX competitions are sprints around a serpentine track of 400 yards with dirt jumps to negotiate. Races are between 900 and 1,200 feet.

Dirt jumps are part of BMX racing. (National Bicycle League photo)

Cycling has long been a wheel experience. (*The Wheelmen* photo)

BMX racing quickly caught on. The National Bicycle League was founded in 1974 to provide sanctioning for BMX races. The organization also sanctions free-style competitions, which are fancy trick-riding exhibitions. Free-style competitions are held on flat surfaces and on ramps with steep curves.

NBL has about 18,000 members. Fees are $15 for a thirty-day trial, $30 for a regular annual membership. Members receive a monthly magazine, *Bicycles Today*.

More information is available from:

National Bicycle League
211 Bradenton Ave., Suite 100
Dublin, OH 43017
(614) 766-1625

Bicycle riding has long been part of American popular culture, but the late nineteenth century, in which so many advances were made in the modern bicycle, has been overlooked. To help preserve the history and tradition, highwheel enthusiasts in 1967 founded the Wheelmen, a national nonprofit organization. Members learn lost skills, retell lost stories, and research and write articles on cycling, particularly from 1876 to 1900.

Many of the 1,000 members have salvaged more than 5,000 antique bicycles from barns, attics, and cellars. Several members have private collections of bicycles, photos, literature, and other memorabilia that rival the collections of best museums.

The Wheelmen ride in parades, put on demonstrations, hold races on highwheelers, and participate in events that also promote modern cycling. Local clubs operate in state divisions styled after LAW of the 1880s. Officers take their titles from the old LAW, starting with the commander, who in 1991 is Marge Fuehrer of Ambler, Pennsylvania. She follows in Kirk Munroe's wheelmarks.

Membership dues are $20 a year. Members receive *The Wheelmen* magazine, published twice a year, and *Newsletter*, published four times a year.

Information is available from:

The Wheelmen
Marge Fuehrer, Commander
1708 School House Lane
Ambler, PA 19002
(215) 699-3187

CHAPTER 7

PUBLICATIONS

WITH CYCLING once more the sport of the nineties, consumer demand has encouraged publishers to roll presses again with specialized publications. The seven cycling periodicals in the United States have a combined circulation of about 800,000. Current titles such as *Bicycling, Bicycle Guide, Winning Bicycling Illustrated,* and *Velo-News* aren't published as frequently as the dozen weeklies such as *The Bicycling World, American Cyclist, Cycling Gazette,* and *The Bearings* that long ago preceded them. But the modern electronic communications era has more information sources competing for attention than a century ago, when the only medium was print, and long-distance messages were sent by cable or carrier pigeon.

Today's largest-circulation cycling magazine, *Bicycling,* epitomizes the American dream. It started as a mimeographed newsletter in northern California and became an ad-rich East Coast magazine with covers that boast, "World's No. 1 cycling magazine." As it changed ownership and grew—to 385,000 circulation at the end of 1990 with a staff of forty, including a West Coast bureau—*Bicycling*'s metamorphosis reflected the revival in American cycling. It also reflects the visions of its early leaders: a couple who transformed it from a local newsletter to a national four-color magazine, and a publisher who took it over when it was losing money and made it a highly profitable property of a publishing company that in 1990 had revenues of $240 million.

Bicycling is a glossy magazine that runs up to 250 pages an issue, thick enough for binding like a book. It is aimed at recreation riders and is published ten times a year, selling for $3.50 an issue. Such a slick publication would have been impossible to predict when Peter Rich turned the handle to roll the drum of the mimeograph machine in his bike shop, Velo Sport, in Berkeley, California. He wanted to put out a newsletter to spread what information he picked up among Bay Area cyclists.

"I used to print up something called the *Velo Sport Newsletter,* in 1961," Rich recalled thirty years later. "It was a mimeographed newsletter, just eight pages, and it came out when I got around to it. I printed up race results when I heard about them. In every issue I tried to put in two or three little articles with tips like keeping your legs warm when it's cold; how to use certain kinds of equipment. At that time, all there was available on racing in the English language was *Cycling and Mopeds*, now called *Cycling Weekly*, which came from England. The rest of the racing publications came from France and Italy."

Northern California in the early 1960s had a growing band of adventurous cyclists, including Rich, who made racing forays to Europe, where cycling reigned as king of sports. Rich and others brought back impressions of how to improve the level of the sport where they lived. Local riders from four clubs formed the Northern California Cycling Association to coordinate their weekend races and draw up a master calendar.

"I saw there was need for an NCCA newsletter," Rich said. "So in 1962 I changed the name of *Velo Sport Newsletter* to the *Northern California Cycling Association Newsletter*."

The next year the newsletter ventured into a magazine format, measuring 5 inches by 7 inches, a small size that gave it a tentative look compared to established magazines like *Esquire*, published in tabloid size. Copies of the newsletter sold for 25 cents and began making their way nationwide.

"Cycling was a tight-knit group," observed Pete Hoffman, one of the early editors, who lives in Palo Alto, California. "If you raced, you knew everybody across the country. The United States had about 1,500 racers at the time. Now there's at least that many just in California."

The new cycling publication was the first introduced for nearly fifty years. In the first wave of American cycling publications, *Bicycling World*, founded in 1879, was the principal magazine, and it lasted the longest,

thirty-six years, until it folded in 1915. The *Northern California Cycling Association Newsletter* was a regional publication, but it quickly gained readers around the country. The only other publication that could have met the need the newsletter was filling was *American Bicyclist and Motorcyclist*, a trade journal for manufacturers, distributors, and retailers, all preoccupied in the early 1960s with the juvenile market.

"Only one half of one percent of the bicycles sold in the United States at that time were to adults, and that one percent wasn't much," recalled Keith Kingbay, who was then working promotions for the Schwinn Bicycle Company.

Racing cyclists appreciated having a publication of their own, which prompted the newsletter's contributors to change the title in 1964 to *American Cycling Newsletter*. In 1965 it became *American Cycling*, and increased to 35 cents an issue.

As the publication developed, people worked as volunteer editors and contributors, including Hoffman and Rich. Bob LeMar of Burlingame, who ran Tri-City Blueprint Company, designed and printed the publication for free on his offset press. A. Robert Fisher, father of mountain-bike pioneer Gary Fisher, took action photos that enhanced the magazine's look. All this contributed to keeping the magazine in business.

By 1965, Hoffman and his wife, Sandy Kelly Hoffman, took over the publication. "We decided we could make it go," Hoffman said. "We had a lot of enthusiasm and great faith in the sport of cycling. We could see it was growing and getting better in America."

"We had a huge attic room in a house in Oakland that was our publishing office," Sandy said. "We lived body and soul for bike racing and for the magazine. We really believed in cycling. To me, there is nothing to compare with a line of bicycle racers making a turn. The way they sweep around, leaning through the turn, the sound of the gears and the tires on the road, riders at the front calling over their shoulders to get a breakaway going. It's pretty exciting."

Hoffman said he was inspired by the love of the sport he participated in and the knowledge that American cycling had roots that went back several decades. "When I started riding, northern California still had a couple of board tracks around."

Hoffman wrote articles, edited contributions, took photos, and designed the pages. Sandy typed copy, proofed galleys, handled subscriptions, went after advertisers, and wrote some editorials. A brunette with long straight hair, she posed for photos, including some covers.

In 1966 *American Cycling* enlarged its format to 8½ by 11 inches. Ironically, big-league magazines like *Esquire* began decreasing to the same size. The new *American Cycling* also introduced four-color covers. It went up to 50 cents a copy.

"The magazine grew like Topsy," Sandy said. "People were starved for information. Riders were scattered around the country, and the primitive handouts that came and went from time to time were always read cover to cover. When something about cycling was put between two covers, people appreciated it. Peter Rich's newsletter was read closely, but four months could go by before the next issue came out. That was a reason we wanted to get involved with the magazine. The magazine became a way of linking everybody together."

Readers were out there, but a stable of regular contributing writers and photographers proved elusive.

"We would publish good reports from anyone, but we weren't getting enough of them," Hoffman said. "We were also pretty naive editorially. We had a down-home style. There was no paid staff. The cycling industry didn't help much. They were pretty much in the dark about what was coming up. De-railleurs were seen as a fad. Schwinn was the only exception—they were very supportive and took out full-page ads. But the other manufacturers couldn't see the benefit of the publication."

Hoffman was confronted with a publisher's dilemma: how to increase circulation to attract more ads. "Because of the economics, we had to get into articles on touring and family cycling," he said. "The direction we had in mind was to have a good national racing publication, but we didn't achieve that goal."

Editorial content expanded to features on touring and family rides, which helped raise circulation in 1968 to 12,000. But after a growth spurt, circulation reached a plateau.

"We weren't attracting advertising," Hoffman said. "There were no clothing ads like in today's cycling publications. The Japanese manufacturers hadn't come into the market here yet. The only American manufacturers advertising in our magazine were Schwinn and Huffy. We needed editorial and photo contributions from professionals. It was time for us to make a major decision and we thought pretty hard about it. Finally we decided to take out an ad in *The Wall Street Journal* to announce the sale of the magazine."

About fifty companies responded, but only Harley M. Leete, a local entrepreneur, offered to buy it. "Harley was not an athlete," Hoffman said. "He had polio as a kid and got around on crutches with arm braces. His interest in the publication was to build a publishing empire. Some of the money from the sale, which wasn't much, really, I turned around and gave to Bob LeMar, who had published it for free for several years. I stayed on the magazine as editor."

With the August 1968 issue, publisher Leete and editor Hoffman covered all bases by entitling the magazine *American Cycling: The Magazine of Touring, Racing, and Family Bicycling*. In December the name was

Pete Hoffman holds copies of American Cycling, *which became* Bicycling!, *complete with exclamation mark, framed behind him. Hoffman stands in front of a Velo-Sport Bicycles poster, from the Berkeley shop where the publication began as a newsletter in 1961.* (Pete Hoffman photo)

shortened to *Bicycling!* Its cover ambitiously touted "The World's Greatest Bicycle Magazine."

"We were a four-color and worldwide publication," Sandy said. "We had subscribers in New Zealand, China, Australia, Japan, plus some European countries. Not a lot, but we were sending them out. That was pretty good for a storefront operation."

The Hoffmans stayed with the magazine for another year, when Leete sold it to a group of investors in Marin County. "At that point my wife and I were totally burned out," Hoffman said. "We went through some lean years that I wasn't proud of, and were working pretty hard."

By then they also had a son, Peter, born in November 1967. When Leete sold the publication in 1969, the couple felt they had taken it as far as they could.

"The fun was starting it," Sandy said. "After a while it became not so much fun. We had to go after advertising. That wasn't bike racing—it was a business. The excitement wasn't there anymore."

Hoffman and his wife had been taking weekend trips up in the Sierra Nevadas for several years. "After the publication was sold, we just had to get away, get out of Oakland," Hoffman said. "We moved 150 miles northeast, up in the Sierras to Nevada City."

While they were preparing to leave the publication and the sport, Bob Rodale of Emmaus, Pennsylvania, saw his first bicycle races at the 1968 Olympics in Mexico City, where he competed as a skeet shooter on the U.S. Olympic team. He returned to his home in eastern Pennsylvania and began looking into how he could get more involved in recreation cycling.

Rodale's family owned a small publishing business in Emmaus, outside Allentown. He was editor of *Organic Gardening and Farming*, which his father, Jerome Irving Rodale, had founded in 1942 to promote farming without pesticides or petrochemical fertilizers. The younger Rodale joined his father's company in 1949. He graduated from Lehigh in 1952, when he took over *Organic Gardening and Farming*, and subsequently became editor of *Prevention*, a magazine that promotes health and nutrition.

Rodale, thirty-eight when he returned from the Mexico City Olympics, turned his attention to recreation cycling. He thought that a local cycling track such as one he saw at the Olympics would benefit area recreation riders, and looked into constructing such an outdoor track. He donated family land to surrounding Lehigh County to build a cement velodrome that measures 333 meters, about one-sixth of a mile, in nearby Trexlertown. The track was completed in 1976, the year his publishing company brought out a book, *American Bicycle Racing*, a collection of articles that describes the sport in America.

In late 1977 Rodale heard that *Bicycling*, which had risen to 50,000 circulation, was for sale and submitted a bid. Another bidder was Bill Fields, a sales representative who represented several magazines, including *Bicycling*.

"*Bicycling* magazine in 1977 was owned by the C.M. Publishing Company in San Rafael, California," Fields said. "C.M. stood for Capital Management. It was two guys who bought *Bicycling* from a sheriff's auction in the early 1970s. My bid for the magazine was $350,000. Rodale bid $600,000, so he bought it. Today it's probably worth $30 million to $40 million."

Rodale signed the papers on the last day of 1977, and early the next year moved the editorial office east to Emmaus, where it is today. He espoused health and fitness themes in his new magazine. A trim man who wore a neat beard, Rodale practiced health and fitness himself and regularly was seen pedaling on roads around Lehigh County. He was also instrumental in arranging for the junior world championships, for cyclists eighteen and younger, at the Trexlertown track in 1978. Many of the riders who competed there went on to win medals at the 1984 Los Angeles Olympics. One was Mark Gorski of Indianapolis, who won the Olympic matched sprints. Rodale continued to follow cycling at the Trexlertown track, especially on Tuesday evenings when the juniors raced.

Under Rodale, *Bicycling*'s circulation rose steadily. He kept the magazine focused on cycling as a lifestyle, particularly for beginning riders. The magazine adopted its current format articles covering all phases of bicycle touring, bicycle repair and maintenance, new products, fitness, and nutrition.

As the publication grew, Rodale introduced surveys to find out which articles appealed to subscribers. "Twice a year we survey our readers," explained Joe Kita, senior managing editor. "We have a whole survey department that prepares questions. The survey staff makes sure the questions are phrased just right. We ask our readers which articles they read first, which ones they skipped, started but didn't finish, and ones they read all the way through. The survey questions go to a certain number of subscribers about the same time as the issue is shipped to them, and we send them something like a $2 bill to make it worth their while."

Other cycling publications came along but didn't get large enough to compete successfully against the burgeoning *Bicycling*. One magazine was *Two-Wheeled Trip*, pub-

Under Robert Rodale, Bicycling *went from 50,000 circulation in 1978 to 385,000 in 1990, to claim the largest circulation of any bicycling magazine in the world.* (Rodale Press Publications photo)

Bicycling magazine

lished in San Francisco in 1972, which lasted only two issues. Another was *Bike World*, which Bob Anderson of Mountain View, California, founded in 1972. It was a monthly that claimed 20,000 circulation when Rodale bought it in 1979. A third publication was the tabloid *Competitive Cycling*, which Jim McFadden of Santa Monica, California, published from 1973 until it folded in 1980. He wrote with wryness and insight that readers appreciated.

In the early 1980s, more and more fitness-conscious Americans were taking up bicycle riding. *Bicycling*'s circulation grew to 170,000 in 1983 and gained considerable advertising. "I could see I was working myself out of a job," said Fields, who continued selling advertising for the publication after he lost his bid to buy it. "My commissions were approaching $500,000 a year, and I knew that Rodale would form his own in-house sales staff."

In 1984 Fields founded *Bicycle Guide*, a magazine that comes out nine times a year and in 1990 had 174,000 circulation. "*Bicycle Guide* doesn't compete toe-to-toe with *Bicycling*," Fields said. *"Bicycling* is aimed at entry-level recreation cyclists. I like to think of *Bicycle Guide* as a thinking-cyclist's publication, for riders who are beyond the novice stage, from midlevel up."

Bicycle Guide covers cycling from an enthusiast's point of view in touring, mountain biking, and racing. It features new products, technical articles on equipment, rides in the United States and Canada, and profiles on cycling personalities. *Bicycle Guide* is known for the *Buyers' Annual* every May, which rates the entire new line of bicycles sold in North America. It is also known for its wry sense of humor. A 1987 issue devoted to the variety of bicycles and components from Japan puckishly listed all staff names in the masthead in Japanese characters.

A magazine that began in 1983 was *Winning Bicycling Illustrated*, which became the racing publication that Pete and Sandy Hoffman had in mind back in the 1960s. *Winning* editor Rich Carlson, who occasionally placed in Northeastern races that were written up in the Hoffmans' publication, describes *Winning* as a magazine for readers interested in racing or top-level fitness and recreation rides. *Winning* is a slick four-color publication with vivid action photos that capture the major international events. Published eleven times a year in Allentown, *Winning's* circulation in 1991 was 75,000.

"It started on my dining room table as the official race program for the U.S. Professional Cycling Championship in Baltimore," explained Jack Simes III, executive director of the U.S. Professional Cycling Federation. Simes, who was race director, worked with publisher Jean-Claude Garot of Brussels, Belgium, in assembling the publication.

Seventy professional racers from fifteen countries were competing for $100,000 in cash prizes, including $25,000 to the winner,

in the richest one-day race in the world. The 62.5-mile race around Baltimore's inner harbor drew 80,000 spectators in the June 1983 event, the second year it was held.

The publication Simes laid out on his dining room table with Garot featured the requisite short biographies and head shots of top riders. What distinguished it was that Garot had access to Belgian star Eddy Merckx (rhymes with "works"), the greatest cycling champion of all time: Merckx's passion for winning earned him the soubriquet "Cannibal." He was a household name across Europe, but a mystical figure in the United States. Garot had an exclusive English translation of Merckx's story reviewing his career from 1961 to 1977, replete with dramatic photos. Merckx was shown riding in the rain, with mud-splattered legs at the head of the pack, over slick cobblestones the size of bread loaves, during the annual 160-mile one-day spring classics. He powered over snow-capped Alpine summits in the July Tour de France. Merckx, tall and dark-haired, contorted his face in pain as he pushed his considerable physical abilities beyond the limit. He had sacrificed school, leisure time, and conventional family life for his career of monumental efforts. His 400 victories include 5 Tours de France, 4 world championships, and a lion's share of the one-day spring classics, some—such as Italy's prestigious Milan–San Remo—as many as seven times each. Merckx was the Muhammad Ali and Babe Ruth of Bicycle Racing. Crowds lined the road for hours in all kinds of weather just for a glimpse of him as he pedaled past. Americans finally had Part I of an exclusive look at his reminiscences.

Garot published *Winning* in Brussels and shipped it to the United States in time for the USPRO race on June 5. Merckx went to Baltimore to watch the event and comment on it for the local television station broadcasting two-and-a-half hours of live coverage. He had invested in a company manufacturing

Eddy Merckx bicycles, which he supplied to some American professionals. Garot wrote in the inaugural issue, "Cycling's time has arrived." Demand for Part II of Merckx's reminiscences and results of the June race led to a second issue of *Winning* in September, after which the magazine was launched.

The USPRO race enjoyed local success, with some national broadcast exposure that contributed to its moving to Philadelphia in 1985, where it became the 156-mile Core-States USPRO Championship.

"We cover the sport all around the entire world," Carlson said. "Most of that coverage is from Europe, where most of the top racing is done. Trying to coordinate our deadlines with the different languages and six or seven time-zone differences between here and Europe can be nerve-racking. But it is gratifying, especially to watch the growth of American professional racing. In 1985 there were two racing teams in the United States, and in 1991 there are seven. We also have seen a lot of growth in the number of professional races. It is rewarding to see American pro cycling grow into its own. It emulates European racing, but it is unique, too."

Winning was founded in time to chronicle Greg LeMond's successes in Europe, particularly his remarkable first world road-racing championship later in the summer in Altenrhein, Switzerland. Yet a remarkable newsletter with limited circulation that described LeMond's early assault in Europe is *European Cycling News*, which Kent Gordis published in 1978.

Gordis, whose parents lived in Geneva, Switzerland, and Berkeley, California, is fluent in French and English. He was in LeMond's first races in the mid-1970s, when they were in their early teens. They became close friends and LeMond, from Reno, frequently stayed in Gordis's home in Berkeley for races in the Bay Area.

Bicycle racing still resembled what Gordis

called a secret society in America. He had had enough of reading French publications like *Miroir du Cyclisme*, which arrived three months old in San Francisco bookstores, so he started his own newsletter, *European Cycling News*, in English, for other cyclists. When he traveled to Europe, he translated French cycling articles and wrote his own race stories, included what he saw, and generally entertained himself writing a newsletter published on his allowance.

In the spring of 1978, Gordis prepared to go to Yale while LeMond explored full-time cycling. That spring Gordis accompanied LeMond, who turned seventeen on June 26th, on his first trip to Europe—two months in Switzerland, France, and Belgium, to race against leading juniors. LeMond had been competing in twenty-mile events in the United States, but European races were about sixty miles long, two or three times a week, and considerably more competitive. LeMond discovered why Europeans dominated cycling. Races were rigorous: courses included long stretches over cobblestones, subjected riders to hard headwinds, and riders formed coalitions against LeMond to launch relentless attacks designed to force him to chase one breakaway after another. Yet LeMond summoned more from himself and won consistently.

Gordis's account of LeMond's trip in the August 1978 issue, supplemented by photos that Gordis's family took, makes for lively reading and provides insight into the depth of substance of young LeMond. Other junior U.S. riders rode with LeMond in races that spring, including Gorski, but all had retired by the time LeMond won his second Tour de France. Gordis presciently wrote in 1978 that LeMond would win the world championship.

After graduation from Yale, Gordis worked briefly as *Winning*'s editor. He covered LeMond's world championships in 1983 and 1989. Gordis co-wrote *Greg LeMond's*

Complete Book of Bicycling (G.P. Putnam's Sons, 1987), and frequently works as a network television producer covering the Tour de France and other cycling events.

The other American journal of competitive cycling is *VeloNews*, based in Boulder, Colorado. The publishing industry's *Folio: SourceBook 1991* listed *VeloNews* as the fastest-growing publication in the country, with a hefty 66.3 percent growth rate. *VeloNews*, a tabloid published 18 times a year, had a circulation of 35,000 at the end of 1990.

Behind the rapid growth of *VeloNews* is editor John Wilcockson, the dean of American cycling journalists. A majority of the reporters who have covered races in the United States have written for him, and virtually every author who has published a book in this country on competitive cycling lists him in the acknowledgments.

Wilcockson is an Englishman who veered into cycling journalism after he felt the pull of the sport when he saw the Tour de France for the first time in 1963, while he still was a student studying civil engineering at the Imperial College of Science and Technology at the University of London. England then took immense pride in countryman Tom Simpson, who had won a spring classic, Belgium's Tour of Flanders, in 1961. The next year Simpson wore the coveted yellow jersey as race leader of the Tour de France for a day on his way to finishing a respectable sixth overall.

Many years had passed since England was identified with a champion cyclist. Bill Bailey had won the world amateur sprint championship four times between 1909 and 1913. After World War II, Reg Harris won a silver medal as a sprinter in the 1948 London Olympics and turned professional. He won the world sprint championship three years in a row from 1949 to 1951 and, after a bronze medal in 1953, came back to win again in 1954. During Harris's reign, the emphasis in

cycling was shifting from track racing to the roads, and Simpson excelled in the long road-races to become England's first modern cycling hero.

The year that Simpson won his first classic was the year Wilcockson took up the sport. As Simpson moved up the professional ranks in Europe and generated increasing coverage in his homeland, Wilcockson improved to become one of England's best amateurs, achieving a Category I license. In 1965, when Wilcockson graduated with a college degree, Simpson won the world professional road race in Nürburgring, West Germany, and capped the season with his victory of the Italian autumn classic, the Tour of Lombardy.

Simpson was a legend throughout Britain's pubs and cycling clubs when Wilcockson started his first professional job out of college. During the day, Wilcockson designed bridges and highways; after work he trained in the evenings and raced on weekends. In the 1967 Tour de France, Simpson collapsed on the thirteenth stage. It was a hot afternoon and he was in a small breakaway group pedaling up Mont Ventoux, an extinct volcano in southern France. His death that afternoon shocked the cycling world. The shock was worsened when an autopsy showed he had been taking amphetamines, a Faustian bargain he made in his attempt to win the Tour de France.

The year of Simpson's death was also the last year of Category I racing for Wilcockson, who had started contributing free-lance cycling articles to *Cycling Weekly* and other publications. At the end of 1967, he decided to go into cycling journalism full-time as assistant editor of England's *International Cycle Sport*.

"I chucked engineering," he said. "I took a 50 percent cut in salary to begin as a writer."

His first big assignment in the spring of 1968 put him on his own. "I was told to go to the Continent and get some stories," he re-

John Wilcockson, dean of American cycling journalists, during a cheerful tête-à-tête with Greg LeMond minutes before the start of a stage in the 1989 Tour de France. (Cor Vos photo)

called, mildly amused years later at the vagueness. "I went to Spain, Belgium, and France to interview riders, talk to the teams, and cover early-season races."

Bicycle races are dazzling to watch. A phalanx of motorcyclists, headlights flashing on and off, beep horns, blow whistles, and fan out across the road to secure it for the approaching riders. A lead car with a race commissar standing up through the sunroof, facing the riders, follows. Then the riders, lean and tanned, swiftly pass by in a blur of vibrant-colored jerseys, clean-shaven legs pumping smartly, wheels flashing in the sunshine. Close behind is an extended procession of bumper-to-bumper press cars and team cars, festooned with spare wheels and extra bicycles on roof racks. Riders who were dropped from the pack, either from mechanical problems that have been corrected or because they missed a key move earlier, chase on their own or in small groups in the caravan flow. It's like a rolling circus.

Races are as challenging to cover as they are to ride, especially at the top international level. Following them in the season, which begins in mid-February and runs straight through October, means spending two hundred nights in hotels and living out of a suitcase. It is a nomadic life, traveling from Spain to France to Belgium to Holland to Italy to Switzerland to Germany, and back, again and again. Occasionally there are a few days' respite between the one-day spring classics in northern Europe, but stage races, like the Tour de France and its counterparts in Italy and Spain, go for three weeks each, usually with just one or two days off. (The 1991 Tour de France, 2,465 miles long from July 6th to 28th, has no rest day.)

For reporters, work means spending six or seven hours a day in a car, often traveling in a long caravan trailing the pack, listening to a radio tuned in to race officials near the action who broadcast in French, Flemish, Italian, Spanish, Dutch, or German. Most of the drive is tame for motor vehicles, but occasionally the cyclists, more adept on steep descents, heighten the drama.

"Riding in the press caravan in the Tour de France can be really frightening," observed photographer Louis Viggio, a native of Peru who lives in Boulder. "Going down those narrow, twisting roads in the Alps and the Pyrenees, the cars are literally on two wheels at sixty miles an hour and faster to keep up with the riders. There is no time to think about what you're doing. The roads have no guardrails, either. It's a miracle that every one of the vehicles doesn't fly straight off the roads. You get the feeling that the hand of God is following the whole Tour."

For the conclusion of each tour stage, or a

one-day race, reporters scramble out of their cars, which speed ahead to the finish, to see how the race ends. That sets off another scramble to interview riders for precious quotes. American sports reporters covering baseball, basketball, or football have the benefit of interviewing athletes who speak regional variations of the same language. But interviewing cyclists who come from at least fifteen countries means being fluent in French and having some familiarity with Flemish, Dutch, Spanish, and Italian.

Getting an athlete who has been competing for four to six hours without a rest to discuss how the action unfolded is an acquired tool of the journalist's trade. Frank Litsky of *The New York Times*, covering the CoreStates USPRO race in Philadelphia, explained that his ideal way to know for sure what happened during the 156-mile event, which lasts six hours, would be to stop the entire field after three hours and interview every rider.

"That way we could learn how the race had gone up to that point," he said. "At the finish, the winner can't always tell you how he did it. These are top professional athletes who move instinctively. The champions are brilliant at what they do. That's why they win. But they move automatically. Afterward, they make stuff up to fit what the outcome was, like modifying the equation to justify the answer."

Wilcockson covered major league cycling for *International Cycle Sport* through 1972 and learned the intricacies of bicycle racing. He traveled on Europe's highways and rural roads, stayed in capitals and backwater towns. Through experience he honed the skill of looking at the distance a breakaway has on the pack and knowing what the lead is, to within five seconds, without checking his watch. He knows who a rider is just from a glance at his style, which saves time looking for a competitor's number and consulting the race program. Wilcockson worked with the network of riders, team directors and mechanics and doctors, race impresarios and officials, reporters and editors, all of whom he drew from—the way a painter selects a brush or particular pigment—to file stories under deadline pressure.

After *International Cycle Sport* he moved on to other publications. He became the first cycling correspondent for *The London Times*. Americans were introduced to his articles in *Bike World*. The articles were published regularly and opened a door to the world of European racing, about which even avid American cyclists knew little.

All this put him in the position in the early 1980s of witnessing LeMond's progress. LeMond had turned professional in late 1980 to compete the next year in Europe, where he succeeded in making a name for himself just as Major Taylor, Bobby Walthour, Sr., and Frank Kramer had done decades earlier. But LeMond's early accomplishments were overlooked in the United States. His 1983 world championship road-race triumph, the first ever for a U.S. rider, was acknowledged in two sentences at the back of *Sports Illustrated*.

When *Winning* was established that year, Wilcockson became editor of the United Kingdom edition in London, and in 1984 he moved to Allentown to take over as magazine editor-in-chief.

For the next three years he continued to travel extensively across the Atlantic, assign domestic stories, and edit copy. He was helping build up *Winning*, and breaking in a cadre of free-lance journalists. LeMond was succeeding Taylor, Walthour, and Kramer the way Simpson succeeded Bailey and Harris. The American media became more receptive to LeMond's accomplishments. *Winning* was the leading publication in the United States following LeMond and other U.S. riders competing domestically and abroad. When LeMond won the Tour de France in 1986, the first non-European to win the event since it was founded in 1903, he became an instant media figure even in the United States. Under Wilcockson, whose connections with the LeMond family went back many years, the unexpected celebrity obligations of LeMond's stardom became material for an article on a fourth week of the tour. LeMond's visit to the White House was only part of that week in Wilcockson's international perspective.

In early 1987, Wilcockson left *Winning* and became a one-man news service. By then American cycling had elevated considerably. European editors were interested in reports on races. Wilcockson filed stories in English as well as French. Frequently when covering an event such as the CoreStates USPRO Championship for a number of publications, he resorted to pseudonyms, including Gunnar Jakobsen. That ruse appeared to increase the number of foreign journalists covering cycling in North America.

VeloNews had been around since 1972 when Barbara George founded it in her home in Brattleboro, Vermont. She and her husband, Robert, were cyclists who limited their racing to New England. "I won the New England road championship for women in 1973," she said in deadpan. "But I was the only woman riding in it that year."

She began the publication in response to telephone calls from other cyclists seeking information. "There wasn't any way to find out what happened in races last week, and what races were available for the next week," she said. "So we started our own publication. The first year it was called *Northeast Bicycle News*. The next year we changed the name to *Cycle News*. After a couple of years, we found out there was a motorcycle magazine with that name, so in 1975 we began publishing *VeloNews*."

Growth was rapid. Like the Hoffmans before them, the Georges relied on information other cyclists sent. *VeloNews* developed its schedule to publish bimonthly during the

summer and monthly the rest of the year. Robert George, a professional photographer, acquired a national reputation for his photos. After 1978, circulation remained level at about 12,000. Barbara expanded *VeloNews* into book publishing.

"There have been a lot of books published on cycling since 1980," she said. "But when I got into cycling, all that was available in this country was a translation of *Cycling*, which the Italian Central Sports School, called CONI, published in 1972. It covered general conditions and riding techniques. In the late 1970s, *VeloNews* started publishing books from articles we ran in the magazine."

VeloNews was up for sale in 1988 when Wilcockson and a group of investors bought it that November. Circulation was less than 14,000. In February 1989 *VeloNews* moved to Boulder. Wilcockson drew from his editorial contacts to expand race coverage worldwide. Ad space jumped. "We had 700 advertising pages in 1990," he said, "compared to less than 200 pages in 1988."

Barbara George remains in book publishing with Vitesse Press Bicycling Books in Brattleboro. Vitesse Press is located in a three-story, nineteenth-century pipe-organ factory, with slate sides and a slate roof. In 1991 Vitesse Press listed more than twenty titles, covering a variety of subjects from bicycle repair to ways to become a better cyclist.

"I am pleased with what has happened with *VeloNews*," Barbara George said. "I enjoy publishing books. There certainly is a lot more information available on cycling now than there was in the 1970s."

Survival in publishing, however, is always an individual effort. Shortly after *Bicycle Guide* and *Winning* made their debut, two other cycling magazines from Southern California also were introduced. *Bicycle Rider* was published in Agoura, and *Cyclist* was published in Torrance. Neither found a

Mountain Bike Action

niche. *Bicycle Rider* went out of business in 1986. *Cyclist* lasted until 1988.

Yet the more than $3 billion a year spent on cycling-related products encourages more publishers to keep trying. Roland S. Hinz, president of Hi-Torque Publications, Inc., in Mission Hills, California, introduced two monthly cycling magazines for young, upwardly-mobile readers devoted to off-road sport.

Mountain Bike Action started in 1986 and in 1990 claimed 51,000 circulation. *Folio:*

SourceBook 1991 ranked the magazine close to *VeloNews* in greatest percentage increases in total circulation, with a 48 percent boost.

Hinz established *BMX Plus!* in 1978. The magazine has readers in more than sixty countries, where BMX and free-style bicycles are popular. Claiming a circulation of 55,000, *BMX Plus!* on its cover proclaims, "The world's largest BMX racing & freestyle magazine!"

The grandfather of them all is *Ameri-*

can Bicyclist and Motorcyclist, published monthly by Cycling Press in New York City. With 10,000 circulation, it boasts that it is the world's largest bicycle trade journal.

It certainly is the oldest. In November 1979 the magazine celebrated its centenary. Staff researchers were surprised to discover they actually were two years late. *American Bicyclist* is the direct descendant of *Bicycling World*, started in 1879, and at least ten other publications that subsequently were merged and consolidated over the years. But research showed that *Bicycling World* itself was the offspring of the short-lived *American Bicycling Journal*, founded in December 1877.

"Rather than change so long-accepted a tradition (and have a 100th anniversary arithmetically irrelevant to our 75th and 90th)," the editors wrote in the November 1979 issue, "we elected to stay with the traditional date."

With constant competition for reader interest and advertising revenue among cycling publications and the rise of mountain bikes in the market, Robert Rodale moved to keep *Bicycling* at the head of the newsstand rack. Hank Barlow of Crested Butte, Colorado, in 1985 started up *Mountain Bike Magazine*, which Rodale bought in 1988. Tim Blumenthal, on the staff of *VeloNews* for many years in Brattleboro, was hired in 1989 as editor of *Mountain Bike*, which is published in a limited edition of some forty-five pages in *Bicycling*.

"This is a publishing experiment," Blumenthal said. "It began in 1990 to entice regular readers to cross into mountain biking, which is a fun part of cycling." About 45,000 copies go out to subscribers as *Bicycling Plus Mountain Bike*.

Rodale, meanwhile, kept expanding his publishing empire. He acquired health-related magazines such as *Runner's World* and *Backpacker*. In September 1990 he was in the Soviet Union to develop plans for a long-term joint-venture agreement to publish *The New Farmer*, a Russian-language magazine for Russian farmers. He was killed in a car crash in Moscow September 5th on the way to the airport to fly back home.

Rodale's death was national news. Taking over as chief executive officer of Rodale Press, Inc., is his wife of thirty-nine years, Ardath.

The following is a list of the national cycling publications, with 1991 annual subscription rates:

Bicycling
$17.97 for one year (ten issues), United States; $22.97 Canada.
33 East Minor St.
Emmaus, PA 18098
(215) 967-5171

Bicycle Guide
$14.90 one year (nine issues) United States; $18.90 Canada.
711 Boylston St.
Boston, MA 02116
(617) 236-1885

Winning Bicycling Illustrated
$23.95 for one year (eleven issues) United States; $39.95 Canada.
1127 Hamilton St.
Allentown, PA 18101-9959
1-800-441-1666

VeloNews
$24.95 for one year (eighteen issues); $33 Canada and Mexico.
1830 North 55th St.
Boulder, CO 80301-2703
1-800-888-6087

Mountain Bike Action
$18.95 one year (twelve issues) United States; $23.95 Canada.
10600 Sepulveda Boulevard
Mission Hills, CA 91345
(818) 365-6831

BMX Plus!
$17.98 for one year (twelve issues)
  United States; $22.98 Canada.
10600 Sepulveda Boulevard
Mission Hills, CA 91345
(818) 365-6831

American Bicyclist and Motorcyclist,
Industry affiliated, United States, $28
  for one year (twelve issues); non-
  industry affiliated, $58 for one year;
  Canada $44 for one year.
80 Eighth Avenue
New York, NY 10011
(212) 206-7230

REGIONAL PUBLICATIONS

Regional cycling publications tend to have avid readerships because they are about people and rides the readers know personally or have heard about through friends. These publications contribute to the vitality of the local cycling community. They give attention to local personalities, pass on detailed ride calendars, tell about local tour rides and races, and frequently carry coupons from area merchants offering discounts on products or services.

Featured here are some of the more prominent regional publications. For more information, check with your local bike shop.

The Bicycle Paper, published in Redmond, a suburb of Seattle, Washington, goes out to six Seattle-area bicycling clubs as part of their membership dues. That arrangement helps the publication as well as cohesiveness among clubs, which are sharing information. A tabloid, *Bicycle Paper* calls itself "The Voice of Northwest Cycling," and has a circulation of 7,000.

In late 1990, Barclay Kruse of Redmond sold *Bicycle Paper* to devote more time to prepare a bid for Seattle to host the world cycling championships in 1994 or 1995. "Staging the world's has been a longtime dream," he told *Bicycle Paper*, "and I am eager to move on to that challenge."

The Seattle cycling community supports an outdoor track, the Marymoor Velodrome, on which Kruse plans to hold the world championship track races. He bought the paper from its founder, Peggy Steward, in 1986 to go with his writing and promotions business, called Northwest Classics. With Northwest Classics, an allusion to the prestigious one-day races during the spring in northern Europe like the Tour of Flanders, Kruse organized more than sixty grassroots and national events in 1990. They included the road and velodrome cycling races of the Goodwill Games.

Kruse sold *Bicycle Paper* and Northwest Classics to Dave Shaw, former president of the League of American Wheelmen. Shaw is also a former president of the Cascade Bicycle Club. He has written articles for national and regional publications.

Subscriptions to *Bicycle Paper*, published eight times a year, are $8 a year. More information is available from:

The Bicycle Paper
7901–168th Ave., N. E.
Suite 103
Redmond, WA 98052
(206) 882-0706

Outdoors-oriented California has *California Bicyclist*, which publishes a northern edition for San Francisco-area cycling and a southern edition for the rest of the state. Emphasizing health, touring, mountain biking, racing, biathlons, triathlons, and fitness, *California Bicyclist* is a tabloid published eleven times a year—monthly except for February. It averages 175,000 circulation a month.

Founded in 1985, *California Bicyclist* is part of the Yellow Jersey Group. *Texas Bicyclist*, which started in April 1989 and has

50,000 circulation, is another publication in the group. Dale Butler, editor and general manager, explained that the tabloids share feature stories of 2,500 words each, have regional news on three pages, and more pages devoted to ride calendars. Administration of the publication is through the San Francisco office.

"Our publications are popular because people involved in cycling have a good chance to see their name in print," Butler said. "We're also in the middle between manufacturers and local bike shops. They consult with us all the time, commenting on things, giving us complaints. We pass this information along to help improve cycling."

Florida Cyclist was introduced in October 1989 but folded in July 1990, Shaw said. "We reached a circulation of 70,000, but Florida's economy is depressed and forced us to close the issue," he said. "We may reopen it in 1991, maybe as a quarterly."

These publications are distributed free in local bike shops, health clubs, and other locations. "We discourage paid subscriptions," Shaw said, "because we want to encourage people to go into the bike shops and health clubs to pick up their copies." Subscriptions are $30 a year for eleven issues.

More information is available from:

California Bicyclist, Northern Edition
490 Second St., Suite 304
San Francisco, CA 94107
(415) 546-7291

California Bicyclist, Southern Edition
P. O. Box 25697
Los Angeles, CA 90025
(213) 546-7181

Covering Southern California, Arizona, and New Mexico is *Southwest Cycling*, a tabloid published eleven times a year with a circulation of 70,000. It was founded in 1983.

Southwest Cycling covers commuting, touring, racing, off-road and triathlons. The publication enjoyed a special advantage in June 1990 when Southwest talent scored big at the CoreStates USPRO Championship. Kurt Stockton of Santa Barbara, California, finished third behind an Italian and a Frenchman to become the national professional champion. Andy Bishop of Tucson was the next U.S. finisher, in fifth, and Kenny Adams of San Clemente was sixth. Stockton, Bishop, and Adams all automatically qualified to represent the United States at the world championships in Japan later in the summer.

Subscriptions are $18 a year. More information is available from:

Southwest Cycling
301 W. California, Suite 201
Glendale, CA 91203
(818) 247-9384

Regional news interest in Ohio prompted Peter Wray to start up *Bike Ohio* as a tabloid in 1988 to cover all aspects of adult recreation riding and racing. After two years, steadily increasing interest in the publication encouraged him to change the title in 1991 to *Bike Midwest*, including the states that touch Ohio: Indiana, Kentucky, Pennsylvania, Michigan, and West Virginia.

Bike Midwest has 35,000 circulation. It is published nine times a year. Subscriptions are $18 a year.

More information is available from:

Bike Midwest
Box 141287
Columbus, OH 43214
(614) 262-1447

Neil Sandler of Silver Spring, Maryland, found in 1986 when he established *Spokes* to serve metropolitan Washington, DC, that it was filling important middle ground for cyclists and triathletes, between club newsletters and national magazines. He distributed *Spokes* for free to bike stores, fitness centers, and related sporting retailers in Virginia, Washington, and Maryland. Cyclists and triathletes wanted more local information, and additional retailers sought to take out ads.

Circulation started at 8,000 in 1986 and increased to 30,000 in 1990. *Spokes* went from five issues a year to nine in 1991, and circulation jumped again to 50,000. Distribution for the issues, which remain free, expanded from the Potomac area to the Middle Atlantic region, extending from Philadelphia to Richmond.

"Bicycling in the Mid-Atlantic," Sandler said, "is the fastest-growing of all participatory sports."

More information is available from:

Spokes
5334 Sovereign Place
Frederick, MD 20701
(301) 926-0031

Mountain-bike information in magazines struck Maurice and Elaine Tierney of Springdale, Pennsylvania, as having a West Coast influence, so they established *Dirt Rag* in 1988 for mountain bikers on the East Coast. "I like to call it the Eastern perspective in mountain biking," Maurice said.

A tabloid, *Dirt Rag*, has a circulation of 4,000 loyal readers, Maurice said. "We get a lot of feedback from our readers. They submit a lot of articles to us."

In 1991 *Dirt Rag* was available in 255 bike shops, he said. "We cover races, and we cover recreation mountain biking, too. In each issue we have an article about a place to ride, like a certain park or game lands in the East."

Subscriptions are $9 a year for nine issues. More information is available from:

Maurice and Elaine Tierney
460 Maple Ave.
Springdale, PA 15144
(412) 274-4529

Cycle South specializes in Southeast cycling explained Mike Hoffland, editor of the tabloid. "We don't worry about the Tour de France and other big races because that is picked up in the national publications. We focus on what is going on for the Southeast states—Georgia, Florida, North and South Carolina, Tennessee, Alabama, and Mississippi. We have 13,000 circulation."

Copies are distributed through bike shops and at touring or racing events. The paper seeks a balance among touring, mountain biking, and racing.

Subscriptions are $10 a year for six issues. "We plan to go to ten times a year in 1992," Hoffland said.

Information is available from:

Mike Hoffland
2891 Twin Brooks Rd., No. 4
Atlanta, GA 30319
(404) 233-1638

Until the 1970s few books were published in America on cycling. As a genre, sports books rarely were taken seriously or sold well, and cycling was relegated to being a minor sport. Even when bicycle racing thrived in the glory days of the six-day races, none of the riders was the subject of a biography. Only one racer, Major Taylor, wrote his autobiography, which he published at his own expense and sold door-to-door in his last years before he died broke in 1932.

But in the mid-1970s, the sports industry underwent a transformation. Baseball's traditional reserve system was shaken up to allow players to become free agents after five years in the major leagues. Player salaries gushed up to rival municipal budgets. Recreation sports like cycling, running, tennis, and swimming enjoyed tremendous surges in popularity that kept swelling through the 1980s. In 1990 *Advertising Age* reported that the sports industry in America had a gross national product, the measure of goods and services, estimated at $65 to $70 billion a year.

Sports books have poured forth and become a lucrative genre. Cycling books are coming out in unprecedented numbers. Since the late 1970s, approximately 150 new cycling titles have been released. They cover a wide spectrum, from touring to fitness to racing to technical repair books. The overwhelming majority are thoughtful and deserve attention.

Four publishers make a speciality of publishing books related to cycling: Vitesse Press Bicycling Books, *VeloNews* Books, Bicycle Books, and Rodale Press. Their book lists are available upon request:

Vitesse Press Bicycling Books
28 Birge St.
Brattleboro, VT 05301
1-800-848-3747

VeloNews Books
1830 N. 55th St.
Boulder, CO 80301
1-800-234-8356

Bicycle Books, Inc.
32 Glen Dr.
Mill Valley, CA 94941
(415) 381-0172

Rodale Press, Inc.
33 E. Minor St.
Emmaus, PA 18098
(215) 967-6171

Bikecentennial has a bicycle bookstore, with a list of books in *Cyclosource*, Bikecentennial's mail-order catalog. It is available from:

Bikecentennial
P. O. Box 8308
Missoula, MT 59807
(406) 721-8719

In the Northwest, Mountaineers Books has published a series of a half-dozen books that Erin and Bill Woods have written about riding in Washington and Oregon. The books are popular for their maps, lists of parks, campgrounds, food stores, and points of interest.

More information is available from:

The Mountaineers
306 Second Ave., West
Seattle, WA 98119
(206) 285-2665

A book that I regard as an old friend is Taylor's 1928 autobiography, which my father bought for $1.50 in a used-book store. In 1990 a copy in good condition sold for $200. Taylor's story is compelling, and his role as a black pioneer athlete is important. When a movie finally is made of his life, surviving copies will shoot up in value like Van Gogh paintings.

The Fastest Bicycle Rider in the World: The Story of a Colored Boy's Indomitable Courage and Success Against Great Odds is aptly titled, for Taylor had America's social structure stacked against him, but he went to the top. His accomplishments are heroic. He wrote the book in the living room of his home in Worcester, Massachusetts, recalled his daughter, Sydney Taylor Brown of Pittsburgh. "He wrote it himself, without anyone doing it for him," she said. "I remember when I visited he took over the living room with his scrapbook pages and photos."

Taylor describes his career around the United States, Europe, and Australia from 1892 when he began racing in Indianapolis, his hometown, to 1910 when he retired at thirty-two in Salt Lake City. His references to rivals, such as Frank Kramer, who otherwise virtually disappeared, are invaluable. What is remarkable about Taylor's autobiography is that his personal life was crumbling when he wrote it, but there is no hint of that, which reflects the grace under pressure that made him a champion athlete. The modest fortune he had saved from his heyday had dwindled away after investments soured. He and his wife, Daisy, had sold their seven-bedroom home and moved to a smaller residence. They were selling off her fine jewelry,

Major Taylor, here with wife, Daisy, and three-year-old daughter Sydney, later put his personal troubles aside when he wrote his autobiography. From the era when cyclists were the best-paid athletes in the country, Taylor is the only rider to write about his career, which increases the value of his book. (Indiana State Museum photo)

and their marriage was over. Taylor put these problems aside when he labored on his memoir. He was straightforward yet reserved when relating his frustrations, which must have been acute, at being denied service in hotels in restaurants in San Francisco and other cities after a hero's treatment abroad. When his book was published, he and Daisy separated: she moved to New York City; their daughter had already left home. He moved to Chicago with boxes of his books, which were heavy to lug around, to sell on his own.

Christopher Sinsabagh describes Taylor knocking on doors and selling copies to old friends. Sinsabagh grew up in Chicago, where he raced bicycles in his youth and joined the staff of the cycling weekly, *Bearings*, in the mid-1890s. After a few years he wrote for the *Chicago Daily News*. It was a time when reporters in the city Carl Sandburg later called "stormy, husky, brawling" wrote stories in pencil. They commuted around the city wearing a button with a red star pinned to their suspenders to show the streetcar conductors, who let them ride for free. Sinsabagh later moved to Detroit and became nationally prominent for his articles on the automobile industry. In 1940 he published his autobiography, *Who Me? Forty Years of Automobile History* (Arnold-Powers Publishing Company).

Taylor's autobiography was 448 pages long, divided into ninety-four chapters, which Stephen Greene Press condensed to 214 pages in an abridged 1972 edition. Copies still are available in used-book stores.

His life was like an open secret in the world cycling community. Scotsman Andrew Ritchie, who studied art history at Cambridge University before embarking on a photojournalism career, spent more than ten years delving into Taylor's career. Ritchie first wrote *King of the Road, an Illustrated History of Cycling*, a social history of bicycle technology published by Ten Speed Press of Berkeley, California, in 1975. It has abundant line drawings, etchings, and photos of the development of the bicycle and its role in society over more than 150 years.

"I was absolutely amazed that nobody had written a biography of Taylor," Ritchie said. "He's better known in Europe than he is in America."

Ritchie began collecting material about Taylor, which led him to Paris where he probed archives, and to Washington, DC, where he researched periodicals in the Library of Congress. He interviewed Taylor's daughter, Sydney. In 1988, Bicycle Books, of Mill Valley, California, published *Major Taylor: The Extraordinary Career of a Champion Bicycle Racer*. It's a valuable contribution, especially for the photos, which help bring Taylor to life.

Whoopi Goldberg and her business agent, Hector Lizzardi, bought a two-year option on Ritchie's biography of Taylor. "This is not a project to be rushed," Lizzardi said. "This guy has fallen through the floorboards of history, and his story deserves careful treatment."

Like Taylor's story, the competitors who pre-ceded him and those who followed in the twelve decades of organized bicycle racing have been unjustly neglected. When Armando was predicting in 1960 that the sport would take off again in America, a prediction he repeated year after year until he died at the end of the decade, he likely was anticipating that a revival in cycling would embrace legends like Taylor, Kramer, and Walthour.

In 1984 I was having difficulty getting an article published on Art Longsjo of Fitchburg, Massachusetts, who was a speed skater and bicycle racer of legendary proportions in New England for his feat of making the Winter and Summer Olympic teams in the same year, 1956. Seven olympiads later, Dave Gilman, a U.S. Army captain, duplicated the feat when he made the luge team in the Winter Olympics and the kayak team in the Summer Olympics. Members of the media forgot about Longsjo for Gilman, who rightly deserved attention for making two Olympic teams in one year. (With the Winter and Summer Olympics alternating after 1992, Gilman and Longsjo will share a unique distinction.)

After rejections from assorted publications, I sent a query letter to the U.S. Olympic Committee in Colorado Springs, to write a feature for their magazine, *The Olympian*, on Longsjo.

"Great," replied Bob Condron, a spokesman for the Olympic Committee. "Nobody knows anything about Longsjo."

Condron could have been describing any American cyclist. No biographies were available in libraries. Taylor's autobiography, which had limited distribution, is confined to his cycling career. What did he do after he retired? The sport's elder statesmen, like Armando, were disappearing, and I felt the chill draft of the door of the sport closing. By February 1985, when *Olympian* published the Longsjo feature, I was prying open that door.

Among my first interviews was Alf Goullet, a headline cyclist in the teens and twenties. He told stories that sounded like they challenged Pecos Bill digging the Rio Grande. Goullet recalled competing for the summer of 1912 in Salt Lake City, where Jack Dempsey used to work out on the track. "He wanted to be a bike racer more than anything else," Goullet said. "He used to run errands for us."

Goullet regaled me with countless stories—all remarkable Americana, most exhilarating, some sad. He said he lent Taylor, with whom he stood eye to eye, a bicycle for the old timers' one-mile race on the Newark Velodrome in 1917. He recalled the ease of Taylor's victory. "Taylor went back to Worcester in good spirits. Then in the early 1930s we heard he died in Chicago and was buried in potter's field."

I went to the Library of Congress to follow up on what Goullet told me. His recollections not only were sound but also understated. Legends rest on the evanescence of memory. Wyatt Earp, Doc Holiday, and the gunfight at the OK Corral might have become minor footnotes in Kansas history if Bat Masterson had remained a frontier law officer instead of leaving Dodge City to become a New York City newspaper writer. Masterson took with him a stock of stories that Easterners read eagerly. The stories found their way into dime novels when Westerns were a flourishing genre. Goullet, who came to the United States in 1910 already a professional cyclist, was opening the door of his sport when he spoke.

After dozens more interviews with Goullet, interviews with hundreds of other people, and reading miles of newspapers on microfilm, stacks of bound magazines, and assorted personal scrapbooks, I accrued a body of stories that Bat Masterson would have appreciated.

Three books, all out of print, gave helpful background. One is *Riding High: The Story of the Bicycle* (E. P. Dutton & Company), which Arthur Judson Palmer wrote in 1956. Palmer's book, 191 pages long, is a reader's delight, giving a scintillating tour d'horizon of the bicycle's development. More than 250 pictures embellish the book; captions are informative and witty. Photos show John D. Rockefeller standing with his bicycle, crowds of well-dressed adult cyclists pedaling in New York City at the turn of the century, and a paved cycleway that ran from Pasadena to Los Angeles in 1900.

In 1964 came *The Turned Down Bar* (Dorrance & Company) in which Nancy Neiman Baranet wrote about her racing experiences in the United States and Europe in the 1950s. She was a pioneer racer who subsequently devoted more than a quarter-century to the U.S. Cycling Federation.

Rodale Press came out with *American Bicycle Racing* in 1976. Edited by James McCullagh, with contributions from four other writers, it lacks the panache of Palmer's book twenty years earlier, but still is worthwhile.

Another book, re-released in 1989, is *50 Years of Schwinn-Built Bicycles: The Story of the Bicycle and Its Contributions to Our Way of Life*. It was published in 1945 to commemorate the fiftieth anniversary of the bicycle company that long was the biggest producer of bicycles in the United States. The book, ninety pages, was intended for the trade industry but is available for general consumption.

Interviews, newspapers, magazines, scrapbooks, and a limited number of books all helped me compose the story of American bicycle racing through the lives of the riders and promoters from the 1880s through the 1980s.

America went through gradual yet substantial changes in the twelve decades of modern cycling, but the characteristics of champions present and past are similar. Longsjo's family, originally from Finland,

Publishers Weekly *called* Hearts of Lions, *"A significant contribution to American sports history."*

and friends agreed the one word that applied to him was *sisu*, Finnish for guts. Longsjo, Goullet, Taylor, and LeMond all share *sisu*. My book, which W. W. Norton & Company published in 1988, is a social history of American bicycle racing entitled *Hearts of Lions*.

The title elicited an unexpected response after the book was reviewed in *The International Herald-Tribune* in Paris. Weeks later came a light-blue aérogramme which my publisher relayed from a Brussels suburb. "Dear Sir," the aérogramme opened, "I am writing to inquire for more information on your book, 'The Red Organs of the Kings of the Animals.'"

Eric Heiden wrote the book's foreword—in pencil, on three-hole, lined paper during a break between classes at Stanford University's Medical School. "If you don't like it, you can throw it in the trash," he said with characteristic modesty, "and my feelings won't be hurt."

I like his foreword for the way it captured the spirit of the story. At a book signing, a middle-aged man approached me with an expectant look on his face. "Are *you* Eric Heiden?" he demanded. Surprised at the question, I promptly confessed I wasn't, which produced a look of profound disappointment.

For a moment, I realized too late, he was planning to go home to tell his wife and family that he had met the great athlete who won five gold medals in speed skating at the 1980 Lake Placid Olympics and several bicycle races, including the 1985 CoreStates USPRO Championship. Hastily, I explained highlights of the research that I put into writing the book. After I poured forth a stream of information on the book's revelance, focus returned to the man's eyes.

"Of course you're not Eric Heiden," he exclaimed, relief registering on his face. "I didn't think Eric was going bald."

Racing makes up only a small portion of the sport, and many books are on recreation cycling. Seven Palms Press, of Tucson, published three that are fun to read and enhance enjoyment of cycling.

Around the World on a Bicycle, by Thomas Stevens, is a one-volume abridged edition of Steven's two-volume 1887 books. Jay and Gail Rochlin, who run Seven Palms Press as an avocation, sifted through nearly 1,000 pages of original text to reduce it for a single volume they brought out in 1987 to celebrate the centenary of Steven's epic around-the-world ride. They also reproduced the engravings that illustrated Steven's original work in their original size.

When Bikehood Was in Flower, by Irving A. Leonard, is subtitled "Sketches of Early Cycling." It's a small, engaging anthology that tastefully takes a reader back to early cycling. Stevens makes an appearance, as do Margaret Valentine Le Long, and a couple, Fanny and William Workman. They all were intrepid, high-spirited adventurers, leading the way for those who make RAGBRAI, TOSRV, and other rides. Published in 1983.

A Certain Bicyclist, by Paul Niquette, is an off-beat guide to the post-petroleum age. Published in 1985.

If these books are not available at your local bookstore, they can be ordered from:

Jay & Gail Rochlin
Seven Palms Press
Box 3371
Tucson, AZ 85722
(602) 299-6515

Changing Gears: Bicycling America's Perimeter, by Jane Schnell. She is a kindred spirit of Stevens and Le Long. At age fifty-five, Schnell retired from an office job at the Central Intelligence Agency in Langley, Virginia, and embarked on a 12,000-mile ride around the inside perimeter of the United States. She started in Detroit in July 1986 and went west in a counterclockwise route that took thirteen months. Schnell did what many of us have only thought of doing. Her book is a delightful diary of the open road— emphasizing the trip, not the arrival. If this 1990 book that Milner Press of Atlanta published is not in your bookstore, it can be ordered from:

Peachtree Publishers
494 Armour Circle, N. E.
Atlanta, GA 30324
(404) 876-8761

The Noiseless Tenor: The Bicycle in Literature, by James E. Starrs. A real collector's book that should be released in paperback. Starrs, a professor of law and forensic science at George Washington University in Washington, DC, has read widely and traveled considerably on his bicycle. The book combines his interests in literature and cycling. William Saroyan wrote the foreword and refers to the bicycle as the "noblest invention of mankind." Henry Miller wrote that his bicycle was his best friend. Ernest Hemingway, Ring Lardner, Stephen Crane and other authors cited bicycles in their writing.

Professor Starrs has gleaned references in literature to the bicycle and put them in his book. Illustrations by Frederic Remington and Marcel Duchamp enhance an already classy publication. Cornwall Books published *The Noiseless Tenor* in 1982.

The Mighty TOSRV, by Greg and June Siple. Greg Siple plays down the stature of TOSRV, but the Tour of the Scioto River Valley has a hardiness that led to its longevity. *The Mighty TOSRV*, published in 1986, looks back at the first quarter-century of the ride. The book has an undergraduate feel of joy and involvement. All aspects of the 210-mile two-day ride are covered, and the black-and-white candid photos over the years, and many before the ride started, give a vivid feeling of what it is like to be part of the mighty TOSRV. Copies are available from the publisher:

The Columbus Council of American
  Youth Hostels, Inc.
P.O. Box 23111
Columbus, OH 43223-0111
(614) 447-1006

My Life on Two Wheels, by Clifford L. Graves, M.D. In the 1950s and 1960s, Dr. Graves was a national leader advocating adult recreation cycling. By the 1970s he had many others taking up his position. He traveled widely on his bicycle around the United States, Europe, and even China. Graves, a surgeon who lived in posh La Jolla, California, organized the International Bicycle Touring Society. For many years its members set the standard of traveling to exotic locations for new places to ride their bicycles, staying in four-star hotels and dining in fine restaurants.

During World War II, Graves was a U.S. Army physician when caught behind enemy lines in the Battle of the Bulge. In his autobiography, he describes uncrating the bicycle he had transported with his gear, soon to

One of the most popular cycling writers in the country is Maynard Hershon, and this collection of fifty-two columns shows why.

pass himself off as a local Belgian waving at a column of German tanks that roared up the road he was on. Published in 1985, shortly before his death.

Copies are available from the publisher:

Manivelle Press
P.O. Box 2220
La Jolla, CA 92038

Pedaling Across America, by Don and Lolly Skillman. How three Oregonians carried 153 years and 702 pounds across the Continental Divide and the Great Plains, against headwinds, eighteen-wheel trucks, and fatigue to make it over the Appalachians after 4,146 miles to Virginia Beach, Virginia. They were fueled by pancakes and the kindness of some kindly folks. Vitesse Press, 1988.

Bicycling Across America, by Robert Winning. He pedaled across the United States in 1986 and wrote a book that is a guide to help others. "The point of the ride was the ride," Winning explains. He has advice on everything—from tires and tubes to where to find the best restaurants that have bottomless cups of coffee and piles of food. Winning's book includes route maps with elevation profiles for each segment. Wilderness Press, 1988.

Tales from the Bike Shop, by Maynard Hershon. One of the most popular cycling writers in the country is Maynard Hershon, and this collection of fifty-two columns shows why. Bike shops, where Hershon worked for nine years, are a world of their own, and he knows his territory. His voice is his own—kind, sympathetic, and not hesitant at skewering equipment fanatics or fitness junkies.

Fit & Fast, *by Karen E. Roy and Thurlow Rogers.*

Roadside Bicycle Repairs, by Rob Van der Plas.

Jef Mallet's illustrations go with the tone of the book, published in 1989. This is a book that occasionally sells out in bike shops, but copies are available from the publisher, Vitesse Press.

Fit & Fast: How to be a Better Cyclist, by Karen E. Roy & Thurlow Rogers. For year-round development, here is a guide for riders at all levels. Everything from setting up a year-long training plan to getting the most out of a limited workout to developing safety skills is covered in this book. Two dozen photos, tables, and illustrations are included. Vitesse Press, 1989.

Eugene Sloane has spent considerable time interviewing bike-shop owners and managers, such as Al Stiller, who ran stores in Chicago and suburban Detroit, to come up with a few books. *Eugene A. Sloane's Complete Book of Bicycle Maintenance*, with information on bicycle care and maintenance, was published in 1984 by Simon & Schuster. In 1988 came two new titles: *Eugene A. Sloane's On the Road Guide to Bicycle Maintenance*, and the more modestly titled, *The All New Complete Book of Bicycling*, which has information on selecting and fitting a bike,

clothes, commuting, touring, and maintenance.

One of the most successful books on cycling is *Richard's New Bicycle Book*, by Richard Ballantine. Many call it the last word on buying, taking care of, and repairing any bike. First published in 1972, this Ballantine book came out in its fourth revised edition in 1987. That's testimony. *Fin-de-siècle* art helps give it a distinguished classic tone.

Bicycling Magazine's 300 Tips for Better Bicycling. Considering how long *Bicycling* magazine has been around, their editors have many good tips to pass along so we get the point. Published 1991.

DeLong's Guide to Bicycles and Bicycling, by Fred DeLong. DeLong has been writing about repairing bicycles longer than anyone writing about the subject today. This is a comprehensive book that covers recreation riding and compares different kinds of equipment, from one who knows. Chilton Book Company, 1978.

The Bicycle Commuting Book, by Rob Van der Plas. If you're considering riding a bicycle to work rather than driving, this will give suggestions on how to ease riding in traffic. Van der Plas is a veteran commuter in cities around Europe and northern California. Bicycle Books, 1989. A companion book is Van der Plas's *Roadside Bicycle Repairs*, which gives dozens of illustrations showing how to handle all common repairs and adjustments while out on the road. Bicycle Books, 1990. Van der Plas also mastered mountain-bike riding for another title, *The Mountain Bike Book*. It's a guide to selecting, riding, and taking care of mountain bikes. Bicycle Books, 1990. Van der Plas also wrote *The Bicycle Fitness Book*, to cover nutrition, selection of equipment, and enjoying riding. Bicycle Books, 1989.

The Woman Cyclist, by Elaine Mariole and Michael Shermer. Elaine Mariole won the 1986 RAAM—3,100 miles from Huntington Beach, California to Atlantic City, New

Jersey—and she knows a lot about cycling. She co-authored the book with Michael Shermer, a veteran RAAM rider and book author. They cover recreation cycling, touring, mountain biking, and racing for women. Contemporary Books, 1988.

Cycling Endurance and Speed, by Michael Shermer, with a foreword by Eric Heiden. For novice riders and others who want to improve their performances. Shermer has competed in several RAAMs and passes along some of what he learned in the school of long miles. Contemporary Books, 1987.

Bicycling Fuel: Nutrition for Bicycle Riders, by Richard Rafoth, M.D. I wanted to eat the cover of this book. The bananas, apples, salad, bread, and cheese all looked so appetizing. The reader learns what to eat, what to leave. *Bicycling Fuel* gives nutritional advice for recreation as well as racing cyclists. Bicycle Books, 1988.

Barnett's Manual: Analysis and Procedures for Bicycle Mechanics, by John Barnett. This book is meant to be used by mechanics—for the workbench, not the library shelf. It's got a plastic ring binding that lets the book lie flat on the workbench, no matter what page it's open to. If grease gets on the page, not to worry. Pages are coated and can be wiped clean.

The manual grew from ten years of seminars that Barnett gave at the Barnett Bicycle Institute in Colorado Springs. The Institute gives two levels of training for bicycle mechanics—one for ninety-six classroom hours of training, the other for forty-eight hours. This is the manual that is used. If you can't make the course, *Barnett's Manual* is amply illustrated for effective self-education. Vitesse Press, 1989.

Edmund R. Burke, the eminent exercise physiologist who earned his Ph.D. from Ball State University, is in wide demand for his writing, now compiled in several volumes. *The Two-Wheeled Athlete* is a collection of thirty-six articles giving practical advice as well as scientific theory on training for cycling and sports medicine. Vitesse Press, 1986. *Medical and Scientific Aspects of Cycling* is edited by Burke and Mary Margaret Newsome, 1988. Experts write on the latest advances in cycling. The publisher is the Human Kinetics Books, a division of Human Kinetics Publishers, of Champaign, Illinois. Dr. Burke edited *Science of Cycling*, which Human Kinetics Books also published in 1986. Researchers and coaches write on biomechanics, and include information on preventing injuries.

Greg LeMond's Complete Book of Bicycling, by Greg LeMond and Kent Gordis. From someone like Greg LeMond, *lui-même*, the three-time Tour de France champion and two-time world champion, a book on cycling should be shaped with a rounded top, like tablets. It's helpful for aspiring racers as well as those who want to improve by taking recommendations from America's greatest-ever road racer. LeMond is a stickler for getting the maximum benefit from the way a cyclist sits on the saddle and holds the handlebars. His advice on positioning alone is worth the price of the book. G. P. Putnam's, 1990, in paperback.

From *Winning* every year comes an oversized book in a series, *The Fabulous World of Cycling*, which Eddy Merckx writes with *Winning* editor Rich Carlson about the past season. In 1991, *LeMond's Tour, Italy's Year* takes a look with Merckx's own special insights into Greg LeMond's third Tour de France triumph and the return to glory of Italian cyclists, whose international performances had been in a slump for much of the 1980s. These annual volumes are chock-full of vivid photos.

Graham Watson is an Englishman whose speciality is photographing great bicycle racers and their events. *Visions of Cycling* is a sumptuous photo essay of a book, with a foreword by Greg LeMond, that covers the working year of top-level professional

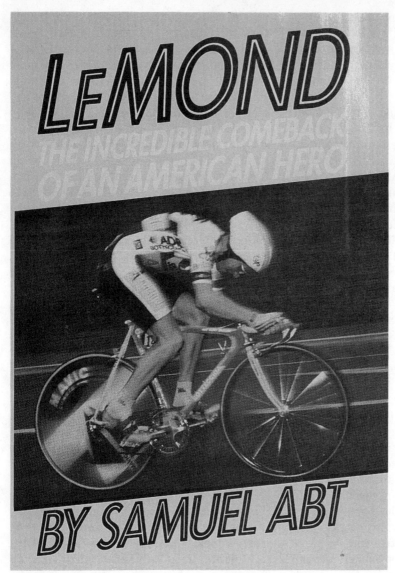

LeMOND
THE INCREDIBLE COMEBACK OF AN AMERICAN HERO
BY SAMUEL ABT

In LeMond: The Incredible Comeback of an American Hero, *author Samuel Abt provides insight into the man and the world of professional cycling. Abt writes with the grace of a cyclist sweeping a turn.*

cyclists—February through October. Watson's photos are consistently distinctive. He began his career as a society photographer in London, with clientele drawn chiefly from royalty and the aristocracy of Britain. After five years of portrait photography, he aimed his lens at bike racing. In early 1978 he published his first cycling photo—of Eddy Merckx in the Tour de France, and has been

photographing the sport steadily ever since.

VeloNews published *Visions of Cycling* in 1989. The next year came *The Tour de France and Its Heroes*. The tour dates to 1903 and was a headline event from the start. *Le Tour*, after all, was created by the sports newspaper, *L'Auto*, now called *L'Equipe*, to promote circulation. Watson's coverage spans from 1978 to 1989. His photography matches the heroics of the riders in Le Tour.

When the 1989 Tour de France started, nobody listed LeMond among the prerace favorites—not even LeMond, who had won it in 1986. He was hoping to make the top twenty.

A shooting accident in April 1987 while he was hunting wild turkey in northern California nearly killed him. Dozens of shotgun pellets tore into his right side, shoulder, legs, and back. The blast broke two ribs and collapsed a lung. Surgeons cut him open to remove pellets that threatened his vital organs. More than two dozen pellets remained embedded, mostly in his back and legs, and two are still in the lining of his heart.

But on the final day of the 2,025-mile 1989 Tour, LeMond rode the perfect ride up the Champs-Elysées to win. His comeback made world news.

In *LeMond: The Incredible Comeback of an American Hero*, Samuel Abt provides insight into the man and the world of professional cycling, and writes with the grace of a cyclist sweeping a turn. Random House published the book in 1990, a sequel to Abt's 1985 book, *Breakaway: On the Road with the Tour de France*, which took the reader every pedal stroke of the route of the 1984 Tour, LeMond's first. Abt also covers in this book the first women's Tour, which Marianne Martin of Boulder, Colorado, won.

Abt, who came from New England and is a deputy editor for the *International Herald-Tribune*, knows bicycle racing well, understands the personalities of the riders, and conveys the sport to readers new to the sport and experienced. In 1989 Bicycle Books published *In High Gear*, in which Abt describes the world of professional bicycle racing. He is the first American writer ever to do that.

In June 1991 Bicycle Books published Abt's fourth book, *Tour de France: Three Weeks to Glory*, which describes LeMond's 1990 Tour de France triumph. Some one hundred photos contribute to Abt's prose.

CHAPTER 8

BICYCLING ON FILM

THE ABUNDANCE OF BOOKS on all aspects of bicycle riding, unfortunately, doesn't extend to videos. In large part this is because producing a video is a collaboration involving many people, compared with writing a book, ordinarily an individual effort. Videos also cost substantially more than books to produce.

One of the best videos for introducing novices to cycling and helping guide their development is *Sport Cycling*, but it was a victim of its budget. "The video cost $100,000," said Michael Shermer, author of the 1987 book of the same title (Contemporary Books) on which the video is based. "The people in the company that did it went first class on everything. But the costs drove them out of business."

Sport Cycling video, like the book, takes a rider step by step from selecting a bicycle and getting the proper fit, to nutrition, clothing, and equipment. It is especially good for helping motivate riders—novices as well as veterans seeking to improve their performances.

"The key in going from a complete novice to a pretty decent rider is setting goals," explained Shermer, who has a Ph.D. in science and the history of science. "The first step is to write down what your goals are and how you are going to approach them. To ride 100 miles, you have to start with shorter rides, like 25 miles, then go up to 35 miles, to 50 miles, and so on."

Shermer, who has motivated himself across the United States several times as a competitor in RAAM, finds a silver lining in failure. "Failures are the most important thing we can do. Failing tells us what to do next. The greatest successes come after the greatest failures. Look at Babe Ruth. He hit the second greatest number of home runs ever, but he also has the greatest number of strikeouts, too. Thomas Edison failed 6,000 times trying to find the right filament to create the electric light bulb. He kept track of what he did in notebooks, many of them. But we never hear about those failures when we're in school. What I encourage in the video and the book is to turn failure

John Marino's ride into the Guinness Book of World Records *prompted the video* Psychling *that is distributed as a motivational film. Of universal interest, it emphasizes that a positive attitude leads to self-confidence and then to achievement.* (John Marino photo by Vito Torelli)

around—look at what goes wrong and try a different approach."

Sport Cycling is forty minutes long, in color, and in stereo. A limited number of the videos are available for $19, which includes shipping, from:

Michael Shermer
2761 North Marengo Ave.
Altedena, CA 91001
(818) 794-3119

John Marino's 1980 ride across the United States in 12 days, 3 hours, and 41 minutes is the subject of the video *Psychling*, which CRM McGraw-Hill Films distributes as a motivation film. Complete with an eleven-page leader's workbook, *Psychling* uses Marino's ride as an example of positive thinking to set a goal, no matter how daunting that goal is, and achieve it.

His accomplishment, the workbook points out, required the physical effort of swimming the English Channel eighteen times, or run-

ning in forty-three consecutive marathons, or doing nearly one million push-ups in a row.

Dr. Larry May of the University of California at Los Angeles Medical Center examined Marino and found him in the same shape as any endurance athlete. The message of the film, which makes it of universal interest, is that a positive attitude leads to self-confidence and then to achievement.

Psychling is twenty-five minutes long and in color. It is available from:

CRM McGraw-Hill Films
110 Fifteenth St.
Del Mar, CA 92014
(714) 453-5000

Also available from:

CRM Films
2233 Faraday
Carlsbad, CA 92008
1-800-421-0833

Olympic cyclists Connie Carpenter and spouse Davis Phinney attempt to pass along some of what they know about cycling in the 1987 video *The Complete Cyclist*. This seventy-five-minute color video covers a lot of material in its attempt, as the narrator contends, to be "the most comprehensive tape about cycling ever produced." Topics like touring bikes, racing bikes, mountain bikes, bike fit, training, clothing, and maintenance are snapped off like roll call.

Carpenter, the gold medalist at the 1984 Los Angeles Olympics in the women's road race, and Phinney, bronze medalist in the 100-kilometer (62.5-mile) team time trial and two-time stage winner in the Tour de France, have a lot of knowledge to impart. The tape is at its best when Phinney discusses his stretching routine and getting started on a training program.

The Complete Cyclist is available through local bike shops.

An award-winning video is *Cycling for Success With the 7-Eleven Team*. This fifty-minute color video came out in 1987 and was voted "Best Sports Instruction Video" at the American Video Awards.

The video features the 7-Eleven racing team members, who go over skills they have honed. Eric Heiden has a segment on bicycle handling. Alex Steida discusses applying the brakes under a variety of conditions. Ron Kiefel has an important segment on cornering. He suggests practicing in a safe area, such as a parking lot. Jeff Pierce tells about how climbing up hills is a skill that can be learned.

Cycling for Success is distributed through the 7-Eleven convenience-store chain and bike shops.

There are also videos devoted to safe cycling and using a bicycle to commute to work. The Los Angeles Police Department in 1989 produced a twelve-minute film, *Be Safe on Your Bike*, which demonstrates basic skills needed for safe bicycle riding. The video is available for a donation of $50 for VHS, $100 for 16mm from:

The Los Angeles Police Department
4125 S. Crenshaw Blvd.
Los Angeles, CA 90008
(213) 485-7742

Tim Kneeland & Associates, of Seattle, produced a video and slide show, *Bicycle Safety First*, in 1989 to encourage safe and responsible cycling. "We developed the video and slide show because there wasn't one we could use," Kneeland explained. The thirteen-minute color video costs $42.99, including postage; the slide show costs $64.49, including postage. They may be ordered from:

Tim Kneeland & Associates
200 Lake Washington Blvd., No. 101
Seattle, WA 98122-6540
1-800-433-0528

In 1990 The National Traffic Safety Institute, a private corporation in San Jose, California, produced a thirty-minute video, *Share the Road*, in cooperation with the Almaden Cycling Touring Club. The video costs $49.95, plus UPS shipping. Copies are available from:

The National Traffic Safety Institute
275 N. 4th St.
San Jose, CA 95112
(408) 297-0873

Dr. Donald Eldredge, a pediatrician in the Rochester, New York, suburb of Pittsford, was instrumental in producing a seven-minute animated video aimed at children aged four to eight to encourage them to wear helmets while riding a bicycle. The video, *Elephants Never Forget*, emphasizes that an elephant doesn't forget to follow the basic safety rules of riding, which means wearing a helmet.

The Rochester Junior League financed expenses of producing the video in 1990, Eldredge said. *"Elephants Never Forget* is designed to show beginning riders," he explained. "It's a simple story and short enough that the teacher can show it to the class, then discuss it, then show it again."

Copies are being distributed through:

Bob DeRoo
2511 East Henrietta Rd.
Rochester, NY 14623
(716) 334-1083

Heads . . . You Win is a ten-minute color video that the Chapel Hill, North Carolina, League for Safe Bicycling produced in 1990. This VHS video is available for a $50 donation from:

The Chapel Hill League for Bicycle
   Safety
Box 16513
Chapel Hill, NC 27516
(919) 933-4870

The Environmental Protection Agency has a video, *Bicycling to Work*, to encourage people to leave the car at home and commute to work on a bicycle. Uncle Sam produced the twenty-minute video in 1984. Copies are available for free by sending a blank tape or requesting loaner copies from:

Ross Ruske, Bicycle Coordinator
United States Environmental
   Protection Agency
401 M St., N.W.
Washington, DC 20460
(202) 382-2671

The American Automobile Association has videos and 16mm films on commuter safety for purchase. Titles include *Bikes Go with the Flow, Bicycling on Three Wheels,*

and *Bicycle Border Patrol*. For more information, get in touch with:

AAA Foundation for Traffic Safety
1730 M St., N.W.
Washington, DC 20036
(202) 775-1456

The League of American Wheelmen is another source of videos. LAW rents them for $10 each, plus a deposit. One of LAW's videos for rent is *Bicycle Safety Camp*, a lively rap message that David Levine & Associates produced in 1989. It lasts twenty-five minutes. It is aimed at youngsters aged six to twelve. Other LAW videos for rent include *Bicycling Safety First, Build Your Own Bike Wheel*, and *Cycling in Delft, Holland*. For a complete list and more information, send a stamped, business-sized envelope with your address on it to:

League of American Wheelmen
6707 Whitestone Rd.
Suite 209
Baltimore, MD 21207
(301) 944-3399

Rides themselves have become so popular they are the subject of videos. The Hotter'n Hell Hundred in Wichita Falls, Texas, in August is such a big event that television coverage of the day's program of rides, as well as bicycle races in downtown Wichita Falls, is broadcast to an estimated 20 million households in Texas and Oklahoma.

Copies of the program are offered in a forty-five-minute video that the Wichita Falls Bicycling Club makes available for the 1989 and 1990 editions. Copies are available from:

Hotter'n Hell Hundred Video
Wichita Falls Bicycling Club
P.O. Box 2099
Wichita Falls, TX 76307
(817) 692-2925

What's good for Texas is good for Washington. The Seattle-to-Portland Bicycle Classic ride of 205 miles in 1989 was filmed and made into a seventy-minute ride. It is available from:

John Fountain
10247 Ninth Ave., South
Seattle, WA 98168
(206) 767-9834

Bicycle racing has long attracted Hollywood. In 1934 Warner Brothers released *Six Day Bike Rider*, a comedy in which one of life's failures impresses his girlfriend by entering a six-day bicycle race. Warner Brothers was the right studio to make a cycling movie: two of the brothers, Harry and Albert, owned a bike shop as young men in the 1890s in Youngstown, Ohio, where they competed in local cycling events.

Six Day Bike Rider stars Joe E. Brown, a native Buckeye and a popular film comedian known for his elastic face and slapstick style. Brown, forty-two when the movie was released, was a good athlete. At nine he had

Bobby Walthour, Jr., on the right, defeated reigning world sprint champion Pete Moeskops of Holland in this 1925 Match race in Newark and subsequently went to work for MGM movie studios. Walthour used his athletic experiences to dub a deep sigh of fatigue for the 1939 movie classic, Gone With the Wind. *(Russell Mamone collection)*

been a circus acrobat, and he later played semi-professional baseball. During the filming, Brown used a bicycle racer as a double in action shots. Six-day racers like Bobby Walthour, Jr., and Fred Spencer were hired to ride around the steeply banked wooden velodrome for the camera. (Walthour subsequently went to work for MGM, where he was in charge of the film library. He was called upon to use his experience and dub a deep sigh of fatigue for *Gone With the Wind*.)

The movie entertained America in the depths of the Depression. Critics regard *Six Day Bike Rider* as one of Brown's better films. Copies of the black-and-white film, sixty-nine minutes long, are difficult to find.

Attempts have been made to make a movie out of the novel *The Yellow Jersey*, by Englishman Ralph Hurne. Simon & Schuster published it in 1973 in the United States; Weidenfeld & Nicolson published it in the United Kingdom. Out of print, the novel is appreciating in value. The protagonist is a thirty-seven-year-old racer near retirement who coaches a younger rider with more talent than the protagonist ever had. At a crucial point, the protagonist makes a break in the Tour de France, which takes on the proportion of a character itself in the novel, and winds up in the yellow jersey.

In 1985 it looked like *Yellow Jersey* was a sure bet to make the leap from novel to movie for Cannon Films. Colin Welland, who wrote the screenplay for *Chariots of Fire*, wrote the screenplay for *Yellow Jersey*. Michael Cimino who directed *The Deer Hunter* was hired. Dustin Hoffman was cast as the protagonist. Hoffman took up cycling and even went to watch the 1985 Tour de France. After $1 million was spent on salaries and shooting 150,000 feet of 1985 Tour footage, the project faltered.

Hoffman, forty-eight at the time, lost interest. Cannon Films got into financial problems. Production stopped.

The next year, Greg LeMond fulfilled author Hurne's premise that a non-European would finally win the Tour. In 1989 LeMond won for the second time, and his comeback after his near-fatal shooting accident drew the attention of Warner Brothers Television. A script was written for an ABC Television movie. George Mullen, an actor twenty-seven years old who bears a striking resemblance to LeMond, was hired. In late 1990, however, ABC Television executives nixed the project.

"We were shocked and dismayed," said Warner Brothers vice president Art Horan, who was behind the project. His great-uncle, Harry Horan, won two six-day races in the 1920s and competed against Walthour, Jr., Spencer, and Goullet.

French film director Louis Malle announced his interest in early 1991 to make a film of the 1992 Tour de France as a documentary through LeMond's perspective. Filmgoers are familiar with Malle's features such as *Atlantic City* and *My Dinner with André*. Less well known is Malle's nineteen-minute film, *Vive le Tour!* (Long Live the Tour), released in 1962. It has an English narration and is available in 16mm from:

New Yorker Films
16 West 61st St.
New York, NY 10023
(212) 247-6110

"The idea is to dramatize the Tour," said Marty Elfand, a producer who works with Malle. "We want to shoot the Tour as it unfolds, through Greg's eyes. If he wins, he wins, and if he loses, he loses. I don't think anybody in America understands what a tremendous event the Tour de France is. What goes on, the day-to-day drama for three weeks, is what gives the race its drive. There's no need to complicate the story with a love interest. We can do a whole movie just on the Tour."

While it looks like a movie on LeMond is years away, videos are available on his triumphs, which have considerable drama. Kent Gordis, his former racing partner, directed *1989 World Championship*, a color video of forty-eight minutes on LeMond's world championship in Chambéry, France. The first sixteen minutes shows previous footage of LeMond winning amateur and professional races. That sets the stage for a fiercely competitive 164-mile world championship race in southeastern France on rain-slick, twisting roads. Down the hills, at the base of the Alps, racers hit speeds of sixty miles an hour.

After nearly seven hours of racing, LeMond was in a breakaway of five leaders in the closing miles. He countered a series of attacks that a Frenchman, a Dutchman, and a Soviet rider launched in their all-out bid for victory. In the sprint to the finish, LeMond won by a wheel.

Videos also are available on LeMond's three Tour de France wins. The films, *1986 Tour de France, 1989 Tour de France*, and *1990 Tour de France*, all can be ordered from:

Famous Cycling Videos
704 Hennepin Ave.
Minneapolis, MN 55403
1-800-359-3107

Famous Cycling Videos also sells two racing films that afficionados regard as classics. *La Course en Tête* (Head of the Pack) is the Eddy Merckx story. This color feature film of seventy minutes was a big hit in Europe in the early 1980s when it was released. It offers a rare film portrait of Merckx, an extraordinary endurance athlete, at his best. Producer of *La Course en Tête* is Louis Malle's brother, Vincent.

A *pièce de résistance* that evokes drama and action as well as tactics is *Sunday in Hell*, a documentary on the 1976 Paris-Roubaix, the most prestigious one-day spring classic. The race in northern France dates back to 1896 and is called "Queen of the Classics." Its rough roads, with stretches of cobblestones that jar the riders for hours between conventionally paved roads, also earned the race the name "Hell of the North."

Sunday in Hell captures the battle between Merckx and other giants of the sport in this 165-mile classic. It is a video that collectors of the genre include in their library.

On this side of the Atlantic, the stage race that flourished the longest in North America was the Tour du St. Laurent, which was artfully filmed in *Sixty Cycles*.

The 11th annual event in 1965 covered 1,500 miles in twelve days. Photographer Jean-Claude Labrecque filmed it in color. Riders from thirteen countries coursed through villages in Quebec near the St. Laurent River with European names like Coaticook, Beauceville, and Thetford-Mines.

Sixty Cycles, twelve minutes long, was released in 1966 and played around Canada and the United States as a short that preceded feature movies. Audiences seeing a bicycle race on film for the first time were entertained by the way Labracque filmed it. A jazzy soundtrack by Booker T and the MGs put the audience in the right mood for the documentary, now important for showing one of the last years the Tour du St. Laurent was held.

The film is available in 16mm. McGraw-Hill distributes the film, which many libraries carry.

Donald Trump was in college when *Sixty Cycles* was filmed. He never got into bicycle riding, but he became a real estate tycoon and put his name on a stage race in 1989 and 1990. Now his name is on a ninety-minute race video, *1990 Tour de Trump: Taming the Devil*. The 1,130-mile race, America's long-

While Hollywood waits to make a movie on Greg LeMond, videos of his Tour de France and world championship victories are available. (Photo courtesy of Famous Cycling Video, 1-800-359-3107)

est, became a battle between Soviet amateur Vladislav Bobrik and professional Raúl Alcala of Mexico. The Tour de Trump raced eleven days through six Middle Atlantic and Northeast states.

On the penultimate day up steep winding roads in upstate New York's Catskills, the race ascended a hill called Devil's Kitchen. There the race was determined, and the video derived its name.

Presented in a documentary style for serious cycling fans. Copies are available for $42.95 including postage from:

Winning Magazine
1127 Hamilton St.
Allentown, PA 18102
1-800-441-1666

Cycling is compelling to see on film, but the sport has also recently inspired audio performances. John Tesh, co-host of television's syndicated *Entertainment Tonight*, covered the Tour de France for five years. The race prompted him to compose and record soundtracks on his Synclavier. His music during the Tour's coverage won him an Emmy Award.

"A TV show spills out on your carpet and is gone the next day," Tesh said, "but an album can make some history, and there is no more dramatic event to capture than the Tour de France."

Two soundtracks, *Tour de France* and *Tour de France: The Early Years*, are available on compact disk for $17 each, on cassette for $11.98 each, covering postage and handling, from:

Private Music
9014 Melrose Ave.
Los Angeles, CA 90069
(213) 859-9200

Indiana has the unique distinction of being the home state of two of the three U.S. racers who won the world professional sprint championship: Major Taylor of Indianapolis won the 1899 world's in Montreal, and Frank Kramer of Evansville won the 1912 world's in Newark. (The third rider was Iver Lawson of Salt Lake City, who won the 1904 world's in London.)

Taylor and Kramer are the subjects of radio plays, fifteen minutes each, that Media Indiana of Indianapolis broadcast as part of a weekly program, "The Nineteenth State." The program reaches a statewide audience of 200,000 listeners. The Museum of Broadcasting in New York City selected the tapes on Taylor and Kramer for their archives.

ABC Television's Chris Schenkel narrates the radio plays. Written by Rodney Richey and produced by Stan Sollers, the stories catch the imagination and vividly evoke the period when the two Hoosiers ruled the board tracks. Both radio plays are on a cassette available for a donation of $8 per episode, includes postage, from:

The Nineteenth State
P.O. Box 501049
Indianapolis, IN 46250
(317) 879-1900

Of all the cycling movies, the one that filmgoers readily associate with the sport is 1979 Academy Award winner *Breaking Away*. The movie rode from the celluloid into the hearts of audiences everywhere. It continues to delight viewers who rent the video or see it on television.

Film critic Roger Ebert called it, "A sunny, goofy, intelligent little film about coming of age in Bloomington, Indiana."

An unsuccessful television series followed in 1980, trailed by a pack of films that didn't catch *Breaking Away*. Steve Tesich, a graduate of Indiana University, where he received a degree in Russian literature, won an Oscar for his movie screenplay. But his next cycling film, *American Flyers* in 1985, didn't get off the starting line at the box office. It is memorable chiefly for being one of Kevin Costner's first movies.

Breaking Away's appeal and its box-office success make it the leader of cycling movies. It is actually two stories intertwined into one, and intertwined in such a way that the movie transcends the boundaries of a simple cycling movie and becomes one of universal appeal.

The story deals with four adolescent boys just out of high school in the early 1960s, breaking away from adolescence and heading, bewildered and reluctantly, into adulthood. One of the four, played by Dennis Christopher, aspires to race bicycles in Italy.

Audiences enjoy watching this cyclist of nineteen, who still lives at home with his parents in Bloomington, become Italian in his own mind. He emulates Italian cycling legends like Fausto Coppi, Gino Bartali, Felice Gimondi, and Erocle Baldini. Assuming the air of Continental élan, he greets his parents with, "Ciao mamma, ciao papa." He studies Italian phrases from a book and learns more by playing Italian opera records. He renames the family cat Fellini and feeds it from a Cinzano ashtray.

All this is a long way from a Midwesterner who couldn't tell an olive tree from a fig tree. But behind the reconstituted dots that fill the screen and tell a story that goes to the heart lies the real model for the movie's bicycle racer. He is Dave Blase (called Dave Stohler in the movie), whose ersatz Italian persona cloaked his shyness and helped him meet girls.

Blase, once the quixotic personality that Christopher portrays, was a popular racer in the 1960s with Olympic aspirations. He won several Indiana district championships when the state was producing national-class riders like Karl Napper, Olaf Moetus, and Dave Mercer, a time not long before the appearance of national champions Steve Dayton and the Stetina family of Wayne, Dale, and Troy.

In 1962, when Blase was a senior at Indiana University in Bloomington, he rode on the four-man Phi Kappa Psi team with fraternity brother Steve Tesich in the university's Little 500. The race was 200 laps on stock bikes (balloon-tired bicycles with no derailleurs) around a quarter-mile cinder track that Tesich made immortal in his screenplay and transformed into the setting of the movie's climax.

"The Little 500 part was close to being true," Blase said. In the movie, as in the real 1962 event, the team Blase and Tesich rode for was considered an underdog. Several other fraternities had what were considered better teams. "We won by a thirteen-second margin, although in the movie it came down to a sprint," Blase said. "That was to make it more dramatic."

Friends heartily agree that the character depicted in the movie strongly agrees with Blase's personality in his undergraduate days. On training rides he sang Italian opera. Blase was known to drop out of group workouts when he got distracted over how the woodwinds joined the strings in a Rossini overture. In one race, Blase and breakaway partner Napper had a comfortable lead in a breakaway when Blase suddenly lost a contact lens and stopped to look for it, thereby giving up possible victory.

After college graduation, Blase became a teacher, but he kept riding. In 1965 Tesich finished second to Blase in the Indiana district's ten-mile championship. Blase that year was preparing for the 1968 Olympic trials in an effort to make the team bound for Mexico City. Just weeks before the trials, however, he was injured in a stage of the Tour du St. Laurent and missed riding the trials.

Tesich cut back his cycling to devote more time to screenwriting. Blase said he felt Tesich "never really tasted success in bike racing. With just a little more training and a little more effort, he might have made it."

Yet Tesich had gathered considerable material from racing and applied himself to make it as a writer. In the early 1970s, Blase learned from a Phi Kappa Psi brother that Tesich had written a story about him. The story was called *The Eagle from Naptown*, with Naptown being a colloquial reference to Indianapolis, Blase's hometown.

In the same period, Tesich, from industrial northwestern Indiana, wrote another story about class conflict involving the privileged against the poor. Both stories interested movie director Peter Yates, but neither was strong enough on its own for a movie. Tesich then merged the two stories, and the result was what Yates thought had a genuine movie plot.

When the cameras began shooting, the working title was *Bambino*. It wasn't long before the title changed to *Breaking Away*.

"I got a call from Steve Tesich, who said they wanted to use my name in the movie, and I said okay," Blase recalled. "Then I was supposed to get a release form that never came. It turned out that 20th Century–Fox's legal department didn't want to use my actual name because the story was based on bits and pieces of my life. Generally, the way Dave Stohler was acting in the movie was the way Steve Tesich knew me in college."

The movie helped launch Tesich's screenwriting career. His other screen credits in-

Actor Dennis Christopher learned to ride like a racer for the movie The Eagle from Naptown, *which was renamed* Breaking Away. (Twentieth Century–Fox photo)

clude *The World According to Garp* and *Eleni*. He is the author of a novel, *Summer Crossings* (Random House), and plays that include *Baba Goya*, *Square One*, and *Speed of Darkness*. He lives part of the time in an apartment in New York City and the rest of the year in a log cabin in Conifer, Colorado.

Blase lives in Indianapolis where he teaches in the city's Arlington High School. He is active in veterans racing and in 1983 won a bronze medal in the veterans' national championships for the kilometer (three-fifths of a mile) time trial. Blase has served as president of the club he helped found in the early 1960s, the Speedway Wheelmen. He is also active in involving secondary-school students in a development program at the Major Taylor Velodrome in Indianapolis.

Although he never achieved his Olympic goal, the Eagle from Naptown who loved Italian opera still can be seen on television, portrayed by an actor who shows him leading his team to victory in the Little 500.

CHAPTER 9

How to Watch a Bicycle Race

The pack of racers whips past. Bare legs in black shorts pump like pistons. Narrow tires hum the sound of speed over the pavement. The racers, in a bouquet of jerseys, are bent low over the frames of their bicycles and bunched together so tightly that it looks like you could walk across their backs.

As suddenly as they came, they are gone.

Two minutes later the pack charges by again. A rider you didn't notice before is fifty yards ahead and the pack is in full pursuit. It doesn't seem possible, but everybody is riding faster—the pack is stretched in a long tight line resembling "crack the whip." You wonder if the breakaway rider will last. That keeps you watching—to see what happens next.

It's another criterium, a race held around a circuit of streets closed to traffic. This is the kind of race repeated in city after city across America, the sort of race that all of today's racers, including Greg LeMond, grew up riding.

Criteriums are the bread and butter of American racing. To many cyclists and racing afficionados, racing is associated with criteriums. They evolved from horse tracks, typically half-mile dirt tracks, where the sport started in the early 1880s. Popularity of the wheel sport in the early 1890s generated tracks designed specifically for bicycle races. The shorter the tracks, the steeper the banking on the turns, with reduced banking on the straights. Labor was cheap and wood was inexpensive and in ready supply. After the mid-1890s, most tracks were constructed out of spruce or pine; six laps to the mile became a popular size. Board tracks, called velodromes, flourished with paying customers until the Depression.

When World War II broke out, demand for raw materials led to dismantling the few remaining board velodromes. After the war,

America was a nation of automobiles. Bicycle races became endangered. One event in suburban Chicago that became a casualty in the clash with cars was the fifty-mile race from Elgin to Chicago. It had started in 1926 and in postwar years verged on becoming an American classic. But by the mid-1960s, traffic forced even this venerable race out of existence.

The kind of bicycle race that would survive the onslaught of cars was one in which cyclists had the roads to themselves. Bicycle races and automobile drivers just never coexisted. Motorists never like to give up the roads, especially on holidays and weekends, prime times for driving cars as well as competing in bicycle races. This led race officials to meet with police and local government officials to close off traffic from streets, making up a short circuit for the riders. Thus criteriums were created.

One of the model criteriums became the Tour of Somerville, a fifty-mile event around a grid of downtown streets closed to traffic on Memorial Day in the New Jersey town of Somerville. First held in 1940, the Tour of Somerville quickly took on national importance. It is America's oldest annual bicycle race. Somerville's population of 15,000 more than doubles on race day, when 40,000 spectators line the course.

The Tour of Somerville is characteristic of the majority of criteriums nationwide. Somerville's course is slightly more than a mile around—forty-four laps for fifty miles in the men's main event for professionals and top amateurs, seventeen laps for the women's twenty-mile race. Riders negotiate three right-angled turns and one sweeping turn every lap. Speeds are consistently high in criteriums; Somerville's fifty-mile course record is one hour and forty-three minutes.

What's the best way to watch a criterium? As the event unfolds, walk around the course in the direction facing the racers. Corners are a good place to stop and watch the action, to see the riders lean at speed into the turns. Another vantage point is at the top of a hill. (Somerville is flat, however.) Walking around the course helps give a feel for the event: what the pavement is like, what turns the riders negotiate, hills they ride up, where they change gears, how they apply their brakes—some of the technical aspects that may help your own riding.

Look for the lead riders. Like any sport, riders of the same team wear team jerseys, which means the better teams will be among riders at the head of the pack. Consistent with all sports, it helps to have some familiarity with the personalities of influential riders, as races tend to reflect the personality of the top riders.

A fundamental factor in bicycle racing is drafting, where riders at the front take the brunt of wind resistance while all riders behind them are pedaling with 25 percent less resistance. That contributes to cycling being such a tactical sport.

What tactics should spectators watch for? Watch to see who attacks off the front of the pack. The breakaway rider may be attempting to draw a reaction from a rival team, which promptly will counterattack with riders sprinting to chase down the breakaway rider.

There are also the independent entrepreneurs, riding without the aid of teammates. These loners attack because they've got nothing to lose. They may get lucky and steal away while teams watch one another to see who reacts first. Or they may draw enough riders to bridge up to them to make the breakaway succeed. With riders working smoothly together in a relay to alternate drafting behind one another, a breakaway of four or more riders often can hold off the pursuing pack. All these possibilities contribute to the racing stew.

How can a spectator tell if the pack is going hard or taking it easy? Generally, the slimmer the pack, the faster the race. When the

When the speed is high, the field strings out wheel to wheel. (Seth Golzer photo)

When the pace eases, riders bunch up and spread across the road like a swarm of bees. (John Pratt photo)

Lisa Goldsmith chases a premium, a prize within the race, which helps spark the event—for spectators and riders. (John Pratt photo)

speed is high, the field strings out wheel to wheel in a line as long as the number of riders in the race. (In criteriums, lapped riders are pulled out of the race.) Riders are bent low and hold on to the drops of their handlebars. When the pace eases, riders bunch up and spread out across the road like a swarm of bees. Some may even rest with their hands on top of the handlebars.

Ironically, it's not uncommon for riders to crash when the pace is slack. They tend to lose concentration and do something careless.

The best riders are constantly evaluating the race. Unlike the kindred sport of running, bicycle racers of widely varying specialities can mix in a criterium. Running power-sprinters who specialize in 50-meter and 100-meter dashes ordinarily don't compete against marathoners. But their counterparts in cycling frequently mingle in criteriums. In criteriums, power sprinters try to save their explosive speed for the finish; endurance riders try to keep the speed high to wear down the sprinters.

Contributing to the charm of criteriums are premiums, referred to as premes, often spelled primes under the impression that the word is French. Premiums grew out of six-day races in Madison Square Garden. Fans would offer cash or merchandise prizes for the first across the line for the next lap, or next half-mile, or whatever struck the fancy of whoever offered the bonus. In one Garden six-day, Bobby Walthour, Jr., won a Pierce Arrow, a luxury car equivalent to an $80,000 car in today's market.

In addition to the prizes that the cyclists

compete for, premiums stoke the criteriums. Fred Mengoni watched a lone breakaway rider churning away with a tantalizing lead in front of the pack of 180 in the 1989 Tour of Somerville and promptly offered a $3,000 premium to anyone who lapped the field. The competition was too fast that day for anyone to get away for good. But premiums of $20 to $200 on nearly every lap heated the pace and enriched many jersey pockets.

Premiums also make the 250 yards leading to the finish a good place to stay fixed to watch the criterium. Riders chasing the premiums sprint over the last 250 yards for the line. With entry fees of $15 to $30 per race, many riders try to win premes to help cover expenses.

What's the best way to watch the finish of a race? As Shakespeare wrote in *The Tempest*, "What's past is prologue." Most bicycle races, no matter what their length, are decided in the last 250 yards. The bigger the race, the more difficult it is for spectators to get a spot at the finish line. But the sidelines in the last 250 yards are just as good. Spectators watch where the key moves are made that decide the final dash to the line as racers hit speeds of forty miles an hour and faster.

The vast majority of breakaway riders get caught by the pack in criteriums. But every once in a while a breakaway escapes free. You never know when the breakaway you watch is going to get caught—or succeed and turn into the winning move. That's what keeps spectators watching.

Another category of racing is the stage race, which ranges from two days to three weeks. A European tradition, stage races are taking root in the United States.

America's premier stage race started out as the amateur-sanctioned Tour de Trump in 1989 and 1990. When Donald Trump was asked before the start of the 1989 event in Albany, New York, if he would consider changing the name to the Tour d'Amérique or some other soubriquet that would omit his identity, he smiled and shook his head. "We could if we wanted to have a less successful race," he replied, provoking spontaneous laughter from the 120 high-spirited media people from around the United States and Europe. "My name is the difference between a press conference like this and speaking to only one reporter."

The stage races in 1989 and 1990 were broadcast on NBC Television and ESPN. That gave the events a national audience beyond the estimated 3 million spectators who lined the race course through the Middle Atlantic and Northeast states.

As Trump brashly predicted, the races were successful. Top racers like Greg LeMond and many European household names of the sport competed. The race generated worldwide coverage. Cities like Richmond, Virginia, and Allentown, Pennsylvania, were datelines for stories that were read in more than forty countries that were following the race's daily action.

What Trump didn't count on, however, were business reversals that led to his pulling out of title sponsorship after the 1990 edition. But the Du Pont Company, an international conglomerate, took over as title sponsor. Du Pont increased the prize list to $300,000—the Tour Du Pont is one of the richest bicycle races in the world.

In 1991 the Tour Du Pont became a race with professional sanctioning. The Fédération Internationale du Cyclisme Professionnel, the sport's professional governing body, included the event on its already-crowded calendar. Officials also awarded the race FICP points, which riders as well as teams compete for to determine world rankings. FICP points are considered key to ensuring that the top riders, whose salaries often depend on their rankings, compete.

Tour de France director Jean-Marie LeBlanc, who watched the final days of the Tour de Trump in New York City and Boston, attended the November 1990 press conference in Washington, DC, where Du Pont and race officials announced the 1991 event, May 9th to 19th. LeBlanc told the gathering that the Tour Du Pont could be "one of the great cycling events. After only two years, the United States has proved itself."

LeBlanc's presence at the press conference, in the National Press Club, was equivalent to a blessing from the Pope. The United States had come a long way in becoming recognized as a peer among major cycling nations.

What's the best way to follow a stage race? Unless you want to commute the event's entire distance, such as the 1,100 miles of the Tour Du Pont, the best way is to keep track of the daily action through network television and print coverage.

The day-to-day action is exciting, but to the uninitiated it can lead to confusion, especially since there are two sets of results daily. One set of results covers the order finish of that particular stage, or leg, of the event. In addition, an overall order is announced. Just bear in mind that the overall order, often referred to as "general classification," is based on the total elapsed time of the race up to that point. The winner of the overall event is the rider with the least elapsed time.

It is not unusual for a stage winner, such as Greg LeMond in the 1990 Tour de France, to win the overall event without capturing a single stage. LeMond succeeded in finishing consistently high, accumulating the best time of all the competitors in the 1990 Tour de France.

Author John Gardner once observed that most stories are founded on the premise of either a stranger coming to town, or embarking on a journey. Stage races involve both elements. A good stage race has a medley of three main riding tests. The first is time trialing, in which riders compete individually against the clock, what the French call the test of truth. The second is hill climbing. The

third is the relatively flat stage that goes from one city to the next and ends in a spectacular mass pack sprint. Individual riders with particular talent can excel for a day. The overall champion is the best all-around rider.

Because stage races go from city to city, often with the race lead changing from day to day, television coverage is difficult to beat. Tim Blumenthal, *Mountain Bike* editor and a veteran scriptwriter for television networks covering stage races, points out how an hour is needed to edit one minute of pictures and music for broadcast.

"Stage races are unquestionably the toughest telecasts," he said. "The racing is superfast. Tactics and flow are subtle and unpredictable, and the actual event is three times as long each day as a running marathon."

Aside from television, what is the best way to watch a stage race? Depending on where you live and the course, pick a day that takes in hills. Drafting helps make riders equal on flat stretches, but it means less in climbing as the force of gravity takes over. Select a spot at the top of a hill, or leading to the top, to watch. Because the race roads are closed to traffic, be sure to get in place early. Take a picnic basket to enjoy during the wait. Consider the wait an investment because when riders arrive they will string out to give you a chance to see each rider individually. If you still have time, get in your car and drive to the finish.

Witnessing an event gives a feel for it. Television coverage and newspaper and magazine articles help fill in the additional details.

Another category of racing is the old American standard of track racing on velodromes. For spectators, velodromes have the advantage of having all the action on the enclosed elliptical track.

A variety of programs are offered during

What has always made track racing exciting is close competition and good sightlines, such as in this 1920 race in Newark. Alf Goullet, on the left, sprints against Eddie Madden of Newark and Oscar-Egg of Paris. (U.S. Bicycling Hall of Fame photo)

the racing season, typically from May through September. Around the United States are nineteen velodromes. They are constructed with good sightlines for spectators to watch the action. The best spot is to sit over the finish line, but anywhere around the track is good.

More information on velodromes and their seasonal programs are available from:

Alkek Velodrome
Alkek Velodrome Racing Association
2999 South Wayside
Houston, TX 77023
(713) 578-0858

Alpenrose Velodrome
4318-SE 8th Court
Gresham, OR 97080
(503) 661-5874

Baton Rouge Velodrome
354 Stanford Ave.
Baton Rouge, LA 70808
(504) 767-1847

Brown Deer Velodrome
P.O. Box 12889
Milwaukee, WI 53151
(414) 963-2126

Dick Lane Velodrome
1431 Norman Berry Drive
East Point, GA 30344
(404) 329-4500

Dorias Velodrome
23262 John "R" Street
Hazel Park, MI 48030
(313) 585-3453

Encino Velodrome
P.O. Box 16006
Encino, CA 91416
(818) 881-7441

Kissena Velodrome
44 Clifford Street
Lynnbrook, NY 11563
(516) 593-7939

Lehigh County Velodrome
217 Main
Emmaus, PA 18049
(215) 965-6930

Major Taylor Velodrome
3649 Cold Spring Road
Indianapolis, IN 46222
(317) 926-8350

Marymoor Velodrome
7901 168th Ave., NE, Suite 103
Redmond, WA 98052
(206) 882-0706

National Sports Center Velodrome
1700 105th Ave., NE
Blaine, MN 55434
(612) 785-5600

Northbrook Velodrome
1727 Ivy Lane
Northbrook, IL 60062
(312) 291-2960

St. Louis Velodrome
P.O. Box 15102
St. Louis, MO 63110
(314) 481-1120

San Diego Velodrome
3141 McKinley Street
San Diego, CA 92104
(619) 281-2946

Santa Clara County Velodrome
3148 Jordan Road
Oakland, CA 94602
(415) 531-1400

7-Eleven Velodrome
1775 East Boulder
Colorado Springs, CO 80909
(719) 634-VELO

7-Eleven Olympic Velodrome
800 East Victoria
Carson, CA 90747
(213) 516-4000

Washington Park Bowl
P.O. Box 836
Kenosha, WI 53141
(414) 657-7338

Another category is off-road racing. As in watching criteriums, walk around the course, depending on the length of the course and the kind of terrain. These are races for adventurous riders, often over rugged landscape. Watch and cheer and let the good times roll.

If you've got the bug and want to get in the action, the best approach is to join a club. The U.S. Cycling Federation, which governs amateur cycling in the United States, has approximately 1,100 member clubs. To find a club nearest where you live, get in touch with the USCF:

U.S. Cycling Federation
1750 East Boulder
Colorado Springs, CO 80909
(719) 578-4581

Racing bicycles begins first with the basics of bicycle handling. With a novice's emphasis on fitness and strength, it is easy to overlook the importance of balance and knowing how

Mountain-bike races are good spectator events and are gaining in popularity. (Beth Schneider photo)

to handle a bicycle, at least until the novice falls down and begins to get the point. A typical race starts with anywhere from seventy to 200 riders. Riders must be comfortable cruising in a dense pack.

Top racers devote considerable effort to enhance their bicycle-handling skills. James Carney of Allentown, among the best amateur racers in the country, learned to juggle bean bags to focus his concentration while keeping track of what is going on in his peripheral vision.

"I am one of the better bike handlers and better matched-sprinters," Carney said, and he has race results that back him up. "I got into juggling in 1986 to work my eye-hand coordination. But basically I did it for my confidence. When I make a move in a race, I want to have confidence that I will succeed. Sometimes I have to squeeze through two riders riding close together. Juggling bean bags, tennis balls, whatever is convenient, is

one of the things I do to help my bike handling."

Joining a club also gets riders accustomed to riding with others in a group. The social aspect of cycling also contributes to shared knowledge of the sport as well as information on new products and enjoyment of the sport.

Bicycle road racing is a rapidly growing sport for women. One of the top woman road racers of the 1980s was Jeannie Longo of Grenoble, France. She retired at the end of the 1989 season after conquering the biggest races with such panache that she also captured public imagination on both sides of the Atlantic. France's President François Mitterrand decorated her with the Legion of Honor, the country's highest award. In this country, she was named an honorary citizen of Texas for her racing.

Longo encourages women to get into the sport and not be afraid of developing overbuilt legs. "Riding does not develop big muscles," said Longo, a petite woman. "Since I began riding intensively, my legs have become much thinner."

She recommends training hard to achieve results like those that enabled her to win the world road championship four times. "In fact, if the body does not sweat enough and if I am not completely out of breath, I do not consider the sport satisfying enough for my system," she said. She recommends training at about the same time every day to have a regular rhythm to the training schedule.

For women and men breaking into the sport, her advice is the same: set realistic goals. She suggests that beginners first try to become the best rider in their community or club. Learn more about the sport, paying attention to tactics, and learn the strengths and weaknesses of the best rider in your region, then aim for a berth on the national team.

Training with friends is a nice way to combine socializing with a workout, Longo points out from long experience. But she cautions about becoming dependent on others to make time to get out and train.

"From time to time, I find myself alone for miles, climbing roads through forests, with no disturbances from automobiles," she said. "I enjoy the silence, only slightly interrupted by the singing of birds or the distant cries of woodchucks."

Longo notes that the opportunities for women cyclists are better in the United States than they are in France. "The money provided by the sponsors allows the girls who have chosen cycling as a career to make a living—and sometimes even more," she said. "Many of my friends would love for French cycling to develop in the same way."

What is life like for the top professional cyclist? Two words are most appropriate: constant motion.

The CoreStates USPRO Champion in Phil-

adelphia is a typical example of life for the top professionals who converge from more than fifteen countries for the seventh annual event on June 9, 1991. One of the riders returning is Roy Knickman of Boulder, Colorado, who rides for the Coors Light Racing Team. He is remembered for the way he sparked the 1987 event when he initiated breakaways that shaped the race and determined the final outcome. Although he was outsprinted to the finish and crossed the line in third place, his performance in the 156-mile race was remarkable when his travel schedule is considered.

Only days before his arrival in Philadelphia, he won the final stage of the Criterium du Dauphiné, a demanding week-long race up and down some of the highest peaks in the French Alps.

After a rest of three days, he and his teammates on the French Toshiba-Look team packed up their bikes and equipment and boarded a plane to Philadelphia. Crossing 3,000 miles and six time zones, they arrived at 6 P.M. Saturday. By the time they retrieved their luggage and checked into their hotel, it was 9 P.M., and they still had to eat dinner.

Yet early the next morning, Knickman and his teammates were on the Ben Franklin Parkway starting line with the other 100 riders. At the crack of the starter's pistol, they sped away in the six-hour race under a June sun that sent the temperature up to 90 degrees.

"I raced for seven years before I turned professional," Knickman said in explaining what his life is like in major-league cycling. "Then I had to put it all under the rug and start all over. There is so much to learn about racing."

A major difference between professional and amateur competition is the distance of road races. The CoreStates USPRO Championship's length of 156 miles is standard issue for what pros ride in major one-day European events, compared with amateur events which ordinarily are fifty to 100 miles. What attracts the pros to fly to Philadelphia for the CoreStates is the purse of $110,000, with $25,000 to the winner. It is the richest one-day bicycle race in the world. Paris-Roubaix is the most prestigious, with a purse of $80,000 in 1991.

"Racing with professionals is a different sort of racing altogether," Knickman said. "It is really strategic. You can't react the same way to the same things that happen in an amateur race. Pro racing is more laid-back, but more intense, too."

Over the racing season, pros pedal more than 15,000 racing and training miles—about the same annual distance that the average American drives a car. Between the opening of the season in February and the close in October, riders compete in 130 races in up to a dozen countries.

"You can't race flat-out all the time," Knickman pointed out. "Some of the racing is low-key, usually in the beginning of a race, the opening miles. But when they lay the hammer down in the second half, the pavement really flies by."

The life that goes with the constant travel has unusual occupational hazards. Drinking bad water cost him a major victory in the 1986 Tour de l'Avenir (Tour of the Future), which Greg LeMond had won in 1982. Knickman was leading the important twelve-day, 1,080-mile race when illness forced him out. He needed four weeks to recover.

"I got a bug in my system when I was in Portugal," Knickman said. "Americans who go to Europe to race have a lot of adjustments they have to make. That is what makes it so hard to race there."

Knickman is known for his own brand of hard racing. During the 1987 CoreStates race through Philadelphia's neighborhoods, he attacked fifteen miles into the event and forced the pace. Ten other riders went with him. They gained up to six minutes on the rest of the field until repeated onslaughts up the steep half-mile climb in the neighborhood of Manayunk, where the hill appropriately is called the Manayunk Wall, fractured the breakaway group.

After 110 miles, Knickman attacked again. Tom Schuler of Pewaukee, Wisconsin, and a member of the 7-Eleven team, went with him, subsequently joined by two others—Cesare Copollini of Italy and Jorgen Marcussen of Denmark, both riding for Team Prince.

On the tenth and final climb up the Manayunk Wall, Knickman faltered. He lost contact with the breakaway and started to drop behind. But Knickman is one of the fastest downhill racers in the world. He recovered and caught the breakaway on the descent. At the finish, Schuler beat Copollini, with Knickman a close third.

Reporters from television, radio, newspapers, and magazines deluged Knickman for interviews. He was clearly the favorite rider of the day. The interviews delayed his return to the hotel, where he finally had a shower, changed clothes, and ate a meal to make up for the calories he spent during the six-hour nonstop event.

Before the sun went down, Knickman and his teammates were back at the Philadelphia airport, checking in for a flight to Europe. They flew all night to Geneva.

On Tuesday they started the ten-day Tour of Switzerland. Knickman rode to an impressive victory on the 158-mile eighth stage, which included climbs at more than 6,600 feet above sea level.

"I race because it's fun," Knickman said. "There is a lot to learn. One thing's for sure—it's a demanding sport."

To watch a bicycle race it helps to understand the role of the players. Like a football team in which the tackles, guards, quarterback, and ends all have assigned roles, cyclists are assigned roles as well. And like a football team, each cycling team goes into events with a winning strategy.

A cycling team generally breaks down to a team leader and support riders, known in Europe as *domestiques*. Domestiques from time to time are allowed their moments of distinction, but their main job is to subordinate their performance and ride for the team leader.

This means that if the team leader has a flat tire, a domestique stops with the team leader and either gives up his bike if they are the same size or gives him a wheel change. (A quick-release lever on the hub unlocks the wheel for a fast wheel-change.) One or two other domestiques also will drop back to help work in a relay and pace the team leader back to the pack.

When a team takes the offense, domestiques continue to protect their leader as much as possible from the wind. If another team has established a breakaway, domestiques charge to the front of the pack to work in a relay and bridge the gap.

Conversely, if a team wants to protect a breakaway of its own, that team's domestiques get to the front of the pack and attempt to disrupt a chase. Disruptions take many forms. A rider can get to the front and just stop pedaling to slow the pace. Or ride in a diagonal line across the road, leading everybody in tow. This impedes the rhythm of riders working in a relay to reduce a lead.

Each team also has a general manager, known in Europe as a *director sportif*, who hires the players he needs, plans strategies, and monitors the race as it is under way. The director sportif follows the event in the team car and listens to radio broadcasts from officials in the race. From time to time he tells particular riders what to do as the race progresses. This includes telling a rider on a breakaway whether to work by taking pulls at the front so the others can take advantage of that rider's slipstream and draft, or not to work by refusing to go to the front. It also includes telling particular riders to move up to the head of the pack to lead a chase, or to launch an attack on the next hill, or just to let the other teams take responsibility for leading the race.

Directors sportif tend to be veteran racers familiar with the intricacies of the sport. "I learned more about bike racing tactics after I started working from the sidelines as a manager," observed Mike Farrell of Chicago, who was director sportif of the Wheaties-Schwinn racing team. "It's different when you're watching up close but not in it."

Avid followers of Greg LeMond's career may recall the director sportif who drove up to him during a crucial stage in the 1985 Tour de France when he was on a breakaway and told him to slow down. High up in the Pyrenees, LeMond was away with Stephen Roche of Ireland. They had gained several minutes on the pack, which included Bernard Hinault, overall race leader and LeMond's teammate. At that point, Hinault's race lead was in jeopardy. LeMond had the opportunity to take over as Tour leader. It was a heady situation, the equivalent in football to a receiver being all alone in the end zone waiting for the quarterback to throw him the football for an easy catch to win the Super Bowl.

LeMond argued impetuously that he wanted to keep stretching the lead. He was second overall to Hinault. This was LeMond's chance to overtake the team leader. It was as though he were yelling and waving for the ball.

But his director sportif, Paul Koechli, would hear none of it and repeated his command. They argued passionately until LeMond, with extreme reluctance, yielded. He followed Roche to the stage finish but didn't contribute to stretching the lead.

It was a difficult moment for the American

cyclist. At the finish of the stage, he broke into tears.

Hinault went on to win his fifth Tour de France that year. LeMond finished second but won Le Tour in 1986. And Roche, it turned out, captured the 1987 Tour de France. With that kind of horsepower stretching out a lead in the Pyrenees, it is no wonder why Koechli was so adamant.

The episode illustrates the power that the director sportif exerts over the riders. LeMond was, after all, hired by Hinault, who at age thirty in 1985 had won more than 200 professional events, including a world road-racing championship, the Tour of Italy, Tour of Spain, and numerous one-day classics.

In other cases the director sportif monitors the race and makes adjustments accordingly. This is what happened in the 1987 Core-States USPRO Championship.

After 110 miles of the 156-mile race, Knickman of the Toshiba-Look team had broken away. Tom Schuler of the 7-Eleven racing team responded by chasing after Knickman and catching him. Schuler was a domestique. He was not to work with Knickman in a relay but was instructed to follow and draft in case Knickman rolled up a dangerous lead.

Knickman did create a dangerous lead. He arrived in Philadelphia with his mind made up in advance to ride aggressively. He powered away with Schuler in tow. Schuler, a national-class rider with punch in his sprint, was content to draft behind and take advantage of the decreased wind resistance behind Knickman. Schuler was waiting for the rest of his team to come up to them and take over the race.

But the 90-degree June heat and relentless pace of the race took a toll on everyone but two Team Prince riders. Casare Copollini of Italy and Jorgen Marcussen of Denmark caught the two breakaway riders in the closing miles.

Schuler's director sportif, Jim Ochowicz,

drove up in the team car and apprised him of the situation. Ochowicz told Schuler that the rest of the 7-Eleven team wasn't joining the breakaway. Instead, they would try to control the pack to keep anyone else from joining the breakaway. This left the two Americans to sprint against the Italian and Dane for the $25,000 first prize as well as the national professional championship. Ochowicz told Schuler to win the race for the team.

Schuler started to work with Knickman. When they wound up for the finish on the Ben Franklin Parkway near the Philadelphia Museum of Art, Schuler won the sprint. It was a case of the domestique—a highly competent rider working as a team player—winning the grand prize in a race he entered without ever being considered a contender. What put him in the breakaway was teamwork. The rest he did for himself.

Famous courses have notorious identities. In Grand Prix car racing, the Nürburgring in Germany has a diabolically hilly, twisting circuit. Running has the Boston Marathon, where the event often is decided on a grueling incline 19 miles into the 26.2-mile race that was appropriately christened Heartbreak Hill. In Philadelphia's CoreStates USPRO race held in June, there is the Manayunk Wall, a 285-foot hill that rears up sharply over a half-mile.

The Manayunk Wall, besides being a knuckle-dragger just to walk up, has something for everybody. It is such a formidable part of the 156-mile race that there is a separate purse of $6,000 for the best five riders up it. Points are awarded to the first three riders up the summit on each of the ten laps of the fifteen-mile course, creating a race within the race. The highest Manayunk Wall scorer is declared King of the Wall. The king wins $2,500.

That is only 10 percent of the $25,000 paid to the overall race winner. But for a rider who may lack preparation for the entire event, the Manayunk Wall's competition is incentive enough to gamble. Early breakaway riders who took advantage of the complacent pack have rolled up points for a payday slightly better than the $2,000 awarded to the subsequent ninth-place finisher. It is not necessary to finish the race to win the King of the Wall prize.

Manayunk is a blue-collar neighborhood that commemorated its 300th anniversary during the sixth annual CoreStates USPRO Championship on Father's Day, in June 1990. For the residents the bicycle race has become a festive tradition. The street the cyclists ride up is closed to traffic and transforms the neighborhood into a block party for 10,000 people.

"It feels like the Fourth of July," observed lifelong Manayunk resident Billy Kelly. "And you have to understand that here in Philadelphia, the Fourth of July is a big thing."

"We see people out here we haven't seen all year," added his wife, Marge. "Everybody's out, walking around the streets visiting during the race."

Anita Pieri, who lives on Manayunk Avenue, never saw a bicycle race until this one started going past her home when the CoreStates USPRO Championship was founded in Philadelphia in 1985. "I love it," she said enthusiastically. "It is very exciting to have riders from all over the United States and Europe riding through our neighborhood. There is a lot of neighborhood involvement, with such a festive air."

They were among the spectators standing three and four deep on both sides of the street behind white steel barricades to cheer and applaud the riders. Enterprising locals set up barbecue grills to sell hot dogs and hamburgers. Vendors sold T-shirts with vibrant art work depicting cyclists toiling up The Wall, written in gothic lettering appropriate to a horror movie title. Rock music blared from stereo speakers dragged outside.

When the ninety-five starters in the event were ten miles into the race and turned right from Main Street in Manayunk to Levering Street at the base of the Manayunk Wall, Steve Speaks of Walla Walla, Washington, powered away for the first decisive move of the day.

"I was the only Team Crest rider in the race," he explained afterward. "I was looking for early attacks from the 7-Eleven or Coors Light riders and I wanted to be up there."

He quickly was joined by an Englishman, an Irishman, and an American. It was too early to predict how successful the breakaway would be, but they were welcomed raucously like heroes.

"The crowd at Manayunk is so big, so loud," Speaks said later. "It really was incredible. I have never seen anything like it, except once in a while in the Tour de Trump."

What is known as the Manayunk Wall actually starts in the neighborhood of Manayunk, which abuts Roxborough, into which the race goes and where the hill's summit is, explained Len Konopka, who has lived for thirty years at the top of the hill. "Manayunk holds up The Wall for Roxborough," he said.

After the riders dance on their pedals up the hill and disappear around the corner down the descent, the area is noisy with talk, music, laughter. Pedestrians take to the street and remark how steep the hill is just to walk. Then the atmosphere grows expectant. The street is vacated. A helicopter beats the air overhead, signaling the approach of the leaders. The crowd, in place behind the barricades, begins buzzing. The cry "Here they come!" ripples up the hill. The cry turns to applause, yelling, whistles.

Greg LeMond, who never met a hill he didn't like, commented in 1989 after he rode the race that he liked The Wall. "It's a good hill," he said. "I'd like to see it about a kilometer longer, though." The following month he won the Tour de France.

Early in the sixth lap of the 1990 edition,

after seventy miles, the breakaway was reduced to Speaks and the Irishman. They had extended their lead to a threatening seven minutes and five seconds. That prompted riders from three teams to mount an aggressive chase. Their riders went to the front of the pack and chased hard.

Only one rider has captured the King of the Wall and gone on to win the race. That was Tom Schuler in 1987. He had intended to accumulate points for King of the Wall. While going for points, Roy Knickman attacked and Schuler went to cover the break. He stayed with Knickman and went on to win the event in a new course record of 6 hours, 4 minutes, and 43 seconds.

An unheralded rider in the 1990 race who was doing better than expected up The Wall was Kurt Stockton of Santa Barbara. At six feet one inch and 180 pounds, Stockton has a build more suited to spinning big gears on flat stretches than hopping up hills.

"I struggled up the Manayunk every time," he admitted. "But every time up I was in the lead group."

Stockton, twenty-four, was a former national amateur team member who turned professional to ride the CoreStates in 1989. Two days later he was in the hospital for an appendectomy, which ended his 1989 season. But he was back riding well in the spring of 1990. He shrewdly drafted behind the riders in top teams that waged war with one another at the front of the pack.

Stockton was in the pack that caught Speaks and the Irish rider after the pair of breakaway riders had gone up The Wall for the seventh time. Speaks found his legs were cooked, his muscles curling like potato chips. He completed the lap and headed for a masseur. By then he had won King of the Wall.

As he pulled off the course, riders of the 7-Eleven and Coors Light teams were attacking one another in full cry. They set a tempo that resulted in the top forty riders breaking the record that Schuler had set when he won.

After completing the ten large laps, the lead pack of twelve merged on the Ben Franklin Parkway downtown for a pack sprint to the finish. Italian Paolo Cimini took advantage of American team rivalry to win in a new course record of 6 hours, 1 minute and 44 seconds. He nipped Frenchman Laurent Jalabert, whose share of the $110,000 purse was $15,000.

Three bike lengths behind was Stockton, top U.S. finisher and therefore new national professional champion.

By the time they sped across the line, however, construction crews were at work dismantling the street barriers from the street in Manayunk and Roxborough. Partying continued into the night, but everybody was getting ready to go back to their own jobs the next morning.

Ernest Hemingway admitted that he tried writing many stories about bicycle racing, but never sought to publish them because he felt his writing did not do the sport justice. Hemingway, who grew up in Oak Park, Illinois, a suburb of Chicago, at the turn of the century, became a fan of bicycle racing in the early 1920s while living in Paris. He went often to indoor and outdoor velodrome events, and to the country to watch road races, particularly the Tour de France. Yet when he sat in the Paris cafés where he did most of his writing at the time, he couldn't get his pencil to capture the strange, musky world of the six-day races, or the Tour with its marvels of road racing in the mountains.

"French is the only language it has ever been written in properly and the terms are all French and that is what makes it hard to write," Hemingway said in *A Moveable Feast*. His enthusiasm for the sport, however, prompted him to introduce some of the leading expatriate writers to bike racing. Hemingway often took Sylvia Beach to velodromes. Her famous Shakespeare and Company Bookshop became the veritable

Ernest Hemingway was an avid cycling fan. Yet he couldn't get his pencil to capture the strange, musky world of the six-day races, or the Tour de France with its marvels of road racing in the mountains.
(Barbara Kiwak illustration)

hub of international literature; she published James Joyce's *Ulysses*.

Hemingway, a student of military history, had an eye for strategy which he found attractive in bike racing, particularly at the Vel' d'Hiver (Velodrome of Winter) in Paris. He noted "the effort and the tactics as the riders climbed and plunged, each one a part of his machine." Time after time, Hemingway went back to the Vel' d'Hiver to watch the races and catch the smoky light of the afternoon and the whirring sound the tires made on the wood as the riders passed.

One of his favorite racers was Victor Lin-art, the Belgian motorpace star who won fifteen national championships and four world championships. Hemingway watched Linart, known as "The Sioux" for his distinctive profile, and wrote that Linart at the outdoor Buffalo Velodrome would drop his head "to suck up cherry brandy from a rubber tube that connected with a hot water bottle under his racing shirt when he needed it toward the end as he increased his savage speed."

Hemingway was in the stands at the Paris outdoor concrete track, the Parc des Princes, when the great rider Georges Ganay suffered a wicked fall during the motorpace event.

Hemingway later wrote that the audience heard Ganay's "skull crumple under the crash helmet as you crack an hard-boiled egg against a stone to peel it on a picnic."

Bicycle races do crop up in Hemingway's work. In *The Sun Also Rises*, Jake Barnes visits southern Spain when the early-season Ruta del Sol bicycle stage race is under way. Barnes dines with a director sportif. They briefly discuss Ottavio Bottecchia of Italy, who won the Tour de France twice in the mid-1920s. (Interestingly, Greg LeMond was riding a bicycle named after Bottecchia when he captured his second Tour de France in 1989.)

Hemingway also modeled a short story, *The Pursuit Race*, after a bicycle race. "In a pursuit, in bike racing," he wrote, "riders start at equal intervals to ride after one another." The story is included in *The Short Stories*, available in paperback (Scribner's).

In the summer of 1938, while Hemingway was away covering the Spanish Civil War, his wife, Pauline, followed the Tour de France with their drinking crony, Robert Capa. Capa, who gained fame for the remarkable photos he took of the Spanish Civil War, received an assignment to cover the Tour for *Paris-Match*. A new publisher had converted *Paris-Match* from a sports magazine to a general-interest publication the previous year. Capa took photos of the Tour and its spectators from the rear seat of a motorcycle.

While they were following the Tour, Red Smith was serving a rigorous apprenticeship in American newspapers. By 1960 he was a syndicated sports columnist for *The New York Herald-Tribune* and had become the most widely read sportswriter in the country. That year he ventured to France to see the Tour up close.

Smith was impressed with what he saw. "There is nothing in America even remotely comparable with it," he wrote. "We think the World Series claims the undivided attention of the United States, but there is a saying here that an army from Mars could invade France, the government could fall, and even the recipe for sauce Béarnaise be lost, but if it happened during the Tour de France nobody would notice."

He was intrigued with crowds of men and women of all ages who could wait for two or three hours to see the Tour sweep past. Smith had plenty of company on the Col de Perty, near Gap. It was an obscure location, "a barren knob not close to anything or anybody, yet it looked like the bleachers in Yankee Stadium on a good day with the White Sox."

Hemingway spent years watching the Tour. He wrote about bullfighting in Spain, fishing off Cuba, and big-game hunting in Africa, but writing about bicycle racing in France continued to elude him.

CHAPTER 10

ULTRAFAST, ULTRALONG— CYCLING'S RECORD HOLDERS

DAMON RUNYON, one of the most unique American sportswriters, became a towering literary figure in the 1920s and 1930s. He wrote books and plays that became successful movies, including *Guys and Dolls* and *Pocketful of Miracles*. Red Smith observed that Runyon could do things with the alphabet that made other writers want to throw their typewriters away and dig coal for a living. Runyon also was an ardent fan of the six-day bike races in Madison Square Garden and an unabashed cheerleader for Alf Goullet. After Goullet's dramatic victory in the Garden's December 1921 six-day, Runyon devoted an editorial in *The New York American* to the cyclist, pronouncing him king of the six-day racers and proclaiming, "Long live the king!"

It turned into quite a prophecy—one that outlived both the Hearst newspaper where he worked and Runyon himself, who died at age sixty-two in 1946.

During an interview in his Red Bank, New Jersey, apartment after he returned from a two-mile walk, Goullet was asked what his secret was to longevity. His clean-shaven face went expressionless in contemplation. Finally he shrugged and threw up his hands.

"Steak and eggs for breakfast," he said. "That's what I always liked when I was racing."

It is easy to underestimate his age by many years. Goullet is a patient listener, an excellent raconteur, and is energetic in his gestures. Then he casually recounts something from his life that astounds a visitor, such as when Jack Dempsey polished shoes and ran errands for him and other bike racers.

By the time he retired at thirty-four in 1925, Goullet had won 400 races on three continents as a professional, set six world records, and captured eight Garden six-days with six different partners. The world record he and Alfred Grenda of Tasmania set in the November 1914 Garden six-day still stands.

Another of Alf Goullet's fans was illustrator Robert L. Ripley, who was on the staff of The New York Globe *and covered the world record that Goullet set in November 1914 with partner Alfred Grenda of Tasmania. (*Ripley's Believe It Or Not!*)*

They went 2,759.2 miles—the distance from San Francisco to Buffalo, and 638.2 miles farther than the 1990 Tour de France that Greg LeMond won in twenty-one days of racing.

It is always difficult to compare performances of top athletes from one generation to the next, but we get a good idea of Goullet's performances from his world-record times. His one minute eleven and two-tenths seconds for two-thirds of a mile set on the Salt Lake City Velodrome in 1912 works out to a kilometer time of 1:06.5, significantly faster than the 1:06.8 which the redoubtable

Leonard (Harvey) Nitz of Citrus Heights, California, rode on a lighter, more streamlined bicycle for a bronze medal in the kilometer during the 1987 Pan American Games at the Major Taylor Velodrome in Indianapolis.

Goullet built his reputation racing six-day events. They were grueling events. Racers spun around a pine bowl that measured ten laps to the mile. Ventilation was poor, and the air was thick with tobacco smoke. "I was coughing up mud for weeks," he said.

His fans easily spotted him in the pack: Goullet wore a scarlet silk jersey with No. 5 on the back. He handled his bike gracefully, pedaled fluidly, and had a reputation for making his moves count. In addition to the six-days he won in New York, he triumphed in other sixes in Paris, Melbourne, Sydney, Chicago, Boston, and Newark.

"He was a great all-round rider and very smart, very cagey," recalled Fred Spencer of Rahway, New Jersey, a rival thirteen years his junior whose career overlapped Goullet's. "You never took him cheap."

Goullet retired in glory and was selling life insurance when professional cycling went bust with the Depression in the United States. Like Taylor, Frank Kramer, and the Walthours, Goullet's fame faded. Yet quality has a way of enduring. In 1968 Goullet was inducted into the Madison Square Garden Hall of Fame. The Australian Sports Federation also recalled his career. The Federation in 1986 flew him with daughter Suzanne to Melbourne for induction into the Sports Federation Hall of Fame. His trip was the first back to his homeland in seventy-five years.

When the U.S. Bicycling Hall of Fame was founded in 1986 in Somerville, New Jersey, Goullet was a first-round inductee. Then, in February 1990, the New York Sports Museum and Hall of Fame held its first round of inductions. Goullet was an obvious choice, along with Runyon, Dempsey, Red Smith, Babe Ruth, and eighty-four other local

Connie Young is a study in concentration—and perseverance. She won her fourth world championship in 1990 after her three-year reign was broken in 1985. (Rich Cruse photo)

heroes. The induction, with a banquet and list of luminaries, would have amused Runyon. He knew seventy years earlier when he called Goullet the king of the six-day bike racers that the king would live long—and live well.

The fastest woman cyclist in the world for many years has been Connie Young of Indianapolis. At the 1990 world cycling championships in Maebashi, Japan, she was the only U.S. rider to win a gold medal when she won the sprint title. In addition, Young, twenty-nine in 1990, reclaimed the sprint championship she had won for three years when she reigned from 1982 through 1984.

Her fourth world title came after persever-

ing through a series of nagging setbacks. Ten days before the 1989 worlds in Lyon, France, Young stepped on a broken piece of cement in her driveway and sprained her right ankle. She hobbled around on crutches for four days and was forced to reevaluate her approach to the world's that year. In 1988 she fell on a training ride and broke her right hand. She wore a cast for twelve weeks. "I've had my share of injuries."

Young, who grew up in Detroit, has more than twenty years of experience in athletics. She took up cycling and speed skating at age nine with the Wolverine Sports Club in Detroit. "I learned a lot of the fundamentals of cycling and speed skating there without realizing it at the time," she recounted. "I was having fun. The workouts were more like playing than regular training."

Being in sports helped her organize her time and instilled discipline, she said. "Cycling is the kind of sport you can do your whole life," she added. "It's easy on the muscles and joints."

Predictably, Connie Young rose to become a world-class athlete. Her specialty was the explosive sprint events. She won two bronze medals in world speed-skating championships and made the Olympic speed-skating teams in 1980 and 1984.

She also reigned as national and world cycling champion. When the Olympics opened up to women cyclists and sprint events were introduced in the 1988 Seoul Olympics, Young decided to concentrate on cycling. She made her third Olympic team as a cyclist. She clinched a bronze medal, making her the only U.S. cyclist at the 1988 Olympics to take home a medal.

"Competing at the top international level is very demanding," she pointed out. "You can't make mistakes and win."

Her specialty, the matched sprints, are pure competition—a combination of speed and tactics. Sprint bicycles are stripped down to the frame, handlebars, wheels, chain, and seat. No brakes, no extra gears. Their design hasn't changed for a century. Riders are matched: two cyclists are alone on the track, most often measuring 333 meters (about 340 yards), for three laps. Nearly all the distance is part of the cat-and-mouse game that leads to the final 200 meters, the only part of the race that is timed. Match-race winners are determined on the best of three rides.

Match sprinters progress through a series of heats, with the winners advancing to the quarter-finals, semifinals, and ultimately the final. Many variables can cost a sprinter any race: selecting the wrong gear for the bicycle before getting on the track, hesitating at a crucial point in the match, or underestimating an opponent. Speed is essential

but not the only factor. At the 1986 world championships in Colorado Springs, Young set the world record for the 200 meter flying start (already pedaling at speed from the start) in 11.24 seconds but finished with a bronze medal in the competition.

Young held a three-year reign until 1985, when a French rider beat her in the final for the world championship gold medal. Then in 1986 and 1987 Young fell back to third-place finishes.

Yet she kept her confidence up and was determined to make it back to the top of the sport. At five feet three inches tall and 115 pounds, Young's chief asset is her sharp acceleration. She varies her training and frequently competes in criteriums to help increase her power and stamina. She went to the 1990 world's ready to show the cycling community she was the fastest woman in the world.

Young advanced through matches at the world track championships north of Tokyo, defeating a French rider in the semifinal to qualify for the final. There she was matched against compatriot Renee Duprel of Bellevue, Washington, who is five years younger and also makes the sprints her specialty.

In their first race, Duprel drafted behind Young until close to the finish when she came from behind to nip Young and take the first match. The second was so close that judges had to consult a photo before giving the match to Young. In their deciding match, Young slowed Duprel to a near standstill on the first turn of the last lap. Then Young unleashed her sharp acceleration to open a gap that she held to the line for the world championship.

As world champion again after a five-year hiatus, Young promptly began to plan her training and racing schedule for the next two years toward the Barcelona Olympics, where she will go for the gold in 1992. In the year between, she is looking forward to defending her title at the world's in Stuttgart.

Ripley's —— **Believe It or Not!**

©1985 King Features Syndicate,
Inc. World rights reserved.

8-5

ARTHUR M.
LONGSJO, Jr.
of Fitchburg,
Mass.,

COMPETED IN THE 1956
OLYMPICS IN CORTINA D'AMPEZZO,
ITALY, AS A SPEED SKATER AND
IN MELBOURNE, AUS., AS A CYCLIST,
BECOMING THE FIRST AMERICAN
TO BE A MEMBER OF BOTH THE
WINTER AND SUMMER OLYMPIC
TEAMS IN ONE YEAR !
Submitted by Peter J. Nye,
Alexandria, Va.

THE SILVER
DOLLAR
ISSUED
BETWEEN 1921
AND 1935, IS
THE ONLY U.S.
COIN WITH THE
WORD "PEACE"
IMPRINTED ON IT

Art Longsjo won three North American speed-skating championships, set a national two-mile record, won a national ten-mile cycling championship, and captured every major bicycle race in the United States and Canada. (Ripley's Believe It Or Not!)

"I'm glad to win the world championship again," Young said. "That shows I'm still improving. That gives me a lot of personal satisfaction and motivates me."

The first American to compete in two U.S. Olympic teams in the same year was Art Longsjo (1932–1958) of Fitchburg, Massachusetts. In 1956 he speed-skated in the 5,000-meter (3.1 miles) event in the Winter Olympics in Cortina d'Ampezzo, high up in the Italian Dolomites, and months later rode in the 4,000-meter (2.5 miles) four-rider team pursuit on the velodrome in the Summer Olympics in Melbourne, Australia.

Yet his Olympic feat represents only a small portion of his athletic career. It began when he was an eleven-year-old skating on frozen ponds in central Massachusetts before he branched out to bicycle racing. Both sports share similar leg drive and use the same muscles. He had developed into one of the top junior skaters in the country by the time he turned eighteen in 1950.

When war broke out in Korea that year, Longsjo was called up to take the draft physical. He failed and was classified 4-F for what was diagnosed as a heart murmur, but more likely was an athlete's developed heart.

He went on to win three North American speed-skating championships, set a national two-mile record, win a national ten-mile cycling championship, win the Canadian national road championship years before the United States introduced them, and to capture every major bicycle race in North America.

Especially noted for his humor, Longsjo was addicted to Henny Youngman one-liners. When he made his first Olympic team, Longsjo listed his occupation as "polisher," as in polisher of medals and trophies—all that amateur athletes were eligible for in those days of strict rules.

He once boldly broke away from a pack of cyclists at the base of a long hill, with the pertinent name of Mount Savage, in a race over the Laurentian Mountains near Montreal so he could solo to the summit, get off his bicycle, and casually walk over to the coach of a rival back in the pack.

"Excuse me," Longsjo inquired. "I'm looking for Mount Savage. Can you tell me where it is?" The next rider was not in sight. The coach looked at Longsjo for a moment and smiled. He replied, "I think you just passed it." Longsjo got back on his bicycle and won the race.

He was inducted into the Amateur Skating Union's Hall of Fame in Newburgh, New York, and the U.S. Bicycling Hall of Fame in Somerville, New Jersey.

In Olympic cycling, the rider who won the

most gold medals is Marcus L. Hurley (1883–1941) of New York City. At the 1904 Olympics in St. Louis, Hurley won four gold medals and a bronze. His four victories tied a record of individual golds until swimmer Mark Spitz won seven in the 1972 Munich Olympics.

The International Olympic Committee, however, does not recognize medals from the St. Louis Olympics because of the lack of foreign competition. The 1904 Olympics, not yet the international events they were to become, held that August were part of the St. Louis World's Fair, which commemorated the one-hundredth anniversary of the Louisiana Purchase and the opening of the West.

Hurley was a sprinter who won the quarter-mile, one-third mile, half-mile, and the mile events. He was third in the two-mile. (Winner of the two-mile was Burton Downing of San Jose, California, whose brother, Hardy, is credited with giving Jack Dempsey his start in professional boxing.) Hurley's career is easy to overlook because none of the distances he competed in are part of the format in Olympic cycling, and the IOC—and thus the U.S. Olympic Committee—consider those Olympics unofficial. Yet Hurley deserves a second look—not just in cycling but also in basketball.

Records show that Hurley competed for the New York Athletic Club and wore the club's winged foot logo on his jersey front. Photos reveal that he was tall and lean, with a deep chest, and parted his dark hair down the middle in the fashion of the day.

He was seventeen and had only just completed his junior year of high school when he won the national amateur cycling championship in 1901. He won his second national title in 1902 and enrolled in Columbia University that October. For the next two years he successfully defended his national title as a member of the NYAC cycling team.

After winning his fourth national championship in 1904 in Newark and garnering five Olympic medals in St. Louis, he shipped out August 24th on the U.S.S. *Oceanic* for the world championships in England. The world's were held on a track on the grounds of the Crystal Palace, a glass-and-steel marvel of Victorian architecture, a few miles south of London. From September 3rd to 8th he progressed through a series of heats and qualified for the final, a single race of two kilometers (1.3 miles), on September 10th.

The final for the amateur world championship was a three-rider race. Hurley faced Englishmen A. L. Reed and J. S. Benyon. At the world's the previous year in Copenhagen, Reed and Benyon had finished one-two. They entered the 1904 world's on home turf and were pre-race favorites.

It was a slow race, slightly over eleven minutes, which indicates it was highly tactical. When they wound up for the final dash to the line, Hurley edged defending champion Reed by the width of a tire, with Benyon close behind.

Hurley remains the last U.S. rider to win the men's amateur world sprint championship overseas. (The previous American to win the world amateur title was NYAC teammate Arthur A. Zimmerman, winner of the inaugural world championship in 1893 in Chicago.) The 1904 world's was a showcase for American talent. Bobby Walthour won his first world motorpace championship. Iver Lawson of Salt Lake City won the professional sprint championship.

Upon returning to the United States, Hurley and Lawson were invited to the Newark Velodrome. On September 25th a crowd of 5,000 welcomed them as heroes.

After his return, Hurley—who was to turn twenty-one on December 22nd—enrolled in Columbia's School of Mines and Engineers. He also switched from cycling to basketball, then starting to blossom as a collegiate sport, chiefly in the Northeast and Midwest. He played guard for the NYAC basketball team as well as for the Columbia basketball team.

In 1905 he was captain of the NYAC basketball team that won the prestigious New York City Metropolitan Club Championship. He also was captain of the Columbia basketball team that won the intercollegiate national championship in 1905 and 1906. Newspaper accounts credit him with helping score points that led his team to victory. Hurley was an All-American in both 1905 and 1906.

Hurley was a nongraduating member of the class of 1906, but received his bachelor's degree in mining engineering from Columbia in May 1908, according to records. He became a consulting mining engineer and had a business with offices on tony Broadway.

A bachelor, Hurley lived at the NYAC, where he died of an apparent heart attack in his sleep at fifty-five in 1941. He was inducted into the NYAC Hall of Fame in 1981, where his medals are on display.

The fastest bicycle rider in the world is John Howard of Encinitas, California, who pedaled a specially designed bicycle behind a rocket car to 152.284 miles an hour.

That was on the Bonneville Salt Flats, west of Salt Lake City, on July 20, 1985. Such speed created problems in preliminary rides. Howard's tires were going flat without a puncture at around 100 miles an hour. Examination showed the air was forced to the inside tire-tube walls and leaked out through the valves. Once the valves were replaced, Howard got back in his full-length leather suit, complete with hard-shell helmet, and set the world land-speed record.

What is it like riding that fast? "There is a sense of calm, even with a 540-horsepower vehicle in front of you," he said. "All your survival instincts are on. Your brain is very clean, very concentrated."

Howard's epic ride is part of a tradition of spectacular speed records that have turned riders into legends. In 1899 Charles Murphy of Brooklyn, New York, astounded the world when he pedaled a mile in 57⅘ seconds on a board track laid between rails where he rode behind a train on Long Island, New York.

Flat-out at 152.284 miles an hour, John Howard sets a new world land-distance record on July 20, 1985, west of Salt Lake City. (Al Gross photo)

Charles Murphy, left, pedaled his bicycle behind a train in June 1899 through the minute barrier for the mile, in 57⁴/₅ seconds, four years before the first car drove that fast. (Library of Congress photo)

Murphy's ride on a June afternoon broke the minute barrier for the mile.

Four years passed before the first car broke the minute barrier. Its driver was Barney Oldfield of Toledo, Ohio, who had been a professional cyclist in the League of American Wheelmen and competed against Murphy. The car Oldfield drove was one that Henry Ford designed with national professional cycling champion Tom Cooper of Detroit, who funded Ford.

Murphy's ride was also remarkable for his lack of special equipment. He wore neither helmet nor gloves. Murphy pedaled the standard track bicycle he used in races to win national championships and set seventeen national and seven world records at distances from one to five miles. His feat caught

the public imagination. He was known as Mile-a-Minute Murphy until he died at eighty-nine in 1950. He was in steady demand as an after-dinner speaker. What audiences wanted to hear about was not his championships or records, but about his ride breaking the minute barrier.

In May 1941 Frenchman Alf Letourner rode 108.92 miles an hour in Bakersfield, California. He pedaled behind a race car equipped with a shield on the back that had a window he looked through as he rode.

"To credit Letourner only with his 108 mph ride is surely short-changing one of the true cycling champions of all time," noted Keith Kingbay. "Among his other accomplishments, he won twenty-one (he always insisted twenty-two) six-day races when they were the real thing."

As a six-day racer, Letourner went into the ride with a conventional cyclist's approach. He wore shorts, a long-sleeve jersey, no gloves. His bicycle was fitted with a smaller-diameter front wheel to set his center of gravity lower and improve drafting behind the car. His only concession to safety was a leather helmet.

Like Murphy, Letourner's other championships and records were overshadowed by his famous speed record. "Alfie, to his dying day," Kingbay added of Letourner, who died in France in 1974, "was fighting the breaking of his record."

John Howard also discovered that his land-speed record earned him greater recognition than his many other achievements. "The speed record gave me more coverage than all the other things I did combined," he said.

Howard's ride of 152 miles an hour came after a competitive career that included ruling the roads in the 1970s. He competed in the Olympics in 1968, 1972, and 1976. He won four national road-racing championships. He helped give cycling a boost in the United States when he won the 124-mile road race at the Pan American Games in 1971, a victory that came in the final event of the Games and made for greater news coverage than it might otherwise have received.

All that was a long way ahead for the skinny, six-feet three-inch underachiever in Springfield, Missouri, who crashed in his first road race and ruined his bicycle. "I got my doors blown off by the big guys back in 1966 when I first started," he admitted. But he stayed with it. Two years later he won a berth on the cycling team bound for the 1968 Mexico City Olympics.

Howard dominated competitive cycling in the 1970s as a member of the original national cycling team. After leaving the national team in 1980, he branched out. He became a triathlete and won the 1981 Ironman Triathlon in Hawaii—composed of the 2.4-mile open-water swim, 26.2-mile marathon run, and the 112-mile bicycle ride. His triumph and stature as a champion cyclist gave triathlons a greater standing while they were taking off in popularity. He competed in the 1982 Race Across America, from Los Angeles to New York City, finishing second in 10 days, 10 hours, and 59 minutes.

Afterward he began looking for a formidable challenge, which the land-speed record would meet. Putting together sponsorship to fund the project, designing a bicycle featuring special gearing with two separate but connected drive chains that would enable him to pedal faster than anyone ever pedaled before, and pulling it all off was equivalent to a modern-day labor of Hercules.

"I redirected my training," he said. "I did a lot of power lifting and gained about twenty pounds over my racing weight so that I could handle the bicycle at speed."

His approach entailed months of planning. Everything was in jeopardy when the tires on the bicycle he was riding at close to 100 miles an hour went flat.

"What forced the air out of the valves is called rotorturbulence," Howard explained.

"I had to wrestle the bicycle to keep from crashing."

Like the record rides of Murphy and Letourner, Howard's 152 miles an hour was international news. A cyclist pedaling that fast made people eager to learn how he did it.

Yet Howard didn't stop there. Soon he was off to set another record. In May 1987 he pedaled 539 miles for a new twenty-four-hour distance record. He rode with a rotating group of other cyclists around the Clearwater Sunshine Speedway, a car-racing track near St. Petersburg, Florida, to set the paced distance record.

"I wanted to break the record of 512 miles that I had set in 1983 in Central Park in New York City," he said. "It had rained for eighteen hours in that ride."

Howard was inducted in May 1989 into the U.S. Bicycling Hall of Fame. Another longtime rider, Alf Goullet, was holding a large wood-and-bronze plaque to present to him in front of an audience of 200 as Howard's career highlights were listed. The forty-two-year-old Olympian and Iron Man Triathlon champion began to choke with emotion. His eyes started to water.

Goullet waved the plaque playfully and asked, "How much are you willing to give me for this?" His quip delighted the audience and helped Howard regain his composure.

Records, it is frequently noted, are set to be broken. Howard's 1987 distance record of 539 miles in twenty-four hours didn't last the year. San Diego cyclist Jim Elliott extended the record to 548 miles.

But Howard's 152 miles an hour speed record has proved more challenge-resistant. In 1988 Dutchman Fred Rompelberg, a former professional track racer, made a serious record attempt. He traveled to the site of Howard's record on the Bonneville Salt Flats with a support crew and race-car driver.

Rompelberg's repeated tries reached a tantalizing but frustrating peak speed of 143 miles an hour. He returned to Europe empty-handed and announced he would return to the Salt Flats to try again in late 1990. That return was postponed when Rompelberg suffered a wrist injury. Howard's record of pedaling 152 miles an hour entered the 1990s intact.

For sheer numbers of miles, Michael Secrest of Scottsdale, Arizona, has set a holy trinity of distance-cycling records: 1,216.7 miles in twenty-four hours pedaling behind a truck, a solo ride of 516.2 miles in twenty-four hours around a velodrome, and pedaling alone across the United States in less than eight days.

"It was desire and perseverance and sweat and hard work that went into setting those world records," Secrest said.

They helped increase recognition of Secrest's name in the cycling community, but have the feats translated to lucrative product endorsements?

"There's no payoff," he said with a light laugh. "The bills just keep coming in, and I wonder how I am going to pay them."

Secrest is philosophical about his records and the diligence that went into them. "I always looked at these records as long-term investments, like becoming a doctor and going through eight years of college. Now I have paid my dues and I am giving motivation talks. It is part of my calling to tell people they can set goals and do what they want. I don't have to speak just about myself, but I use what I did to show what can be done. I use myself as an example."

All night, all day, Michael Secrest keeps pedaling: 1,216 miles in twenty-four hours behind a truck, 516 miles on his own in twenty-four hours, and solo across the USA in less than eight days. (David Nelson photo)

Secrest grew up in car country, in Flint, Michigan, in the 1950s and 1960s, when metropolitan Detroit was car maker to the world. He drove trucks. At one point he wanted to drive race cars. He is five feet ten inches tall and weighs 160 pounds, a good fit behind the wheel of a fast car. But in 1980, at twenty-seven, he discovered bicycle riding.

"I found I have a talent for long-distance riding," he said. "I'm the kind of person to develop a talent."

Developing such talent is labor-intensive and requires dedication that borders on mania. For long-distance riders, there is nowhere to go but the Race Across America. In 1983 Secrest was third in the 3,170-mile race from Santa Monica to Atlantic City. That confirmed his talent and encouraged him to keep at it.

The next year the course was shortened slightly, to 3,047 miles, starting in Huntington Beach and going to Atlantic City. Secrest moved up to second place, which he repeated in 1985. In 1986 he had a good chance to win. After six days and 2,380 miles, he was riding a strong second place as he approached Jonesboro, Tennessee.

"It was not dark," Secrest said. "I wasn't sleepy. I felt the front of the bike give out." He struck a pothole that threw him to the ground. He broke his collarbone and was out of the race.

After he recovered, he began to prepare for the 1987 event, over a new course—3,127 miles from the Golden Gate Bridge to the Washington Monument. Secrest played for keeps. He had a support crew of twelve riding in two motorhomes and two cars. A sponsor provided his team with a $25,000 budget. It was a major effort for a trophy and glory, but transcontinental men and women racers are motivated from within.

Secrest had developed a reputation for starting out fast and paying for it later. This time he started the 1987 Race Across America fast and followed through. But he suffered. He pedaled through three nights of subfreezing cold in the mountains of Nevada, Utah, and Colorado. The chill gave him exercise-induced asthma, which he had never experienced before. He arrived bone weary at the base of the Washington Monument, barely able to manage a feeble victory salute to the gathering of about 150 who waited for his arrival at one o'clock in the morning.

"I wouldn't want to ride this course again next year," he said.

His suffering was eased by rest, and recognition that ABC Television's *Wide World of Sports* made him Athlete of the Week. ABC chose him over Martina Navratilova, who had just won her eighth singles Wimbledon championship.

Secrest didn't compete in the Race Across America again, but he knew what he was capable of, and made plans to set the transcontinental record. He mapped out a course of 2,915 miles from Huntington Beach to Atlantic City, and recruited a support crew of seven and two officials from the Ultra Marathon Cycling Association.

A music lover who had relocated to Arizona, Secrest used his transcontinental ride as a fund-raiser for the Phoenix Symphony Orchestra. He raised pledges of $250,000 for the orchestra when he started his ride June 16, 1990.

"I rode to Amarillo, Texas, in sixty-three hours, about 1,160 miles, without any sleep," he said. "In Amarillo, I slept for four hours. After that, I averaged two hours of sleep a day."

Northeast of Amarillo, he stopped briefly in Pampa, Texas, where he has aunts and uncles. "I gave them all a hug and a kiss. Then I caught a tailwind that carried me along."

Through Oklahoma and up to St. Louis, Indianapolis, and Columbus, he endured

100-degree weather with humidity to match. He kept on rolling through rain and sun, day and night, to reach Atlantic City in 7 days, 23 hours, and 16 minutes. He averaged 365 miles a day.

"I'm the first man in the world to break eight days for riding across the United States," he said.

The first record he set was in March 1985, when he pedaled 516.2 miles in twenty-four hours around the Olympic Velodrome in Montreal.

His first record on top of his other stamina feats led Secrest to arrange for the ultimate confluence in speed and distance: a twenty-four-hour paced ride behind a tractor-trailer rig around the Phoenix International Speedway. On April 26 and 27, 1990, he pedaled 1,216.7 miles, for an average speed of 50.7 miles an hour.

"The most demanding part was total concentration for twenty-four hours," he said. "Part of the ride was fun. There were times when I had to put the brakes on to keep from riding into the truck."

A pair of drivers alternated driving the truck. "They had to switch every three hours to keep from going crazy," Secrest said.

After completing his ride, Secrest the ultra-marathoner came up with a new ultra-transcontinental inspiration. "I'd like to ride cross-country behind a truck, and pedal on interstate highways. I figure I could ride my bicycle across the country in less than three days."

CHAPTER 11

COLLECTIONS

WHEN CYCLING WAS the sport of the nineties a century ago, manufacturers couldn't make bicycles fast enough to meet demand. Customers paid cash and waited eagerly for weeks to receive their bicycles. The prestige of being seen on one, and the fun of riding, were worth the wait. Men and women cyclists wore custom-made clothing when they took to the roads. They posed for photos with their bicycles. They bought sheet music to sing new bicycle-related songs, purchased pins and buttons depicting bicycles, and collected other mementos. Twenty years later, America was an automobile culture. The bicycles, cycling clothing, photographs, and other memorabilia were put away in garages, attics, trunks, and closets. Over the decades, much of it was lost.

Much of what remains is in private collections. "As repositories of bicycles, photos, and other related memorabilia, the private collectors are best," said Carl Wiedman of Bloomfield Hills, Michigan. "Museums are the worst. The Smithsonian Institution has an extensive collection of antique bicycles, but they've got fewer than ten bicycles on display."

Wiedman, a member of the Wheelmen and associate editor of their magazine, *The Wheelmen*, has been collecting and restoring bicycles since 1970.

"Most collectors have to restore bicycles," Wiedman said. "Anything can be salvaged. Without question. Any bicycle can be restored, with complete integrity. Restoring bicycles is something I enjoy doing. I fight to keep these things what they were when they were new, not just to fix them up with new parts."

Wiedman was introduced to cycling as a youngster growing up in Buffalo in the 1920s and 1930s, when his parents took him to see six-day races in the Buffalo Coliseum. "I found the six-days were quite exciting. I think the whole six-day era was very important. They had such appeal: big crowds, lots of money spent, such excitement."

By the time he moved to Michigan to study

When cycling was the sport of the nineties, bicycles had social cachet. But most of the bicycles and much of the memorabilia have been lost, including the identities of this father and son. (Smithsonian Institution photo)

metallurgical engineering at the University of Michigan in the early 1940s, the war had ended the golden era of the sixes in North America. He didn't think much about bicycles until 1969, when a friend gave him a vintage highwheeler.

"I was intrigued by it," he said. "I kept it, and then I saw somebody riding one in a parade. I introduced myself and learned the fellow riding it was a member of the Wheelmen. Then I joined the club in 1970."

As a member of the Wheelmen, he encountered a national network of others dedicated to preserving the cycling heritage and restoring bicycles. Wiedman started to attend regional meetings where members discussed a variety of antique bicycles they had restored, rode them in groups like the old League of

*Arthur Zimmerman of the New York Athletic
Club won the first world cycling championship,
in 1893, in Chicago. He poses with his Star
bicycle, designed in the 1880s to prevent falls over
the front of handlebars. (The Wheelmen photo)*

American Wheelmen, and exchanged information. He began buying and acquiring a collection of bicycles and related memorabilia.

"I have original sheet music of about 170 different bicycle songs," he said. "Many of them were written in the era of the 1890s. Most people today are familiar with 'Daisy, Daisy.' But there were many songs written about the newly emerging sport of cycling in America."

Among private collectors, Wiedman is known for the breadth of antique models representing development of the bicycle from the boneshaker to the highwheeler to early safety bicycles and the balloon-tired bicycle, from the 1860s to the 1930s.

"My spectrum is general," he said. "I have

more than 100 bicycles. They cover the development of the bicycle pretty well. My collection doesn't have a lot of any one thing, nor any one-of-a-kind bike."

He has them standing in a three-car garage adjacent to his house and in another large room. A couple of the more unusual bicycles in the collection are the Rover Star and the Eagle, made for about a dozen years in the 1880s and early 1890s. Both makes of bicycle were attempts to reduce headfirst falls that riders of the highwheelers were susceptible to. The Star and the Eagle both had the small wheel in front and the large wheel behind it.

The Star replaced conventional pedals with a treadle that was pumped vertically up and down. The Eagle had the standard pedal arrangement off the big-wheel hub, where the cranks were attached. The Star and Eagle started to disappear when the chain-driven safety bicycles took over.

"None of the bicycles in collections like mine are attractive prey for thieves," Wiedman said. "There is no quick money to be made from them because the field of buyers is so narrow. All the collectors know one another, and they're the only ones buying these bikes."

Lorne Shields of Concord, Ontario, has seen demand for collecting shoot up in the 1980s. "I was collecting before, when cycling stuff from the old days was just junk," he said. "Now there are a lot of people picking up bicycles and whatever else is collectible. It's getting more difficult to find these things."

Shields devoted considerable energy to building his collection. He traveled around North America and to England to buy collections. In 1982 and 1986 he donated an extensive collection to the National Museum of Science and Technology in Ottawa. The Shields collection has vintage four-color posters of bicycle races, photos of cyclists, lithographs, cups and trophies of champions, dozens of rare antique bicycles, and about 3,000 books. The books include approximately 400 trade catalogs, patent books, and a wide variety of cycling-related volumes. Some of the Shields collection is on display; the rest is available to researchers.

"I always collected stamps and coins as a kid in the 1950s and 1960s," he said. "What fascinated me about cycling was that it was such a socializing factor in the last quarter of the nineteenth century. The people involved in making and developing bicycles went into making motorcycles, cars, and airplanes. That set up the transportation of the twentieth century. Bicycles are an incredible social history."

G. Donald Adams, curator of the Henry Ford Museum and Greenfield Village in Dearborn, Michigan, points out that many of the car makers started out building and repairing bicycles in the 1880s and 1890s. "There is a whole long list," he said.

The list includes some who used the same name for their car models that they had first used for bicycles. One was J. M. Pierce, whose Pierce Arrow bicycle had a badge on the front of the frame head stamped TRIED AND TRUE. Frank Kramer rode Pierce Arrow bicycles with nickel-plated frames, before chrome was available, to national championship victories. Pierce Arrow, however, is a name that is associated with the luxury car to most of the public.

Another bicycle manufacturer that went into cars and kept the name from two-wheelers to four-wheelers was the firm of R. Philip Gormully and Thomas B. Jeffery. They made Rambler bicycles, which were immensely popular. Ramblers had gold-foil badges sealed into the paint on the frame head. In the 1890s Rambler bicycle clubs proliferated. The Chicago Ramblers still were around in the 1930s and helped revive the League of American Wheelmen. When Gormully and Jeffery began making cars after the turn of the century, they named them the Rambler, a model that was made for more than six decades.

Some bicycle manufacturers were linked to other products. The Dayton, Ohio, Bicycle & Sewing Machine Company made bicycles that Bobby Walthour, Jr., rode to victory in races. The company evolved into the Huffy Bicycle Company of Dayton. Greg LeMond won the 1986 Tour de France riding Huffy bicycles.

The Iver Johnson Arms & Cycle Works of Fitchburg, Massachusetts, made bicycles and hired Major Taylor to ride them under contract. Taylor wore the name Iver Johnson emblazoned on his jersey front. He was featured in their ads in trade journals.

"Once you understand what these bicycles and the memorabilia are," Shields said, "it helps increase your knowledge of the development of transportation in North America. It also adds to your depth of history."

But for decades anything related to cycling past was relegated to the trash heap. Russell Mamone of Arlington, Virginia, an early member of the Wheelmen when the club was founded in 1967, said he was shocked to discover that antiques dealers involved in estate sales were throwing away antique bicycles without a thought. Dealers were reluctant to help him search for antique bicycles or cycling accessories.

"I would carry photographs of what I was looking for, and the antiques dealers would shake their heads at me," he recounted. "They thought highwheelers were made in very small numbers for circuses or vaudeville. They had no idea bicycles were part of the development of general transportation or that bicycle racing was a sport.

"These dealers knew the value of Wedgwood plates, crystal glasses, English or French furniture. They had big libraries with all kinds of books on everything on antiques in the world. But their libraries had not one piece of paper on the bicycle. Zero. The bicycle didn't exist. This shows how far removed cycling had become. So many decades had passed since there was interest in bicycles that there was no institutional knowledge of them. The information gap was huge."

The information gap started to close fast in the 1980s as collectors caught on to bicycles with big wheels. Highwheelers were selling in the range of $2,500 to $6,000 in 1991, depending on the make of the bicycle and its condition.

Henry Ford and Thomas Edison began collecting together in the late 1920s. They selected bicycles, cars, furniture, and other everyday types of Americana. Inventions of Ford and Edison were permanently changing how Americans lived: Ford's cars in the 1920s were already starting the migration of families to the suburbs from the city; Edison's light bulbs, photographs, movies, and other inventions also were major influences on how people worked and spent their leisure time. Ford and Edison saw the profound social changes that had taken place since they were young men. The inventors started assembling ordinary artifacts that they knew would soon be improved, replaced, and thrown away. The collection became the Ford Museum and Greenfield Village in Dearborn.

"The collection has grown to some 24 million objects," curator Adams said. "It is the second-largest collection in the country, second to the Smithsonian Institution."

Adams has considerable experience restoring bicycles. He published a book on the subject, *Collecting & Restoring Antique Bicycles* (Tab Books, 1981), now out of print but available in used-book stores.

Part of the Henry Ford and Greenfield Village is the bicycle shop that Orville and Wilbur Wright owned in Dayton. "This is the original shop that was moved from Dayton in 1930," Adams said. "The shop is set up as it would have been in 1903 when the Wright

Brothers were making bicycles and doing repairs on them for customers while they also were experimenting with making the first airplane."

The Ford Museum and Wiedman collection feature bicycles that people used for practical, everyday life. David Metz of Freehold, New Jersey, has spent some forty years collecting bicycles, including some that are unique. "When I come upon something that is a one-of-a-kind," Wiedman said, "I pass the information along to David."

Metz has a collection of about 150 bicycles that he has restored, traded, or bought. He also has about 2,000 accessories including miniature kerosene bicycle lamps, sales posters, and photos. His collection is renowned for the 1850 Sawyer quadricycle. Handmade mostly of wood, with steel-rimmed wheels, the Sawyer is a four-wheeler for one rider. Pedals activate a driving mechanism on the rear axle. A steel tiller fastened to both ends of the front axle steers it. Metz also has a custom-built four-seat tandem, twelve feet long, that was built in the 1890s in Philadelphia. Quads, as they were called, were popular attractions at races where foursomes would pace a cyclist to speeds that fascinated audiences.

The most comprehensive collection in the United States is the Schwinn Bicycle Company History Center in Chicago. It contains about 750 bicycles, tracing their development from the Middle Ages to recent times, and about 50,000 pieces of memorabilia.

"We deal with 4,000 people who write letters or telephone us for information every year," said curator James L. Hurd. "The History Center is not open to the public yet. We're looking at a game plan of opening to the public maybe in 1993 or 1994. One place we're considering," he said in 1991, "is a building in Chicago with 30,000 square feet of space."

Schwinn is a name long identified with cycling in the United States. Ignaz Schwinn was thirty-one when he emigrated from Germany where he was trained as a machinist and an experienced bicycle maker. He arrived in Chicago in 1891. Railroads were running long trains of livestock into the city's stockyards every day, making Chicago what Carl Sandburg later called "Hog butcher for the world." The bicycle business was accelerating, and Schwinn wanted to form a company. He met a meatpacker and businessman named Adolf Arnold. In 1895 they formed Arnold, Schwinn & Company, to become one of the more than 300 companies making bicycles in America.

Schwinn designed the bicycles, selected machinery and equipment to make them, and set up the factory. After the turn of the century, when demand for bicycles plummeted, Schwinn bought out Arnold and kept the business going. It was one of the few to survive from the heyday of cycling to the present.

The Schwinn History Center is crammed into a red-brick downtown Chicago loft with 10,000 square feet of space. "We are in the old Chicago Bicycle Supply Company," Hurd said. "In this neighborhood of Desplains and Lake streets in the 1890s, there were thirty bicycle manufacturers. My office overlooks Bicycle Alley, where Gormully and Jeffery made Ramblers."

Succeeding Ignaz Schwinn, who lived into his late eighties, was son Frank W. Members of the Schwinn family had the foresight to start collecting not just Schwinn bicycles but also other makes from this country and abroad. They also collected engineering drawings, trade journals, movies, and art work. Over the years, the collection broadened. Dealers traded their old bicycles for new Schwinns to fill in models that weren't already in the collection. When the Chicago Museum of Science and Industry put its bicycle collection up for sale in the 1950s, the Schwinn family bought it.

The Schwinn Bicycle Company helped lead the American bicycle industry out of a commercial trough in the 1930s. Production of bicycles in the United States had declined every year after 1899, when 1.2 million bicycles were made. Production dropped to 194,000 in 1932.

"The industry had been standardized for so long that you almost had to be in it to tell one bicycle make from another," Hurd said. "In 1932 Schwinn made 25,000 of the 194,000

Balloon-tired bicycles that the Schwinn Bicycle Company introduced in 1933 got the bicycling industry rolling. In 1954, Vic Damone swept Debbie Reynolds off her feet with his balloon-tired bike. (Russell Mamone collection)

Jimmy Michael, left, was a world champion whose unmarked grave was weed-covered in Brooklyn until Frank Schwinn bought a headstone for it, as he did for Major Taylor. (U.S. Bicycling Hall of Fame photo)

bikes in the United States. Then, in 1933, Frank Schwinn introduced the balloon-tire bicycle. People in the industry laughed at him.

"From 1895 to 1932 the standard bicycle tire was twenty-eight inches in diameter, with a tire that was an inch and a half wide. The tire was called a single-tube—the tire and tube were one unit that glued to the rim. When the tire was cut, the tire and tube had to be replaced. The Schwinn balloon tire was twenty-six inches in diameter, two and one-eighth inches thick. The tire and tube were separate. Sales went right up. Balloon-tire bicycles caught on. By 1936 about all the bicycle manufacturers had converted to balloon tires. There were 1.2 million bicycles

made that year—250,000 were Schwinns."

Frank Schwinn was also involved with a group of Chicago-based racers who had survived from the 1890s. In the early 1940s they had formed the Bicycle Racing Stars of the Nineteenth Century Association. Members located Major Taylor's unmarked grave in Chicago's Mount Glenwood Cemetery. In May 1948 they moved his remains to a better resting place, in the cemetery's Memorial Garden of the Good Shepherd. The memorial ceremony included members who had competed against Taylor and younger black athletes, including 1936 track Olympic gold medalist Ralph Metcalfe. Taylor's rivals provided a bronze plaque for his gravesite. Schwinn provided the headstone.

Schwinn also provided a headstone for another neglected world champion, Jimmie Michael. When bicycle riders fascinated the public with the speeds they reached, especially when paced behind four-man racing tandems in the early 1890s, Michael was a gutsy rider who dazzled audiences. He was the fastest person in the world—on two wheels or four.

Michael won the inaugural world motor-pace championship behind a motorcycle on his eighteenth birthday, August 18, 1895, in Cologne, Germany. Michael, a Welshman, was five feet tall and still boyish looking, but he was taken seriously, particularly for the way he delighted crowds with his showmanship. He used flat handlebars and sat upright, but was small enough to still benefit from his pacemaker. When a reporter asked him why he raced with a lucky toothpick perched in the corner of his mouth, Michael credited the toothpick with helping his breathing. In races where he showed up without the toothpick, his riding suffered.

Billy Brady, who managed world boxing champion Jim Jeffries and soon would manage Taylor, was looking for a star attraction for the bicycle races he promoted in Brooklyn. In September 1896 Michael accepted Brady's offer to go to New York for races. Brady then arranged for Michael to compete around the United States. In Chicago, Ignaz Schwinn saw him ride and made sure Michael was hired to compete on a Schwinn World. Michael was Schwinn's favorite rider and set world records on the World.

The Welshman was in such demand that he may have been the best-paid athlete in the world in the nineties. He had a staff of two dozen pacers who traveled with him back and forth across the Atlantic.

While training at the Friedenau track in Berlin in April 1903, Michael fell and fractured his skull. His injury left him with head pains, but he kept training and racing.

In November 1904 he was on a French ship with other European racers bound for New York for the upcoming six-day race in Madison Square Garden when he collapsed and died. The ship's captain wanted to give Michael a burial at sea, but the riders talked the captain out of it. When the ship docked in New York, the cyclists hastily found a resting place for him in the Green-Wood Cemetery in Brooklyn.

The world champion's grave was un-marked and weed-covered until late in the 1940s. Mile-a-Minute Murphy, who had suffered the amputation of his right leg after a motorcycle accident, got around on a wheelchair and found the grave. He prevailed upon Schwinn and members of the Bicycle Racing Stars of the Nineteenth Century Association who had known Michael. In June 1949 Michael's old colleagues held a memorial service. His career and personality were recalled, and the marble monument Schwinn paid for was installed.

The career of Michael and other racers, as well as the recreation bicycle industry, is recalled in the Schwinn History Center. The center contains more than 700 books, 250 movies dealing with bicycles in silent films and talkies, photos, and stories that Schwinn family members and others wrote.

"The bicycle is a piece of Americana that was mostly lost in a time frame," Hurd said. "Our collection has helped reclaim and preserve it."

With the rise in cycling's popularity, two halls of fame were founded independently in the late 1980s for cycling. The U.S. Bicycling Hall of Fame in Somerville, New Jersey, was

Somerville Mayor Michael Kerwin, right, prepares to cut the ribbon to open the U.S. Bicycling Hall of Fame on Memorial Day weekend in 1990 at 34 East Main St. Assisting him, from the left, are Hall of Fame President Frank Torpey and inducted members Alf Goullet, Fred Spencer, and Mike Walden. (Sharon Thompson photo)

established in 1986. The Hall of Fame officially opened its doors at 35 East Main Street in Somerville on May 27, 1990, with Alf Goullet making a symbolic snip of the scissors to cut the oversized red-white-and-blue ribbon and showing that there is a future in American cycling history.

What began as an idea in the mid-1980s has been transformed into 1,000 square feet of office space devoted to framed photos, biographical summaries, national and world championship jerseys, and other memorabilia. One of the bicycles donated to the Hall of Fame was a black Peugeot that Major Taylor brought back after racing in France. Community and civic leaders in Somerville initiated the proposal that led the state legislature in 1988 and 1989 awarding two grants of $100,000 each as seed money.

"I was astonished that there hadn't been a Hall of Fame established for cycling," observed Don Hull, who was hired in April 1988 as the first executive director. Hull previously worked for the Amateur and International Boxing Federation. He started working in 1988 for the Hall of Fame in the back of a Somerville bank that donated space for the project's start.

With the new location on Main Street, Frank Torpey, Hall of Fame president, said, "We now have a solid presence."

The May 1990 ribbon-cutting ceremony also kicked off the induction ceremony for four new members with an awards banquet attended by 150 sports celebrities, afficionados, and members of the media.

Fred Spencer of Rahway, New Jersey, was inducted. He set world records at distances from one-tenth of a mile to twenty-five miles in his career in the 1920s and 1930s. Spencer was so popular that when he won his first of three national professional championships in 1925, President Calvin Coolidge invited him and his six-day racing partner Bobby Walthour, Jr., to the White House.

Spencer, still spry at eighty-five, also was

a renowned six-day racer who competed in 102 of the grueling events. He won four in New York's celebrated Madison Square Garden, and two in Chicago.

Emile Fraysee, a founding member in 1920 of the Amateur Bicycle League of America, which became the U.S. Cycling Federation, also was inducted. Fraysee, of Teaneck, New Jersey, won some 300 races in the early part of the century before retiring to oversee the sport. He served as ABL president from 1929 to 1932 and coached the 1928 and 1932 Olympic cycling teams.

For the post-1945 era, Mike Walden of Detroit was inducted in recognition of the more than 100 national champions and eight world champions he had coached, including Connie Young and Sheila Young-Ochowicz, since the 1940s. Walden said that with cycling's new popularity, coaching will be a crucial issue for the 1990s.

Olympic gold medalist from the 1984 Los Angeles Games Connie Carpenter-Phinney of Boulder also was inducted. She won the inaugural women's Olympic road race to cap her career of twelve national championships, and a gold, two silver, and a bronze medal in world championships. "Without a Hall of Fame," she said, "our riders today won't know where they are going if they don't know where they came from."

Previous Hall of Fame inductees include Goullet, Howard, Taylor (1878–1932), Kramer (1881–1958), and Bobby Walthour, Sr. (1878–1949). (Walthour was also inducted February 1991 into the New York Sports Museum & Hall of Fame in New York City along with Muhammad Ali, Chris Evert, and Roy Campanella among a total of 76 top athletes and sportswriters.)

Another inductee to the U.S. Bicycling Hall of Fame is Audrey McElmury Levonas of Helena, Montana. She won the 1969 world road-racing championship in Brno, Czechoslovakia, to become the first U.S. rider ever to wear the world champion's white jersey, created in 1919, with the band of rainbow colors over the chest.

Jack Heid (1924–1987) is another Hall of Famer. In post–World War II years, Heid was a pioneer cyclist who successfully broke into European racing. The bronze medal he won at the 1949 Copenhagen world championships remained the best men's performance in world's sprints through 1990.

Two other New Jersey natives also are in the Hall of Fame. Fred "Pop" Kugler left the legacy of the Tour of Somerville, which became a focal point for American bicycle racing. He was the first officially inducted member, in 1987.

Another New Jersey native who followed him into the Hall of Fame was Arthur Augustus Zimmerman (1869–1936). Zimmerman won the first world cycling championship, held exclusively for amateurs in 1893 in Chicago, and went on to turn professional. He made a vivid impression wherever he went. The French in particular found him a favorite and called him, Le Grand Zimm. (A member of the New York Athletic Club, Zimmerman wore the club's winged foot logo on his jersey front when he competed around the United States, Europe, and Australia. He was inducted into the NYAC Hall of Fame in 1990.)

Following the example of Somerville, pioneers of mountain-bike riding in 1988 established the Mountain Bike Hall of Fame and Museum in Crested Butte, Colorado. Crested Butte, located at 13,000 feet altitude in the Rocky Mountains, has a long tradition of off-road racing. President of the Hall of Fame is Carole Bauer, who works as retail manager of the popular Bakery Cafe on Elk Avenue. She spends two or three volunteer hours a day at the Hall of Fame, answering telephone calls and correspondence. Bauer also organizes Fat Tire Bike Week held every July for the Hall of Fame.

Soon after it was founded, the Mountain Bike Hall of Fame prompted an article in an Italian magazine which prompted letters—and membership checks—from Italian men and women mountain-bike riders who wanted to join and read the Hall of Fame's newsletter. Cyclists from Japan and Poland also have joined.

The Mountain Bike Hall of Fame and Museum is joined to the town's Mother Earth Natural Foods. Mother Earth staff answer questions from customers about mountain-bike riding and sell $20 Hall of Fame memberships. In 1991 the Hall of Fame had seven bicycles from the original makers, more than 100 photos, and about fifty posters.

Mountain Bike Hall of Famer Charlie Kelly in 1976, shooshing down a Rocky Mountain trail, wearing protective combat boots, a firemen's coat, and kneepads over his jeans—just in case he fell. (Mountain Bike Hall of Fame & Museum photo)

Members inducted into the Mountain Bike Hall of Fame through 1990 were: Jacquie Phelan, Joe Murray, Joe Breeze, Steve Cook, Murdoch, Mike Sinyard, Tom Ritchey, Gary Fisher, Charlie Kelly, Charlie Cunningham, Jeff Lindsay, Eric Koski, Tom Hillard, Wende Cragg, Don Cook, Victor Vincente (né Michael Hiltner), Glenn Odell, Scot Nicol, Cindy Whitehead, Ned Overend, and Steve Potts.

Still in the planning stage in 1991 is the National Bicycle Center in Redmond, Washington. Jerry Baker of Redmond said that a facility in the Seattle suburb is planned for the mid-1990s to provide educational and recreational programs related to cycling history, technology, and safe operation of human-powered vehicles.

"This will take four to five years to get off the ground," Bauer said in 1990. "We plan to have a 250-meter pavilion-style covered board velodrome, with a museum and education facility underneath. We envision a facility to make Seattle a bike capital."

The link between bicycles and motorcycles is well documented at the Indian Motocycle Museum in Springfield, Massachusetts, where the famous Indian motorcycles were made for a half-century. Indian motorcycles used to outsell rival Harley-Davidsons by three to one. Demand for the Indians has kept the museum open to the public long past the company's existence.

Indian motorcycles started out as the American Indian Bicycle, which the country's first national cycling champion, George M. Hendee, made in the 1890s. Hendee had won the first national cycling championship, on a highwheeler, at the League of American Wheelmen convention in September 1882 in Boston. He repeated as national champion for the next four years. In that time he traveled widely, including an excursion to England, which was a major sports power. Hendee was a national hero. His American Indian Bicycles sold well until after the turn of the century, when consumer demand plummeted.

Oscar Hedstrom, a professional bicycle racer with considerable mechanical aptitude, was a good friend of Hendee's and had money to invest. Hedstrom suggested in 1901 that Hendee put a motor that Hedstrom could make on the inventory of bicycles that Hendee was stuck with. Thus the Indian motorcycle was founded to become the country's first American-made motorcycle.

Hendee and Hedstrom became wealthy men as inventions they made for the Hendee Manufacturing Company contributed to the advancement of Indian motorcycles. One of their managers was a tool-and-die maker named Robert Ellingham, who had coached Major Taylor in Taylor's last amateur years and the early part of his professional career, a period that lasted five years.

For five decades, Indian and Harley-Davidson motorcycles dominated all the major races and alternated breaking records. Police at President Eisenhower's 1953 inauguration parade on Pennsylvania Avenue from the Capitol to the White House rode Indian motorcycles.

Months later, the company closed its doors—and a chapter of American motorcycle history. The bicycles, motorcycles, and engines remain on display in Springfield, across town from the Basketball Hall of Fame.

More information is available from:

Charles & Esta Manthos
Indian Motocycle Museum
33 Hendee St.
P.O. Box 3, Highland Station
Springfield, MA 01139
(413) 737-2624

Considerable history is derived from stamp collectors who make cycling stamps their specialty. Bert Schapelhouman of Mountain

Bicycle Department.

LOVELL DIAMOND CYCLES

SOLID, PNEUMATIC, AND CUSHION TIRES.

HIGH GRADE IN EVERY PARTICULAR.

If not called for in 10 days, please return to

JOHN P. LOVELL ARMS CO.

Manufacturers and Jobbers in

Bicycles, Fire-Arms, Fishing Tackle, Base Ball,

And GYMNASIUM GOODS.

P. O. Box 5203—147 WASHINGTON ST., BOSTON, MASS.

E. A. Adams,

West Medway, Mass.

In the 1890s, bicycle manufacturers—such as the Lovell Diamond Cycles—used to mail customers correspondence with advertising on the left side of the envelope. (Bert Schapelhouman collection)

View, California, is an avid collector whose pursuit is relentless. He is regularly on the telephone with international collectors in Tokyo, Sydney, Frankfurt, and London— following leads, exchanging information, and doing research that would make Sherlock Holmes proud. Many of the stamps command considerable sums, but collectors know one another and the pedigree of what they buy.

Philatelists like Schapelhouman also collect envelopes, called "covers," that bike manufacturers used to mail to customers with ornate advertising on the left side of the envelopes.

"In the 1880s and 1890s there were hundreds of small bike-companies," he said. "Some of the covers had elaborate art work, in four colors. Bicycle clubs sent covers, too, to announce a big race coming up. They would mail out covers to club members with these notices on the left side. The stamps are

neatly canceled. All these bike manufacturers and clubs disappeared just after the turn of the century."

Four-color covers sold for up to $500 each in 1991, Schapelhouman said. Regular covers averaged $25 to $150 each.

Some bicycle stamps grew out of necessity, such as the California bicycle stamp, part of American labor history. In early July 1894 train workers who objected to the new Pullman railroad parlor and sleeping cars went on strike. In days before cars and airplanes, railroads were a vital link between cities. Bicycles were becoming popular, and Fresno merchants approached Arthur C. Banta, who had a local store selling Victor safety bicycles. Merchants asked Banta to set up a bicycle relay, like the Pony Express from an earlier era, to carry mail to San Francisco, 210 miles northwest.

Roads were rough—made of dirt and rutted. Many in Fresno were skeptical when

When train workers struck in California in July 1893, merchants in Fresno approached a local bicycle dealer to organize a relay of cyclists to carry mail with privately issued stamps 210 miles to San Francisco. The bicycle stamp is regarded as the first issued as a result of a strike.
(Bert Schapelhouman collection)

they heard of Banta's enterprise. But Banta recruited riders, carefully selected routes, set up relay points, and began the bicycle service on July 7, 1894. In three days, bicycle messengers had the service down to eighteen hours between Fresno and San Francisco. Public confidence in the service went up. The bicycle messengers began carrying more than just mail. A Fresno dentist ordered a set of teeth for a patient. A Fresno photographer ordered nitrate of silver. A merchant ordered shirts. They all arrived by bicycle messenger.

When the service started, a Fresno engraver, Eugene Donze, designed a stamp. "The die was engraved on a copper plate," Schapelhouman said, "and then mounted on a block of engraver's boxwood by O. J. Treat

of the Commercial Printing Company of Fresno, who also did the print."

The California bicycle stamp depicted a cyclist inside an oval that fit in a diamond. It is regarded as the world's first stamp issued as a result of a strike.

The service carried approximately 380 covers between July 7th and 18th when, the strike ended. "Only about forty to fifty covers, or less, are known to be in collections today," Schapelhouman said. They are valued at more than $1,400.

Some of the most prized stamps grew out of the siege of Mafeking in the South African War at the turn of the century. The Mafeking Blue Cyclist stamp has Sergeant Major Warner Goodyear riding a safety bicycle beneath a scroll bearing the legend, "Mafeking

Besieged," in small Roman and sans-serif capitals. Mafeking Blue Cyclist stamps in 1991 were valued at up to $2,000.

Robert Stephenson Smyth Baden-Powell, the British soldier who founded the Boy Scouts, defended Mafeking from the Boers who surrounded the city and bombarded it with artillery. During the siege, from October 12, 1899, to May 17, 1900, British subjects under Baden-Powell sent mail out by bicycle couriers.

"Bicycles didn't make any noise and got the couriers past enemy lines," Schapelhouman said. "The couriers were well paid. Some of them were thirteen or fourteen years old. They were quick and daring. But it was dangerous work. Some couriers were caught and killed."

The correspondence they carried had stamps engraved with fine printing. One stamp depicted the cyclist; one other issue had Baden-Powell on the face. Baden-Powell, forty-three at the time and destined to live another forty-one years, provoked ill-will back in his homeland for authorizing stamps issued without Queen Victoria's portrait. England's queen commanded her portrait on all stamps in the United Kingdom and her empire.

Few of the 18,000 stamps printed during the siege have survived. "These stamps are now extremely scarce, especially in mint condition," Schapelhouman said. "You have a real rarity when you find one actually used on an envelope and canceled in Mafeking during the siege of the town."

Driving up the value of the stamps are collectors whose specialties are sports, cycling, and the Boy Scouts. Specialty collectors seek both the cyclist stamp and the Baden-Powell stamp as a complete set of the issue.

Stamps with bicycles on them are popular worldwide. The first on record are bicycle stamps from Germany in 1886, Schapelhouman said. Countries issue bicycle stamps to commemorate the bicycle as transportation, racing, the Olympics, the Pan American Games, Goodwill Games, world championships, and other events.

"Practically every country has issued cycling stamps," Schapelhouman said. He estimates that since Germany issued the bicycle stamps in 1886, at least 2,000 cycling stamps have been issued internationally.

More information on private collections such as those of Carl Wiedman, Lorne Shields, or David Metz is available from:

Carl Wiedman
Associate Editor, *The Wheelmen*
3515 Walbri Dr.
Bloomfield Hills, MI 48013
(313) 646-2756

or

Marge Fuehrer
Commander of the Wheelmen
1708 School House Lane
Ambler, PA 19002
(215) 699-3187

or

Lorne Shields
Shields Intertrade Corp.
141 Adesso Dr.
Concord, Ontario, Canada
L4K 3C3
(416) 669-4821

Information on the Schwinn History Center is available from:

James L. Hurd, Curator
Schwinn Bicycle Company
Schwinn History Center
217 N. Jefferson St.
Chicago, IL 60606-1111
(312) 454-7400

Collections available to the public include:

The Ford Museum and Greenfield
   Village
Dearborn, MI 48121
(313) 271-1620

Crawford Museum
Western Reserve Historical Society
10825 East Boulevard
Cleveland, OH 44106
(216) 721-5722

Canadian National Museum of Science
   and Technology
Dave Monahan, Curator of
   Transportation
Shields Collection
P.O. Box 9724
Ottawa Terminal
Ottawa, Ontario, Canada
K1G 5A3
(613) 991-3082

Smithsonian Institution
Roger White, Curator of
   Transportation
Museum of History and Technology
Constitution Ave. and 14th St., N.W.
Washington, DC 20560
(202) 357-1438

The California History Center
   Foundation
A Century of Cycling in Santa Clara
   County Exhibit
De Anza College
Cupertino, CA 95014
(408) 864-8712

Collecting bicycles—antiques and even
more recent balloon-tired bicycles—is in an
early stage but maturing rapidly. In response to growing demand for prices and related information, James Hurd and T. A.
Gordon co-wrote the 150-page *Bicycle Blue
Book* in 1990.

"The *Bicycle Blue Book* is the first published on the values of the bicycles," Hurd

said. "Our first printing, in December, was
1,500 copies. At $9 each, they sold out in four
weeks." A second printing followed in February 1991.

The *Blue Book* features line drawings of
bicycles of particular models, tells what the
market value is, and lists a calendar of
events for bicycle shows where collectors can
buy, sell, or trade.

Hurd and Gordon in 1990 also co-authored
*Collectible Elgin, J. C. Higgins and Haw-
thorne Bicycles, 1933–1965*. The authors
spent three years collecting old Sears &
Roebuck and Montgomery Ward catalogs to
compile more than 250 reprinted pages that
give a guide for dating and restoring these
bicycles.

"From 1933 to 1959 there were 38 million
balloon-tired bicycles made in the United
States," Hurd explained. "Another 17 million lightweight bicycles (with tires one and
three-quarters inches thick) were made in
that time. That means there were more than
50 million of these machines passed down—
from older brother to younger brother, to sisters, nephews, and nieces. Now these bicycles are coming out of the woodwork and
they're appreciating.

"When you go for a ride on these heavy
bikes, you roll over a curb and keep on going.
You get the feeling that when your computer
in the office went down, it doesn't matter
anymore. People who buy these bicycles are
buying back their childhood, and it's cheaper
than psychiatry."

Bicycle collecting is a hobby that Hurd
rated in 1991 as being in what he calls the
infant stage. "As a hobby, it turned over in
1990," he said. "It started to come awake in
1991."

The *Bicycle Blue Book* was made for collectors to carry to garage sales to scout for
valuable bicycles. A Schwinn Corvette middleweight bicycle has a *Blue Book* value of
$250 to $400. A 1910 Pierce Arrow Road-
ster, made with shock absorbers on the rear

fork stay, has a *Blue Book* value of $1,500. Depending on styling and condition, other Pierce Arrow bicycles command up to $2,500.

For 1991, Hurd and Gordon planned to keep the *Blue Book* limited to bicycles. In 1992 they are scheduled to publish a 300-page *Blue Book* that would include a small number of posters, sheet music, and accessories such as headlamps, cyclometers, and handlebars.

"Collecting bicycles is just getting started," Hurd said. "But the way things were picking up tempo in the late 1980s, bicycles and cycling memorablia will double and then quadruple in the early 1990s. Collecting bicycles and memorabilia will rate with brass beds and rolltop desks."

Copies of the *Bicycle Blue Book* are available for $9. Copies of *Collectible Elgin, J. C. Higgins and Hawthorne Bicycles* cost $19.95. Both prices include postage and handling. They can be ordered from:

Antique/Classic Bicycle Newsletter
P.O. Box 1049
Ann Arbor, MI 48106

Memberships in the U.S. Bicycling Hall of Fame and the Mountain Bike Hall of Fame and Museum each are available for an annual donation of $20. Information is available from:

U.S. Bicycling Hall of Fame
P.O. Box 8535, 34 East Main St.
Somerville, NJ 08876
(201) 722-3620

Mountain Bike Hall of Fame and
  Museum
Carole Bauer, President
P.O. Box 845
Crested Butte, CO 81224
(303) 349-7382

New York Athletic Club Hall of Fame
Joseph Ingrassia, Chairman
180 Central Park South
New York, NY 10019
(212) 247-5100

New York Sports Museum & Hall of
  Fame
Bill Shannon, President
One Dag Hammarskjold Plaza
Suite 200
New York, NY 10017
(212) 605-8768

National Bicycle Center
P.O. Box 3401
Redmond, WA 98073-3401
(206) 869-5804

Information on bicycle antiques is available from:

Antique/Classic Bicycle Newsletter
$12 a year for six issues
T. A. Gordon, Managing Editor
P.O. Box 1049
Ann Arbor, MI 48106

Information on bicycle stamps is available from:

Bicycle Stamps Club
$24 annual dues, includes *Bicycle
  Stamps* Quarterly
c/o Benoit Carrier, Secretary
C.P. 154 STN: "M"
Montreal, Quebec, Canada
H1V 3L8

Another source for philatelists is:
The Fresno and San Francisco Bicycle Mail of 1894, by Lowell B. Cooper, published in 1982 by Leonard H. Hartman. Copies are $50 and can be ordered from:

Philatelic Bibliopole
P.O. Box 36006
Louisville, KY 40233

INDEX

ABOUT THE AUTHOR

PETER NYE's articles on cycling have been published in *USA Today, The Washington Post, Denver Post, Sports Illustrated, The Olympian Magazine,* and *Women's Sports & Fitness Magazine.* He has been a contributing writer to *Winning Magazine* since 1985. A graduate of Ball State University, Nye did graduate study in economics at The London School of Economics, covered the night police beat for *The South Bend Tribune,* and was editor of *National Voter Magazine* in Washington, DC. He is author of *Hearts of Lions: The Story of American Bicycle Racing.*

(Pam Bishop photo)

Greg LeMond's Complete Book of Bicycling
by Greg Lemond and Kent Gordis

illustrated with over 100 photographs

Greg Lemond, winner of the 1981 and 1985 Coors Classic, the 1983 World Championships, and the 1986 and 1989 Tours de France, is regarded as the top professional cyclist in the world. In his complete book on bicycling LeMond shows how millions of bicyclists in America can become better riders and get more enjoyment from the sport.

Greg Lemond's Complete Book of Bicycling describes and explains everything you need to know about buying, riding, and maintaining a bike, whether you are a recreational rider or a serious racer. Illustrated with over 100 instructive photos, the book discusses determining the proper frame size, how to select the best bike for the best value, what to avoid in buying a bike, seat and handlebar height, safety tips, and much more. LeMond discloses the training techniques that have helped make him the top cyclist in the world and even includes chapters on bicycle maintenance and a brief history of bicycling.

Liberally sprinkled with anecdotes from LeMond's own cycling experiences, this is *the* complete book on bicycling by the hottest cyclist in the world.

Greg LeMond's Pocket Guide to Bicycle Maintenance and Repair
by Greg LeMond

Illustrated with step-by-step photographs and line drawings, this handy guide covers all the essential tips and how-to techniques to keep cyclists on the road.

Included are basic bicycle-maintenance steps to keep bikes in tiptop condition, from adjusting the seat and handlebars to greasing the wheel hubs and checking the brakes. Also covered fully are emergency repairs you can make *on the road* to help you get back in the saddle quickly, with specifics on what tools you should carry for short rides, day trips, and overnight touring; how to change and repair a flat tire (both clincher tires and tubular tires); what to do if a spoke breaks; how to adjust brakes that rub against the tire rim; and much more.

An essential companion for cyclists of all levels—in convenient pocket format to fit in a seat pack or handlebar bag.

Ordering is easy and convenient.
Just call 1-800-631-8571
or send your order to:

The Putnam Publishing Group
390 Murray Hill Parkway, Dept. B
East Rutherford, NJ   07073

Also available at your local bookstore or wherever books are sold.

		PRICE	
		U.S.	CANADA
_____ **Greg LeMond's Complete Book of Bicycling**	399-51594-1	$10.95	$14.50
_____ **Greg LeMond's Pocket Guide to Bicycle Maintenance and Repair**	399-51511-9	7.95	10.59

Subtotal $ _____

*Postage & handling $ _____

Sales Tax (CA, NJ, NY, PA) $ _____

Total Amount Due $ _____

Payable in U.S. Funds (No cash orders accepted)

*Postage & handling: $1.00 for 1 book, 25¢ for each additional book up to a maximum of $3.50

Please send me the titles I've checked above.　　Enclosed is my ☐ check　☐ money order
Please charge my ☐ Visa　☐ Mastercard　☐ American Express
Card # _____ Expiration date _____
Signature as on charge card _____
Name _____
Address _____
City _____ State _____ Zip _____
Please allow six weeks for delivery. Prices subject to change without notice.